Benson John Lossing

An Outline History of the United States

For Public And Other Schools

Benson John Lossing

An Outline History of the United States
For Public And Other Schools

ISBN/EAN: 9783744749411

Printed in Europe, USA, Canada, Australia, Japan

Cover: Foto ©Thomas Meinert / pixelio.de

More available books at **www.hansebooks.com**

BORN
22ᴰ FEBʸ
-1732-

DIED
14ᵀᴴ DECᴿ
-1799-

WASHINGTON.
— from —
the Portrait by Stuart.

CONSTITUTION

AN

OUTLINE HISTORY

OF THE

UNITED STATES,

FOR PUBLIC AND OTHER SCHOOLS;

FROM THE EARLIEST PERIOD TO THE PRESENT TIME.

BY

BENSON J. LOSSING, LL. D.,

AUTHOR OF THE FIELD BOOKS OF "THE REVOLUTION," "THE WAR OF 1812,"
AND THE "CIVIL WAR;" THE "HOME OF WASHINGTON,"
"LIFE AND TIMES OF PHILIP SCHUYLER," ETC.

COPIOUSLY ILLUSTRATED BY MAPS AND OTHER ENGRAVINGS.

NEW YORK:

SHELDON & COMPANY,

No. 677 BROADWAY.

1875.

LOSSING'S SCHOOL HISTORIES

OF THE

UNITED STATES.

I. LOSSING'S PRIMARY UNITED STATES HISTORY. For the Youngest Children. Elegantly Illustrated.   Price $1.00.

II. LOSSING'S OUTLINE UNITED STATES HISTORY. A Complete History of our Country in a Condensed but Attractive form. For Public and Private Schools. It is the most elegantly illustrated School History ever published.

Price $1.25.

III. LOSSING'S COMMON SCHOOL HISTORY. A Full, Complete, and Attractive History of our Country. For Private Schools and more advanced Scholars. Elegantly Illustrated. Over 400 pages. Price $1.75.

Entered according to Act of Congress, in the year 1875, by
SHELDON & CO.,
In the Office of the Librarian of Congress, at Washington.

Electrotyped by SMITH & MCDOUGAL, 82 Beckman St., N. Y.

INTRODUCTION.

This book has been prepared to meet the demands of Teachers and Pupils, and the conditions of our Common School Teaching. They require a book *clear and concise* in all its statements of facts concerning the more prominent events in the History of the United States, with *helps for the memory.* They require a book that shall be *full, and accurate, and attractive,* and at the same time to occupy, in its study and the recitations, as little time as possible in the routine of the school-work. To answer these requirements the Author has bestowed the most careful thought and labor on this work, and has given to it prominent features, which may be defined as follows :

1. As **few words as possible** have been used in giving it a *pleasing narrative form.* **Ideas** are not smothered in **words ;** nor is the living interest in the story dulled by the dryness of a mere chronological form.

2. The narrative is divided into **six distinct periods,** in the natural time and order which events suggest, namely : *Discoveries, Settlements, Colonies, The Revolution, The Nation,* and *The Civil War and its Consequences.* This is the general arrangement of the whole series of the author's Histories of the United States for Schools and Families.

3. The work is **arranged in short sentences,** so that the substance of each may be easily comprehended by an ordinary effort of memory.

4. The **most important events** are indicated in the text by **heavy-faced letter,** so as to impress the vision, and thereby give to the memory powerful aid in the retention

of facts. For the same reason all *proper names are printed in italic letter.*

5. Full questions are framed for every verse.

6. A pronouncing vocabulary is furnished in footnotes wherever required, giving to the teacher and pupil an ever-present index to the method of pronouncing the proper names used in the book.

7. A brief synopsis of topics is given at the close of *each section.*

8. An outline history of *important events* is given at the close of *every chapter,* affording a review of the previous studies, and texts for the exercise of the pupil in historical tabulation or more elaborate composition, as illustrated on pages 32 and 33 of the text. At the close of the volume are **Topical Review Questions.**

9. The work is **profusely illustrated** by *Maps, Charts,* and *Plans* explanatory of the text, and by carefully-drawn pictures of objects and events. *These are very numerous and useful,* and give powerful help to the memory in the comprehension of the narrative, for the eye seldom forgets. The **Colonial Seals** have been copied from impressions taken from the originals, and are accurate representations of those originals.

The **National Constitution**, which, with its several amendments, forms the *supreme law of the land,* is introduced as a part of the lessons of prime importance. It being the guarantee for all the privileges of American citizenship, a knowledge of it should be deeply impressed upon the minds of the young.

With these remarks concerning the general character of this book it is submitted to the public.

Outline History of the United States.

CHAPTER I.

DISCOVERERS AND DISCOVERIES.

SECTION I.

NORTHMEN, COLUMBUS, AND INDIANS.

1. Our Country, called the **United States of America,** extends in a broad, irregular belt across the continent of *North America,* from *the Atlantic Ocean* to the *Pacific Ocean.*

2. This great belt of country is divided into *States* and *Territories,* and contains about forty million inhabitants. Their government is called a Representative one. The people choose a few of their number to make laws for the whole. When these representatives meet for that business, they form the **Congress.** The people also choose one man to enforce the laws of Congress, who is called the **President of the United States.**

3. The President and Congress choose a certain number of lawyers to explain the laws, and these form the **Supreme Court of the United States.** The Government therefore consists of three separate departments, but working together.

4. One is the *Executive Department,* composed of

QUESTIONS.—1. Define the extent of the United States. 2. What can you tell about the divisions and Government of our country? 3. How is the Supreme Court formed? Of what does the Government consist?

the *President* and his advisers, called the *Cabinet.* Another is the *Legislative Department,* and is composed of a Senate chosen by the State legislatures, and a House of Representatives chosen by the people of the several States. A third is the *Judiciary Department,* composed of the judges or members of the Supreme Court.

5. This form of government seems to be the best ever known on the earth. Here, where it exists, the whole country, less than three hundred years ago, was inhabited by copper-colored barbarians and wild beasts, and nearly all covered with forests. You may ask, How has it come to pass that such a people as we are, and such an excellent form of government, have appeared in this land, so lately a wilderness? The wonderful story before us will answer the question.

NORTHMAN.

NORTHMAN'S SHIP.

6. About nine hundred years ago, seamen from *Iceland,* far toward the north pole, came to this country in small vessels and tried to make a settlement in *New England.* How long they stayed we cannot tell. The story of their discoveries, if it ever went abroad, had long been forgotten. An old tower at *Newport, Rhode Island,* is supposed to have been built by these Northmen.

TOWER AT NEWPORT.

QUESTIONS.—4. Of what or whom are the Departments composed? 5. What can you say of our form of Government and its place of existence? 6. What can you tell about early discoveries and discoverers?

Trade of European merchants.

TRACK OF THE NORTHMEN FROM ICELAND AND GREENLAND.

7. About four hundred years ago, the merchants of *Europe* carried on a profitable trade with *India* or *Eastern Asia.* The people of *Italy* had lately obtained the mastery of the *Mediterranean Sea,* over which merchants had gone to Asia from *Western Europe.* The

QUESTIONS.—7. What can you tell about Italian and Western merchants, and their trade with India?

Italians would no longer allow their rivals of *Western Europe* to go over that sea, and the Western merchants sought for another way. It was found by a *Portuguese* sailor. It was around the *Cape of Good Hope,* and so across the broad *Indian Ocean.*

COLUMBUS.

8. At that time learned men believed *the earth to be round,* like an orange, and not flat, like a pancake. Among these was *Christopher Columbus,* of *Genoa,* in *Italy,* who had been a seaman ever since his boyhood. He made a voyage to *Iceland,* where he probably heard of the discovery of a western continent hundreds of years before.

9. Believing that Eastern *Asia* might be reached sooner by sailing westward than by any other way, *Columbus* was anxious to go in search of *India* in that direction. He was poor. His countrymen refused to help him. After much wandering and many trials, he found Queen *Isabella* of *Spain* willing to fit out vessels for him to sail over the Atlantic Ocean on a voyage of discovery.

ISABELLA.

10. *Isabella* was a Christian and a patriot. She wished to send the gospel to the heathen, and to gain fame and riches for

Spain. *Columbus* promised to carry Christianity to the pagans and win honor and wealth for *Spain.* The pious and patriotic Queen said, "I will furnish you with vessels if I have to sell the jewels in my crown to pay for them."

11. Three vessels were prepared, and on the 3d of August, 1492, they sailed from *Palos,*[1] in *Andalusia,* under the command of *Columbus.* They touched at the *Canary Islands.* After a stormy and perilous passage across the *Atlantic Ocean,* the navigators were greeted

THE FLEET OF COLUMBUS.

with the perfumes of flowers at the evening twilight. At dawn the next morning, the 12th of October, they saw land.

12. The ships had arrived at the *Bahama Group* of islands, many leagues eastward of *Florida.* Naked inhabitants, of a copper color, were seen on the beach, and fled to the woods on the approach of the Europeans. *Columbus,* supposing he was on the shores of *Farther India,* called the people **Indians.**

COLUMBUS ON SAN
SALVADOR.

13. Dressed in scarlet, and carrying the banner of the expedition, *Columbus* landed. He was followed by a priest with a cross and the men of the ships. All knelt upon the

Questions.—11. What can you tell about the first voyage of Columbus ? 12. What did he discover ? 13. Describe the scene when Columbus landed.

¹ *pah'los.*

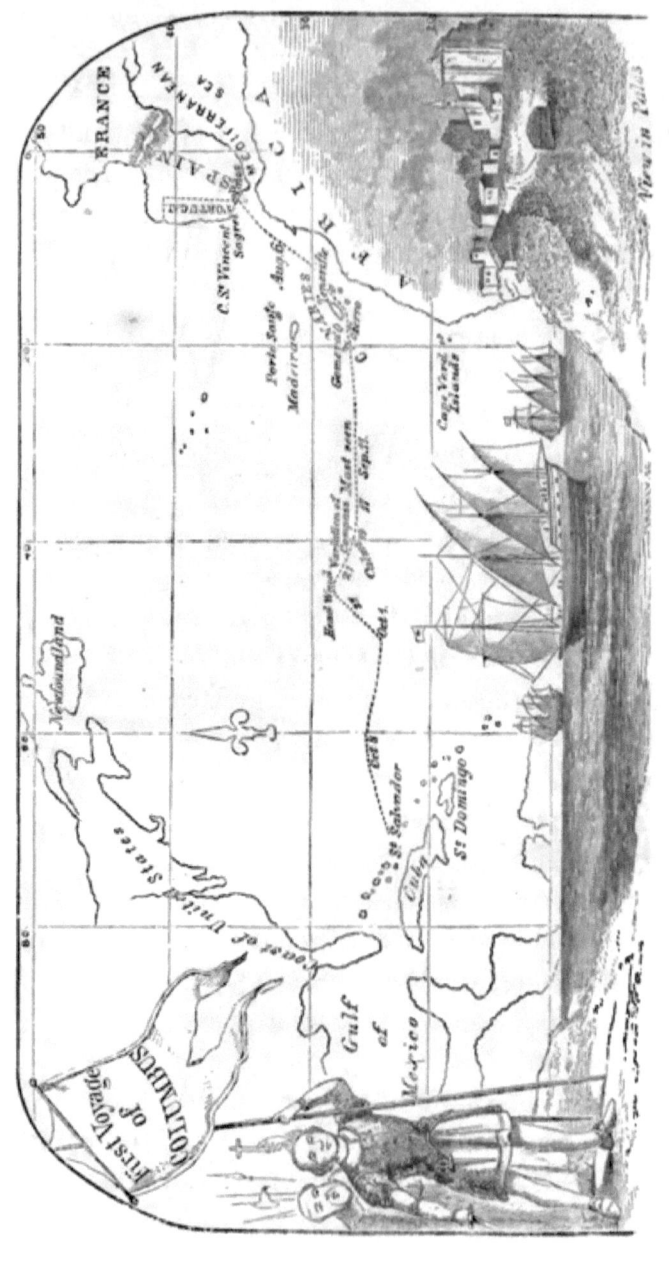

First Voyage of COLUMBUS

Landing of Columbus.

COLUMBUS DISCOVERING LAND.

sandy shore and thanked God for his goodness.   Then *Columbus* took possession of the land in the name of the sovereigns of **Spain,** *Ferdinand* and *Isabella.*

14. The land was an island, to which Columbus gave the name of *San Salvador,* or Holy Saviour.   It is now called *Cat Island.*   He visited other islands of the

QUESTIONS.—14. What was the land that Columbus first discovered, and what else did he do?

GATHERING OF WILD RICE.

Bahama group. Going southward, he discovered *Cuba* and *Hayti* or *San Domingo*, and then sailed for *Spain*. Believing these islands to be a part of *India*, and as they lay westward of *Europe*, he gave them the name of **West Indies**.

15. *Columbus* did not then see the *Continent* of America, which was thinly inhabited by a copper-colored race, who were savages and barbarians, such as he saw on *San Salvador*. Their general appearance was the same everywhere. Their habits varied with circumstances.

SOUTHERN INDIANS.

16. The *Indians*, in the colder parts of America, were dressed in the skins of beasts, and in the warmer parts they were almost naked. They got their food by hunting and fishing. They also raised grain, which we call Indian corn, and a few vegetables.

17. The *Indians* were divided into large and small families. The larger families were known as *Nations*, and spoke different languages. The smaller were known as *Tribes*, and the languages of these also sometimes differed. They lived in huts made of poles and covered with barks and skins, which they called *wigwams*.

A WIGWAM.

18. The *Indians* had no *written language* excepting rude picture-writings, and these were confined to records of war, of alliances,

INDIAN PICTURE-WRITING.[1]

and brave deeds. Their history was transmitted by memory.

19. Their money was made of parts of shells in the form of short tubes, arranged in strings or belts, and was called *wampum.* These were used in traffic, and between nations and tribes, as tokens of alliance or affection. *Wampum belts* were held by sachems, or chief men, as records of public acts.

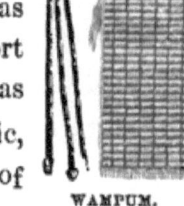

WAMPUM.

INDIAN CHIEF IN MILITARY DRESS.

INDIAN WEAPONS.

20. War was the principal business of the men. The women performed all other labor. They fought with bows and arrows, clubs, hatchets of stone and iron called *toma-hawks,* and knives. They made peace by the action of the chief

QUESTIONS.—19. What can you tell about their money and its uses? 20. What have you to say about the men and their way of making war or peace?

[1] This is part of a record of a war expedition. The figures on the right and left—

men of both parties, who would sit around a large fire after the terms were agreed upon, and smoke the *calumet*, or *pipe of peace.*

CALUMETS.

21. The *religion* of the *Indians* was simple. ' They believed in a great *Good Spirit* and a great *Evil Spirit;* and anything which they could not· understand or control, such as the sun, moon and stars, lightning, wind, fire and water, they thought to be a kind of god.

22. They believed that at death, each one went to a beautiful land, where there was plenty of game. When a man was buried they placed by the side of his dead body,

SCAFFOLD BURIAL-PLACE.

bows and arrows for use in the spirit land. Sometimes the body was laid in a shallow grave ; sometimes placed in the ground in a sitting posture and covered, and sometimes laid upon a scaffold out of the reach of wild beasts.

23. The government of the Indians was simple. The head ruler, or President, was called Sachem, and the head warrior, Chief. The Sachem was at the head of civil affairs. The warriors followed the Chief wherever he might lead. Both were chosen by the people.

24. *Marriage* among the Indians was a contract that

QUESTIONS.—21. What can you tell about the religion of the Indians? 22. What can you tell about the death and burial of Indians? 23. Tell about the government of the Indians.

one with a gun, and the other with the hatchet—denote prisoners taken by a warrior. The one without a head, and holding a bow and arrow, denotes that one was killed ; and the figure with a shaded part below the cross indicates a feminine prisoner. Then he goes in a war canoe, with nine companions, denoted by the paddles, after which a council is held by the chiefs of the Bear and Turtle tribes, indicated by rude figures of these animals on each side of a fire.

INDIANS IN BUFFALO-SKIN BOAT.

might be broken by the husband, who had a right to take and dismiss a wife at pleasure. Women were the slaves of men. They were never permitted to engage in any games, but were allowed to be present, with their children, at the war-dances.

25. The *Indians* were nearly all wanderers, and left the vast continent in an uncultivated state. In this condition the *Europeans* found our country. They brought with them the arts of civilization. Where the *Indians* hunted and fished, are now seen farms, villages, and cities. The race of red or copper-colored men, who have played an important part in the history of the **United States**, is rapidly passing away, and the white or pale-faced men are taking their places.

QUESTIONS.—24. What can you tell about the marriages of the Indians, and the condition of the women? 25. What have you to say about the Indians when Europeans first came? What is their fate?

MEETING OF WHITE MEN AND INDIANS.[1]

26. When *Europeans* came to *America*, they found here eight distinct nations of Indians, named respectively:

[1] This represents the meeting of General Oglethorpe, the founder of Georgia, with the Indians, at Savannah. To-mo-chi-chi, the famous Chief Sachem of the Creek Indians, presented to Oglethorpe the skin of a buffalo, on which was spread out an eagle. He desired Oglethorpe to accept it, because the eagle was an emblem of speed and the buffalo of strength, and the English, he said, were as swift as the bird and strong as the beast. They flew in their ships to the uttermost parts of the earth, and were too sharp for all other people. The feathers of the eagle, being soft, represented love; the buffalo skin was warm, and represented protection. "Therefore," he said, "I hope the English will love and protect our families."

| *Names of the Indian Nations.* | *Voyages of Columbus.* |

Huron-Iroquois,[1] **Algonquins,**[2] **Mobilians,**[3] **Cherokees,**[4] **Catawbas,**[5] **Uchees,**[6] **Natchez,**[7] and **Dacotahs.**[8] There was one of those nations, the **Tuscaroras,** who belonged to the *Huron-Algonquin* people, then located in *North Carolina.* For the position of these nations in our country, see the frontispiece map.

27. In this section we have considered—

(1) *The extent of our country* and its form of government ; (2) its *discovery by the Northmen* and by *Columbus;* and (3) the *character, habits and destiny* of the native inhabitants.

SECTION II.

SPANISH DISCOVERERS AND DISCOVERIES.

1. On his return to Spain, *Columbus* was received with great applause by the sovereigns and the people. The report of his discoveries, printed soon afterward, caused other exploring expeditions to be fitted out in *Spain.* *Columbus* himself made three other voyages across the *Atlantic* and back, in search of other lands.

2. The second voyage of *Columbus* was made in the autumn of 1493. The third voyage was undertaken in May, 1498, and on the first day of August he discovered the continent of **South America,** near the mouth of the *Orinoco River,* a few days after *Sebastian Cabot* had discovered *North America.* The fourth voyage was begun in May, 1502.

QUESTIONS.—26. Give me the names of the eight Indian nations. 27. What have you learned in this section ? Give a general account of these facts.

QUESTIONS.—1. What can you tell about the return of Columbus and his other voyages? 2. What other discoveries did he make ?

[1] *e-re-kwá.*   [2] *ahl-gôn-kin.*   [3] *mo-beel'-yun.*   [4] *cher-o-kees'.*   [5] *ka-taw'-bahs.*
[6] *u'-chees.*   [7] *nat'-chez.*   [8] *dah-kô-tahs.*

Death of Isabella and Columbus. *Americus Vespuccius.*

3. The fourth voyage of *Columbus* was made for the purpose of discovering a strait through which ships might pass from the *Gulf of Mexico* into the *Indian Ocean.* It was not found, and the now aged navigator returned to *Spain.* Queen *Isabella* died a few days after his arrival. Neglected and poor, the great discoverer died the next year, with the belief that he had seen the continent of *Asia* on its Eastern side. He did not suspect that he had discovered an unknown continent.

AMERICUS VESPUCCIUS.

4. *Americus Vespuccius,*[1] a *Florentine,* was in *Spain* when *Columbus* made his second and third voyages. He went with a former companion of *Columbus* to *South America* in 1499 ; and a year after the great navigator had discovered that continent, Vespucius saw it for the first time.

5. In a fraudulently dated letter, written in 1504, *Americus* claimed the honor of the first discovery. A German friend of his, in a printed work, suggested the name of **America** for the new-found continent, in compliment to the Florentine. Thus it was that our country received its title, and *Columbus* was cheated out of the deserved honor of having it bear his name.

6. Immediately after *Columbus* discovered the *West India Islands, Spanish* settlements were made on some

QUESTIONS.—3. Give an account of Columbus after his last voyage. 4. What can you tell about Americus Vespuccius? 5. How came America to be named in his honor?

[1] *ves-pu'-she-us.*

DISCOVERIES FROM 1492 TO 1609.

SPANISH DISCOVERERS AND DISCOVERIES. 23

Discovery of Florida and the Pacific Ocean. Conquest of Mexico.

of them, and expeditions were soon sent out from them in search of other lands. *Yucatan*[1] was discovered ; and in 1510 a settlement was made on the isthmus of *Darien.*[2]

7. *John Ponce de Leon,*[3] an old Spanish soldier in Porto Rico, having heard of a marvellous fountain in an island at the northward, whose waters would restore youth and make it perpetual, sailed in quest of it in 1512. He did not find the fountain, but he discovered a land fragrant with spring flowers, which he called **Florida.** It is yet so called.

BALBOA.

8. The next year (1513) *Vasco Nunez de Balboa*[4] ascended the highlands of the isthmus of *Darien,* and discovered a great ocean, which he took possession of in the name of Spain, and called it the *South Sea.* Six years later (1519) *Magellan,*[5] a *Portuguese,* sailed through the straits that bear his name, and over that sea, which he called the *Pacific Ocean,* because it was so free from storms.

9. Meanwhile *Spanish* adventurers had explored portions of *Yucatan* and *Mexico,* and thought they discovered evidences of much gold in the interior. *Hernando Cortez,* with a fleet and soldiers, went to conquer *Mexico* in 1519. He was successful. In 1521 *Mexico* became a *Spanish* province, and remained so just three hundred years.

QUESTIONS.—6. What followed the discoveries of Columbus? 7. What can you tell about the discovery of Florida? 8. Tell about the discovery of the Pacific Ocean, and its name. 9. What had other Spanish adventurers done? Tell about the conquest of Mexico.

[1] *yu-ka-tan'.*   [2] *day-re-en'.*   [3] *pone'-tha-da-la-on.*   [4] *vasco-noon-yez da bohl-bo'-a.*
[5] *ma-gel'-lan.*

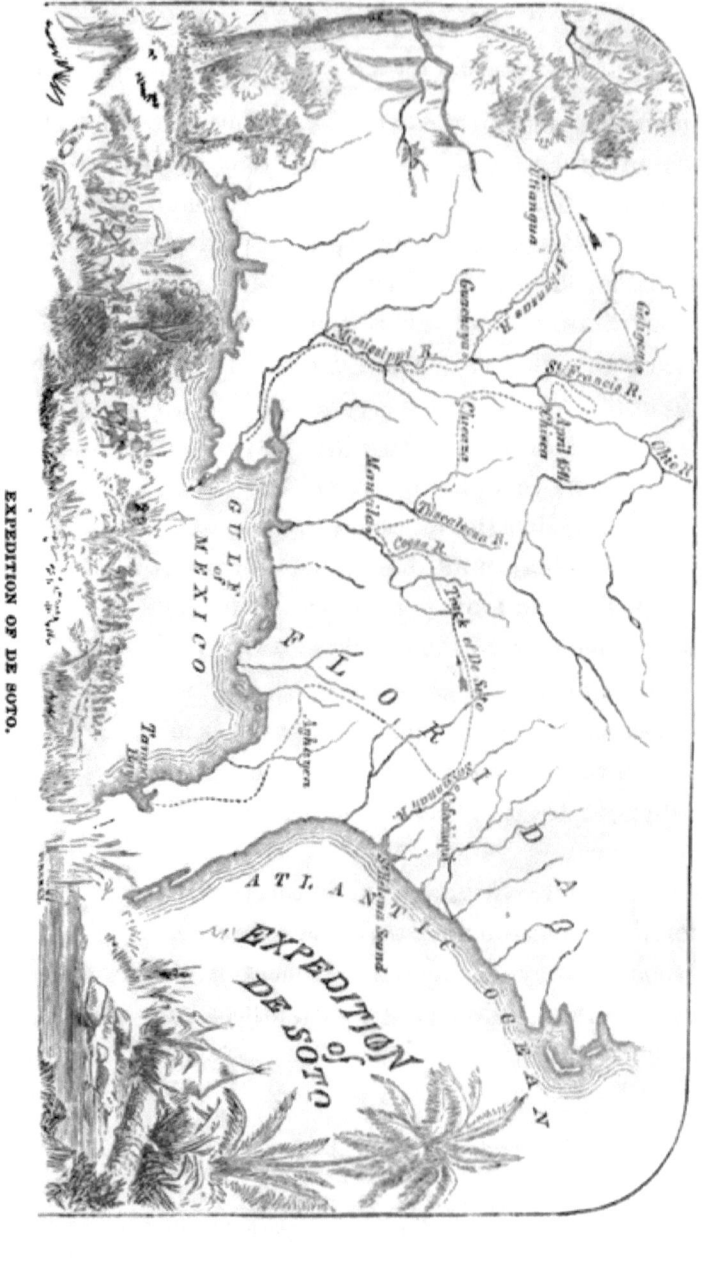

EXPEDITION OF DE SOTO.

10. The conquest of *Mexico* led to explorations northward of it, along the *Pacific* coast. *Cortez*, it is believed, discovered the *Gulf of California;* and in the course of a few years *Spanish* adventurers penetrated to *New Mexico,* up the *Colorado* [1] to the *Gila,* [2] and along the *Pacific* coast to *Oregon.* [3]

11. In 1520 a planter of *San Domingo,* named *D'Ayllon,* [4] went to the coast of *South Carolina* to kidnap natives for slaves. He treacherously carried away many of them. Whilst he was there a second time, and was preparing to make a settlement, the *Indians,* exasperated by his conduct, acted as treacherously as he, and murdered *D'Ayllon* and a large number of his followers.

12. Eight years later (1528) an adventurer named *Narvaez* [5] went from *Cuba* with ships and troops to conquer *Florida.* His cruel treatment of the *Indians* made them unite in efforts to expel him. He was obliged to leave the country in an open boat, and while on the waters of the *Gulf of Mexico,* he and most of his companions perished.

13. The bad conduct of *Narvaez* made the expedition of *De Soto* [6] to conquer *Florida,* a perilous and unsuccessful undertaking. *De Soto* was a rich *Spanish* cavalier and bold soldier, who had assisted *Pizarro* in conquering Peru, and shared with him in the plunder of the Incas.

DE SOTO.

14. *De Soto* had a splendid retinue of

[1] *kol-a-rah'-do.* [2] *he'-lah.* [3] *or-e-gon'.* [4] *da-ile-yone'.* [5] *nar'-rah-eth.* [6] *da-so'-to.*

BURIAL OF DE SOTO.

several hundred *Spaniards,* many of them mounted on horses. After wandering in the region bordering on the *Gulf of Mexico,* and far into the interior, for about two years, from 1539, fighting the *Indians* and searching for gold, he discovered the *Mississippi River.*

15. Crossing that great stream, *De Soto,* with the number of his followers greatly diminished, penetrated the country westward far toward the *Rocky Mountains.* Returning to the *Mississippi* in 1542, *De Soto* died there. His body was buried beneath the muddy waters of that stream. The remnant of his followers made their way, in a small vessel, to Mexico, taking with them some beautiful young *Mobilian* [1] women, their captives.

16. The same year in which *De Soto* died (1542) *Cabrillo* [2] first explored the coast of the present *State of California,* up to the borders of *Oregon.* It is believed that he discovered the *Bay of San Francisco.* Forty years afterward (1582) *Espejo* [3] explored *New Mexico* and founded **Santa Fe.** [4]

17. In this section we have considered—
(1) the *return of Columbus to Spain* and his three other voyages; (2) his *impressions* concerning his discovery; (3) the *voyage of Americus Vespuccius* and his claims ; (4) *discovery* of *Yucatan, Florida* and the *Pacific Ocean ;* (5) the *conquest of Mexico* and explorations northward; (6) *events* on the *coast of South Carolina ;*

QUESTIONS.—14. Give an account of De Soto in Florida, and his discovery of the Mississippi. 15. Give an account of his wanderings and death, and the fate of his followers. 16. What have you to say about explorations of California and New Mexico? 17. What have you learned in this section? Give a general account of the facts.

[1] *mo-beel'-yun.* [2] *kab-reel-you.* [3] *es-pay'-ho.* [4] *santa fay.*

(7) the *attempts of Narvaez* and *De Soto* to conquer *Florida ;* and (8) the *discovery of the Mississippi River.*

SECTION III.

ENGLISH AND FRENCH DISCOVERERS AND DISCOVERIES.

1. *Sebastian Cabot,*[1] son of a *Venetian* merchant in *England,* sailing from *Bristol* in search of a northwest passage to *India* beyond *Greenland,* discovered the continent of **North America,** on the coast of *Labrador,* late in June or early in July, 1498. That was a little while before *Columbus* discovered the continent of *South America.*

2. *Cabot* did not land on *Labrador.* He sailed far up the coast, and then turning southward, he discovered *Newfoundland* and the coasts of *Nova Scotia* and *Maine.* He probably went as far South as *North Carolina.* Then he returned to *England* and told of his great

SEBASTIAN CABOT. discovery.

3. *Cabot* was only about twenty-one years of age when he discovered *America.* That made him famous, and he made other voyages of discovery from *England* and *Spain.* He had told of the great number of codfishes seen off the coast of *Newfoundland.* *English* and *French* fishermen soon went there to catch them, and this led to discoveries and settlements on the adjacent shores.

QUESTIONS.—1. What can you tell about the discovery of America by Sebastian Cabot ? 2. What portion did he discover ? 3. What were the effects of his discoveries ?

[1] *kah'-bot.*

4. A *Florentine* named *Verazzani*,[1] employed by the King of *France,* crossed the *Atlantic* in 1524, and touched the *American Continent* near *Cape Fear,* in *North Carolina.* He sailed northward as far as *Nova Scotia,* entering bays and rivers on his way, took possession of the country in the name of the *French* King, and called the country **New France.**

VERAZZANI.

BANKS OF THE ST. LAWRENCE.

QUESTIONS.—4. What can you tell about the discoveries of Verazzani?

[1] *ver-at-sah'-ne.*

5. Ten years after *Verazzani's* voyage, *Jaques Cartier,*[1] of *St. Malo,* in *France,* sailed for *America.* He first landed on *Newfoundland,* and there discovered and named the *Gulf* and *River St. Lawrence,* the discovery having been made on the festival of that saint. He, also, took possession of that region in the name of the *French* monarch. He was thus the discoverer of *Canada.*

CARTIER'S SHIP.

6. In the following spring (1535) *Cartier* made another voyage to the *St. Lawrence.* From the site of *Quebec*[2] he went up the river in a boat to *Hochelaga,* an *Indian* town. Charmed with the view from a great hill near, he called it *Mont Real* (Royal Mountain), and the *French* city built on the site of *Hochelaga*[3] was called **Montreal.**

7. *Cartier* made a third voyage to the *St. Lawrence* in 1541, with some men, to settle there. He had carried off the *Indian* "King of *Canada*" on his last visit, and the natives were unfriendly. The *Frenchmen* built a fort near *Quebec,* spent a hard winter there, and in the spring of 1542, at about the time *De Soto* was dying on the *Mississippi,* they abandoned the country.

8. *France* was now disturbed by bitter quarrels between the Roman Catholics and the Protestants. As the Roman Catholics were the most numerous, they deprived the Prot-

QUESTIONS.—5. What can you tell of the discoveries of Cartier? 6. What did Cartier do on the St. Lawrence? 7. What did he do on the St. Lawrence on a third voyage? 8. What can you tell about two parties in France?

[1] *kar'-te-ay.* [2] *ke-bek'.* [3] *hosh-e-lah'-ga.*

estants of many privileges in Church and State, and made them discontented.

9. Admiral *Coligny,*[1] an eminent soldier of *France,* was a Protestant. He wished to have his friends settled where they might not be molested. In the spring of 1562 he sent a colony of them to *America* to found a settlement to which others might go. They were led by a worthy man named *Ribault.*[2]

10. The *Huguenots,*[3] as the *French* Protestants were called, landed on an island near the shores of *South Carolina,* where they built a fort. *Ribault* returned to Europe for supplies. Many of the settlers died, and the remnant, fearing starvation, started for home in a weak vessel.

FRENCHMAN IN 1560

11. These colonists suffered from starvation at sea, and the few who were left were about to perish, when they were picked up on the ocean and taken to *England.* Their story of the beautiful land they had abandoned caused *Englishmen* to make attempts to settle in that region.

12. In 1564 *Coligny* sent over another colony, in three ships, under *Laudonniere.*[4] They settled on the *St. Johns River,* in *Florida,* and built a fort there. *Spain* claimed ownership of all that region by right of discovery, and sent *Melendez,*[5] or *Menendez,* a brave naval officer, to drive

QUESTIONS.—9. Who was Admiral Coligny, and what did he do? 10. What were the French Protestants called? Where did they settle, and what did they do? 11. What happened to the Huguenots? 12. What can you tell about another colony sent by Coligny? What happened to them?

[1] *ko-leen'-ye.*   [2] *re'-bo.*   [3] *hug'-nots.*   [4] *law-don'-e-a.*   [5] *ma-len'-deth.*

BUILDING THE FORT.

FRENCH SOLDIER IN
FLORIDA.

away the *Frenchmen*. He laid the foundations of the city of *St. Augustine*,[1] and then proceeded to murder the *Huguenots* on the St. Johns.

13. The *French* King did not resent this cruel massacre. One of his subjects, named *De Gourges*,[2] did. He came with ships and soldiers, in 1567, and destroyed nearly all the *Spaniards*. So ended, for a time, all attempts of *Frenchmen* to colonize *America*.

14. Again *English* navigators tried to

QUESTION.—13. What did a French soldier do?

[1] *aw-gus'-teen.*   [2] *da-goorg'.*

find the northwest passage for which *Cabot* sought. *Martin Frobisher* made three voyages on that errand, but failed.

15. In 1578 *Francis Drake* went through the *Straits of Magellan;* sailed up the *Pacific Coast;* plundered *Spanish* settlements in *Peru;* discovered the coasts of *California, Oregon,* and *Washington Territory* (1579), and made a voyage around the world. He named our Western coast New Albion.

16. *Walter Raleigh,*[1] a wealthy and energetic young *Englishman,* who had been a soldier under *Coligny,* in *France,* was now a favorite of *Queen Elizabeth.* He procured for his step-brother, *Sir Humphrey Gilbert,* the Queen's permission to plant a colony in the warmer regions of *America.*

WALTER RALEIGH.

17. Early in 1579, *Gilbert,* who was an eminent navigator, sailed for *America* with a number of followers. Storms and *Spanish* cruisers drove him back. He sailed again, with emigrants, four years later (1583), stayed awhile at *Newfoundland,* and on a voyage off the coast of *Nova Scotia* he and his ship perished in a storm.

18. *Raleigh* now fitted out two ships at his own expense, and sent them to *America.* They reached the coast of *North Carolina* in July, 1584. The people landed

Questions.—14. What did English navigators do? 15. What can you tell about Sir Francis Drake? 16. Who was Sir Walter Raleigh, and what did he do? 17. What can you tell about Sir Humphrey Gilbert? 18. What can you tell about an expedition sent out by Raleigh?

[1] *raw'-le.*

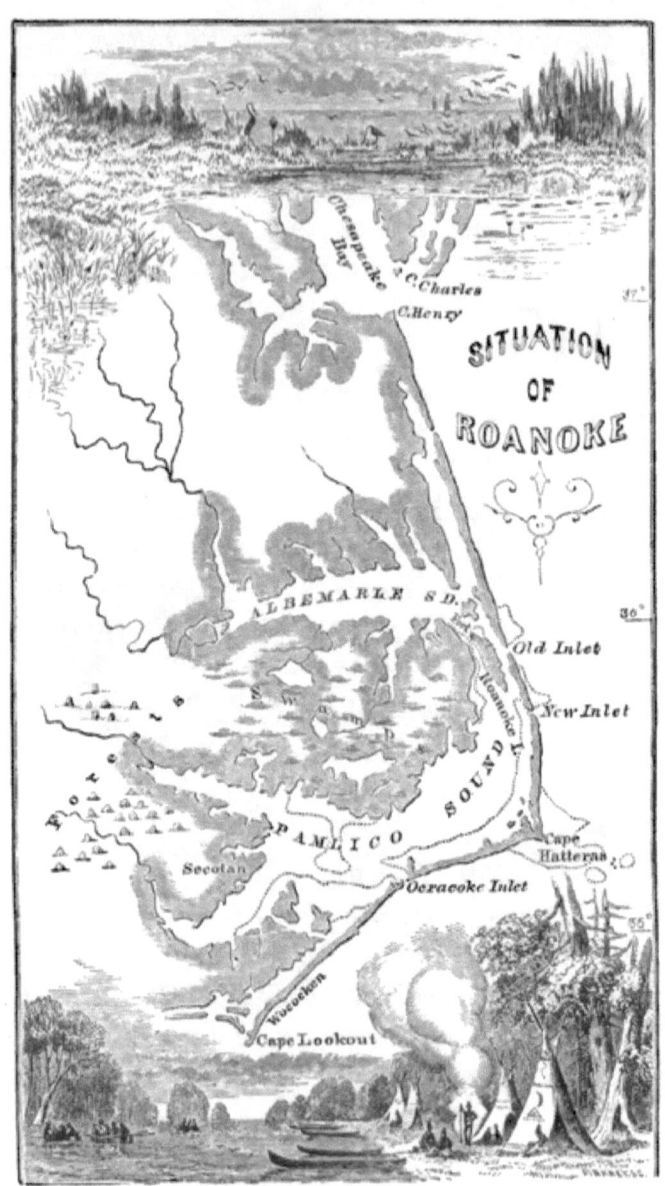

SITUATION OF ROANOKE.

on *Roanoke Island,* and after trading with the *Indians* and exploring the country near, they returned to *England,* accompanied by two native chiefs.

ENGLISH GENTLEMAN, 1580.

19. When *Barlow* and *Amidas,*[1] commanders of the vessels, told *Raleigh* of the beauty and grandeur of the region they had visited, he was delighted. So also was the Queen ; and she gave the name of **Virginia** to this region which *Verazzani* had called **New France** sixty years before.

20. The following year (1585) *Raleigh* sent five ships to America under Sir *Richard Grenville,* with one hundred emigrants, and *Ralph Lane* as governor. They and their governor were gold-seekers, and did not cultivate the soil. They offended the *Indians* by bad conduct, and were in great peril.

21. When they were on the point of perishing from starvation or the weapons of the *Indians,* Sir *Francis Drake* appeared at *Roanoke Island,* and bore the emigrants back to *England.* This was in 1586.

RALEIGH'S SHIP.

22. Learning wisdom by experience, *Raleigh* sent out mechanics and farmers, with their families, to plant a colony. This was in 1587. *John White* was their governor. His daughter and her husband,

QUESTIONS.—19. What effect did the report of the sailors have ? 20. What can you tell about another expedition sent by Raleigh ? 21. How was a colony saved ? 22. What can you tell about a third expedition sent by Raleigh ? What happened in the colony ?

[1] *am'-i-das.*

named Dare, were with him. There she gave birth to a girl, whom they named *Virginia*. *Virginia Dare* was the **first English child** born in *America*.

23. Governor *White* went to England for supplies. He was gone very long, and when he returned the colonists had disappeared, and were never heard of afterward. *Raleigh* did not send any more colonies to *America*.

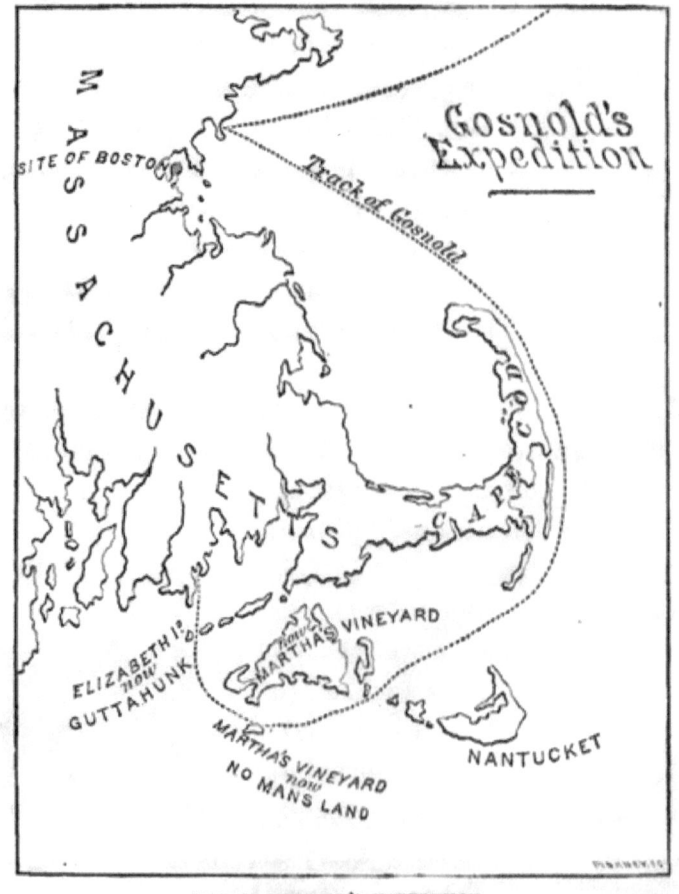

MAP OF GOSNOLD'S EXPEDITION.

QUESTIONS.—23. What was the fate of Raleigh's last colony?

24. In 1602, *Bartholomew Gosnold* crossed the ocean and visited a part of the coast of *Massachusetts*. He discovered a long cape, and because of the many codfishes which he saw there, he named it **Cape Cod.** On one of a group of islands, which he named *Elizabeth,* in honor of his Queen, he attempted to plant a colony, but failed.

25. In 1603, *Martin Pring,* an English sailor, discovered the coast of *Maine* and explored the shores of **New England** westward to *Martha's Vineyard.* In 1605, Captain *Weymouth,* another sailor, visited *Maine,* and there kidnapped some *Indians.* This crime made the natives hate the white people, and they gave the *English* much trouble afterward.

26. At this time the *French* tried again to make settlements in *America.* *De Monts,*[1] a wealthy Protestant, obtained a grant from his King for that purpose, and in 1604 and 1605 he planted a colony on what is now *Nova Scotia,* and called the country **Acadia.**[2]

27. *De Monts* sent *Samuel Champlain* to the *St. Lawrence* in 1608. There he planted a settlement and named the place **Quebec.** It is the oldest *French* settlement in *America,* for the others were short-lived. In 1609, *Champlain* discovered the lake that bears his name.

28. In 1607, some London merchants sent *Henry Hudson* to search for a northwest passage to *India.* He made two voyages, but failed, and the project was abandoned.

29. In 1609, *Hudson* offered his services to the **Dutch**

QUESTIONS.—24. What can you tell about Gosnold's voyage and discoveries? 25. What can you tell about other English sailors? 26. What can you tell about French settlements in America? 27. Tell about the voyage and discoveries of Champlain. 28. What can you tell about Hudson?

[1] *deh-mong'.*   [2] *ah-ka'-de-a.*

East India Company, at *Amsterdam,* in searching for a passage to *India* around the north of *Europe.* They sent him in a small vessel called the *Half Moon.* Ice covered the sea in that direction, and he sailed westward to *America.*

HUDSON.

30. Early in September, 1609, Hudson entered *New York Harbor.*

HALF-MOON.

He explored the river that bears his name as far up as the site of *Albany.* This discovery led to a traffic in furs between the *Dutch* and the *Indians,* and then to the founding of a settlement on the site of *New York.*

31. *Hudson* afterward discovered the great bay in the far north which bears his name. There some of his sailors, who rebelled, put *Hudson* and his son, with seven sick companions, in an open boat, and set them adrift to perish on the deep with cold and hunger.

32. In this section we have considered—

(1) The *discovery of America by Cabot* and *Verazzani ;* (2) the discovery of the *St. Lawrence* and *Canada* by *Cartier ;* (3) the attempts of *Coligny* to *found a colony in Florida,* and the *cruelty of the Spaniards there ;* (4) the voyages of *Frobisher* and *Drake,* the latter to the *Pacific coast ;* (5) the *failures of Raleigh* to make settlements ;

QUESTIONS.—29. What else did Hudson attempt ? 30. What discoveries did he make, and what did they lead to ? 31. What did Hudson afterward discover, and what was his fate ? 32. What have we considered in this section ?

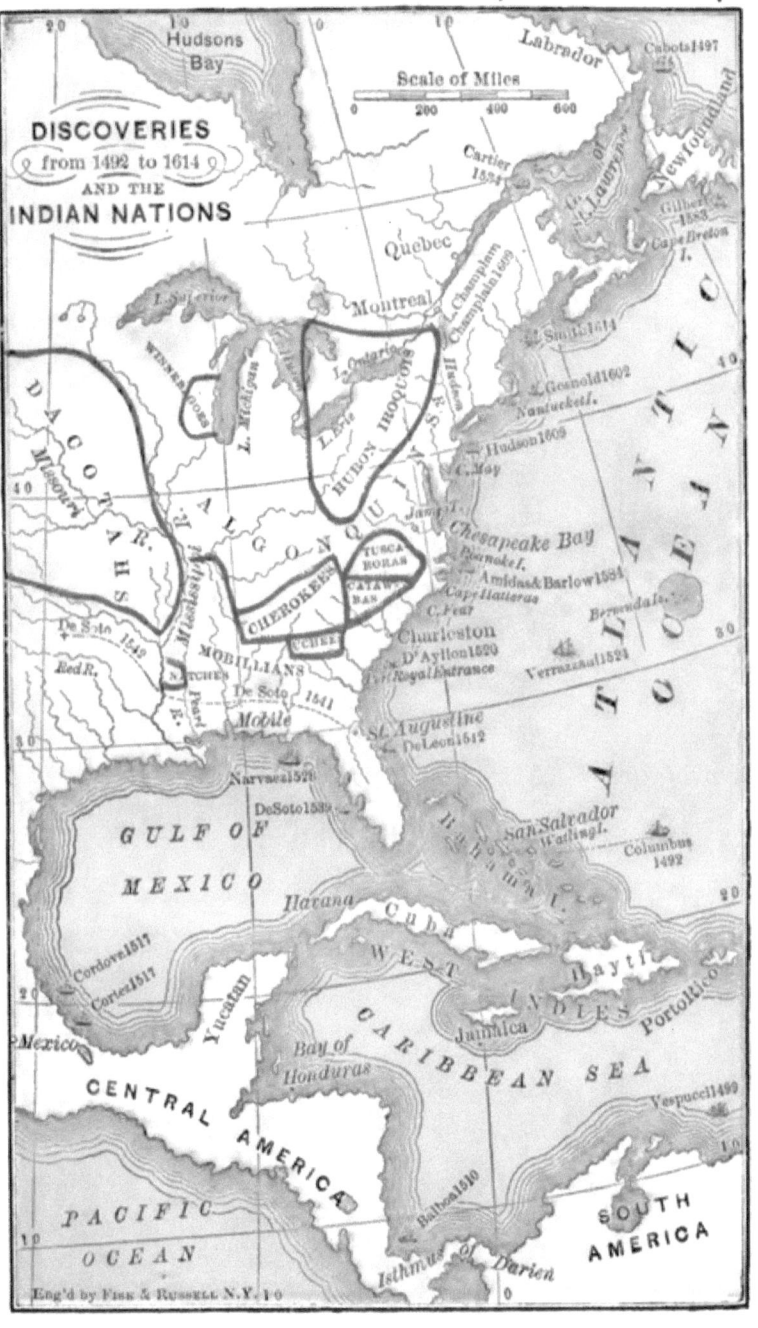

DISCOVERIES

from 1492 to 1614

AND THE

INDIAN NATIONS

(6) *explorations of the New England coasts;* (7) the *French settlements in Acadia* and in *Canada;* and (8) the *discovery of the Hudson River.*

OUTLINE OF IMPORTANT EVENTS FROM 1002 TO 1609.*

1002. America discovered by Northmen.

1492. American islands discovered by Columbus.

1498. North American Continent discovered by Sebastian Cabot.

1498. South American Continent discovered by Columbus.

1499. The American Continent first seen by Americus Vespuccius.

1504. The name of America given to our Continent in honor of Americus Vespuccius.

1510. Settlement made on the Isthmus of Darien.

1512. Florida discovered by John Ponce de Leon.

1513. The Pacific Ocean discovered by Vasco Nuñez de Balboa.

1517–1518. Coasts of Yucatan and Mexico explored.

1519. Straits of Magellan discovered.

1519–1521. Mexico conquered by Cortez.

1520. D'Ayllon visits the coasts of South Carolina and kidnaps Indians.

1524. Verazzani explores the coasts of North America from the Carolinas to Nova Scotia.

1528. Narvaez attempts to conquer Florida.

1534. Cartier discovers the Gulf and River St. Lawrence.

1535–1541. Cartier explores the St. Lawrence and winters at Quebec.

1539–1541. De Soto attempts to conquer Florida.

1542. Cabrillo explores the coasts of California and Oregon.

1562. Coligny attempts to settle French Protestants in Florida.

1564. Coligny sends another colony to Florida. They are massacred by the Spaniards.

1567. De Gourges destroys the Spaniards in Florida.

1579. Francis Drake visits the coasts of California, Oregon and Washington Territory.

1582. Espejo explores New Mexico.

1584. Walter Raleigh sends an expedition to the coasts of North Carolina. The country named Virginia.

1585. Raleigh plants a settlement on Roanoke Island.

* This outline is for the use of the teacher and pupil. The teacher may find in each topic, suggestions for queries, to which answers, without reference to the text, may be given by the pupil, orally or in writing on paper or on the blackboard. The written exercise is recommended as the best for giving essential aid to the memory in retaining facts. A pattern may be found on the next page.

Outline of Important Events.	*Pattern for a Synopsis.*

1586. The Roanoke settlers return to England.

1587. Raleigh sends another colony to Virginia. It was lost.

1602. Gosnold discovers the coasts of Massachusetts and names Cape Cod.

1603–1604. Martin Pring explores the New England coasts.

1604–1605. The French plant a colony in Nova Scotia and call the country Acadia.

1605. Captain Weymouth visits New England and kidnaps Indians.

1608. Champlain founds Quebec.

1609. Champlain discovers Lake Champlain.

1609. Henry Hudson discovers the Bay of New York and the North or Hudson River.

The following is a pattern for the pupil in making a synopsis or outline sketch of a subject :

TOPIC: SIR WALTER RALEIGH.

Walter Raleigh: His Efforts to plant a Colony in America.

PERSONAL NOTES.
- A young *Englishman.*
- A soldier under *Coligny,* in *France.*
- A favorite of *Queen Elizabeth.*

RALEIGH'S STEP-BROTHER, HUMPHREY GILBERT.
- Receives a commission from *Queen Elizabeth.*
- Sails for *America* in 1579.
- Driven back by storms and *Spanish* cruisers.
- Visits *America* and perishes in a storm at sea.

RALEIGH'S NAVIGATORS.
- *Amidas* and *Barlow* sail for *America* in 1584.
- Land on *Roanoke Island* and explore the neighboring regions.
- Return to *England* with a good report.

EFFECT OF THE NAVIGATORS' REPORT.
- *Raleigh* and the *Queen* delighted.
- The Queen names a portion of *New France, Virginia.*

OTHER PERSONS SENT TO AMERICA BY RALEIGH.
- Five ships under Sir *Richard Grenville* sail for *Roanoke* in 1585.
- Emigrants land on *Roanoke Island* and search for gold.
- They offend the *Indians,* and are in great peril.
- They are taken back to *England* by Sir *Francis Drake.*

END OF RALEIGH'S EFFORTS TO PLANT A COLONY IN AMERICA.
- Raleigh sends farmers and mechanics to plant a colony in *America* in 1587.
- *John White* governor of the colony.
- *Virginia Dare,* grand-daughter of Governor *White,* born on *Roanoke Island.*
- *Virginia Dare* the first English child born in *America.*
- While *White* was in *England,* the colony disappears forever.
- *Raleigh* sends no more ships to *America.*

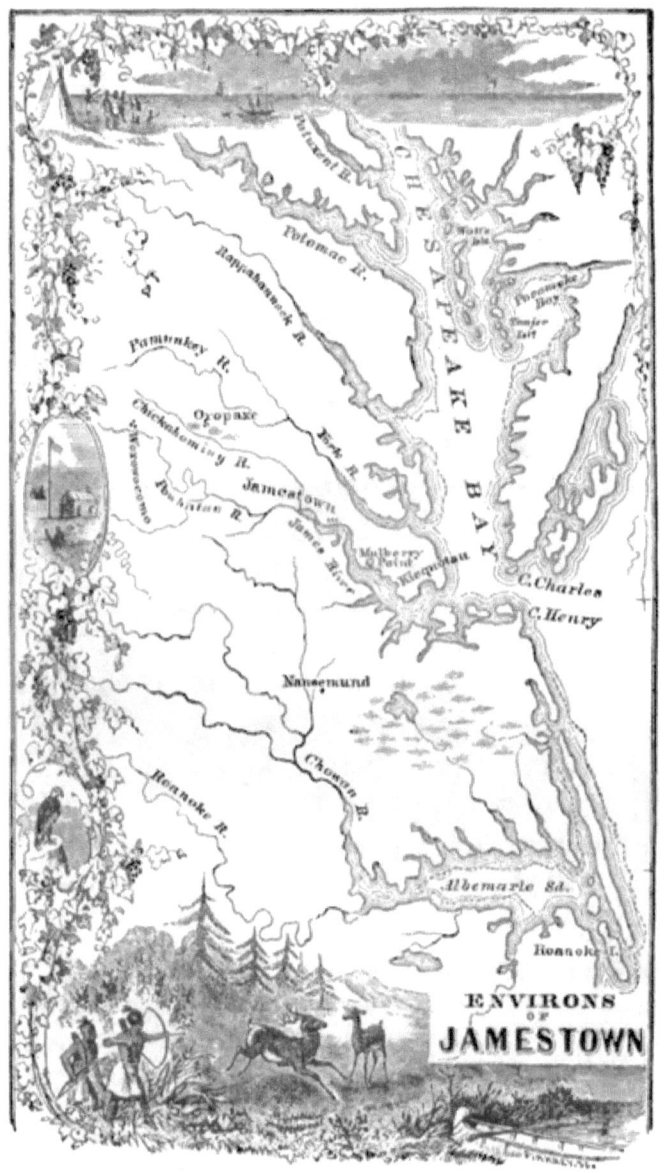

ENVIRONS
OF
JAMESTOWN

42   SETTLERS AND SETTLEMENTS.

Discoveries and Planting of Settlements.   Virginia and its Divisions.

CHAPTER II.

SETTLERS AND SETTLEMENTS.

SECTION I.

SETTLERS AND SETTLEMENTS IN VIRGINIA.

1. We have considered the principal events in the **discovery** of different parts of *America.* By these discoveries different nations claimed a right to the country. These were the *Spanish, French, English* and *Dutch* nations. The *English* claimed a right to the whole region across the continent, in width, from *Cape Fear,* in *North Carolina,* to *Halifax,* in *Nova Scotia.*

2. We will now notice the **planting of settlements** in parts of *America* where *Colonies* and *States* have since existed. We will notice them in the order of time in which settlements were first made, beginning with *Virginia.*

3. This domain was divided into *North* and *South Virginia.* In 1606, King *James* of *England* gave a charter or written agreement, by which a number of persons were permitted to make settlements in *Virginia.* They formed two associations. One was named the **Plymouth**[1] **Company,** and the other the **London Company.**

4. The *Plymouth Company* were authorized to make settlements in *North Virginia.* The *London Company*

QUESTIONS.—1. What have we considered? What can you tell about different claims? 2. How will we notice the planting of settlements? 3. How was Virginia divided? What companies were formed? 4. What privilege had each company?

[1] *plim'-uth.*

were allowed to do the same in *South Virginia*. The *Plymouth Company* made the first attempts at settlement, but failed.

5. In December, 1606, the *London Company* sent Captain *Newport,* with three ships and one hundred and five men, to make a settlement on *Roanoke Island*. The ships were driven by a storm into *Chesapeake*[1] *Bay*. They sailed up a broad river more than fifty miles, and landed at a place which they afterward called *Jamestown*. The river they called the *James.*

6. It was in April, 1607, when the emigrants landed. The King had appointed certain persons among them to govern the colony. Among these was Captain *John Smith,* a great soldier, and *Bartholomew Gosnold,*[2] who had proposed the expedition. *Edward Wingfield* was chosen to be president of this council.

JOHN SMITH.

7. Most of the emigrants were unfit to be the **founders of a colony.** They had come without families, to make a fortune by digging gold, and then to return. Many of them were idle. Some of them were vicious. The president turned out to be a knave.

8. *Virginia* was then inhabited by *Indians*. They were ruled by an emperor called *Powhatan*.[3] He lived on the

QUESTIONS.—5. What did the London Company do? What happened? 6. What can you tell about the emigrants in Virginia? 7. What was their character? 8. What can you tell about the inhabitants and their monarch?

¹ *ches'-a-peek.* ² *goz'-nold.* ³ *pow-hah-tan'*

banks of the *James River,* near the site of *Richmond.* *Smith* and *Newport* visited him there, and were kindly received.

9. In June, *Newport* sailed for England with the ships, leaving a small vessel at *Jamestown.* The idle settlers would not work. The food they had brought with them was gone before the close of summer, for much had been spoiled on the voyage. They had raised almost nothing from the soil, and the Indians, who were unfriendly, would not bring them corn.

10. Famine came and with it sickness. Early in September **one-half of the settlers were dead.** Captain *Smith* went down to the mouth of the *James,* and by his courage and energy compelled the *Indians* there to bring him large quantities of corn, with which he returned to *Jamestown* and **saved the colony from starvation.**

11. When he returned, President *Wingfield* and a few others were about to go away with the small vessel and what was left of the stores, when *Smith,* by force of arms, compelled him to stay. Soon after that *Smith* was chosen to be president of the colony.

12. In October, wild fowl became plentiful on the waters, and corn was procured from the abundant crop of the *Indians.* When order and abundance were restored, Captain *Smith* and a few others went up the *Chickahominy*[1] *River* in a boat, where he was made a prisoner by the

---

QUESTIONS.—9. How did the settlers act? 10. What can you tell about famine and sickness, and the services of Captain Smith? 11. What can you tell about President Wingfield and his successor? 12. What was now the condition of the colony? What about Captain Smith?

[1] *chick-a-hom'-i-ny.*

SETTLERS AND SETTLEMENTS. 45

Captain Smith and Pocahontas.   Arrival of other Emigrants.

Indians. He was taken to another dwelling of *Powhatan,* on the *York River.*

POCAHONTAS.

13. After much consultation, the Indians concluded to put *Smith* to death. His head was laid upon a large stone, and two warriors had raised their clubs to beat out his brains, when *Pocahontas,*[1] the favorite daughter of *Powhatan,* sprang from her father's side, clasped the head of Smith with her arms, and begged for his life. Her request was granted, and *Smith* was sent back to *Jamestown.*

14. The colony was again starving. It was winter. Only forty were living when *Smith* returned, and these were preparing to leave *Virginia,* and go to the *West Indies.* *Smith* again procured food, and they remained. In the spring of 1608, *Newport* came with supplies and a company of emigrants, when the hopes of the first settlers were revived.

15. The new emigrants were no better than the first. They were mostly **gold-hunters,** and would not work. *Smith* turned from *Jamestown* with disgust for a while, and with a few companions he explored *Chesapeake*[2] *Bay* and its tributary streams, in an open boat. In this way, in the course of three months, they voyaged about **three thousand miles.** Smith made a *map* of the country he had explored.

QUESTIONS.—13. Tell the story of Captain Smith and Pocahontas. 14. What did Smith find and what did he do at Jamestown? 15. What can you tell about new emigrants, and what did Smith do in the way of explorations?

[1] *po-kah-hon'-tas.*   [2] *ches'-a-peek.*

THE EXPLORERS AND THEIR BOAT.

16. In the autumn *Newport* came again, with emigrants. With them were two **women**, the first who had ever come from *Europe* to *Virginia*. The men who then came were of the same sort as the others. *Smith* tried to induce them to cultivate the soil, but they would not. *Laziness* afflicted most of the settlers, and at the end of two years they had not more than forty acres under tillage.

17. The *London Company* obtained a new charter in 1609, by which the management of the colony was put in the hands of a governor with a council. Under this second charter, Lord *De la Warr* (*Delaware*[1]) was appointed governor for life. Sir *Thomas Gates*, Sir *George Somers*[2] and Captain *Newport* were appointed commissioners to manage the colony until the arrival of the governor.

18. In June, *Newport* sailed with nine ships and five hundred emigrants. *Gates* and *Somers* sailed in the same vessel with *Newport*. A storm scattered the fleet, and *Newport's* ship was wrecked on one of the *Bermuda* islands.

19. Seven vessels reached *Jamestown* in safety, with most of the emigrants. It was a more vicious company than any which had yet arrived. In the autumn, an accident compelled Captain *Smith* to go to *England*. Left to themselves, the lawless colony so offended the *Indians* that the savages refused to let them have food, and resolved to kill all the *Englishmen*. The settlers were saved by a timely warning from the good and loving *Pocahontas*.

QUESTIONS.—16. Who came with Newport? What about the men? 17. What can you tell about a second charter and appointments under it? 18. Tell about a large emigration to Virginia. 19. What was the character of the emigrants, and how did they act? How were they saved?

[1] *del'-ah-ware.* [2] *sum'-mers.*

EARLY EMIGRANTS.

20. Famine did much of the work which the *Indians* had conspired to do. The winter and spring of 1610 was long remembered as **"the starving time."** Within six months after *Smith* left only sixty of the five hundred settlers were alive.

21. When the commissioners reached *Jamestown*, in June, the prospect was so gloomy, that they resolved to abandon *Virginia*, and go to *Newfoundland*. When they reached the mouth of the *James* in their vessels, they met a small squadron coming in. *Lord Delaware* had arrived with food and emigrants. The whole company were resting at *Jamestown* that night.

22. Now there was a **happy change.** Six ships with three hundred emigrants came in 1611. They were mostly *sober and industrious men,* who tilled the ground and made food abundant. The colony flourished, and in 1613 there were a **thousand Englishmen** in *Virginia,* when an event happened that affected the colony favorably.

23. That event was the **kidnapping of Pocahontas** by Captain *Argall*,[1] a sort of freebooter. Her father was sullen and unfriendly. Food had become scarce at *Jamestown,* and *Powhatan* would not allow any to be carried there. *Argall* declared that he would not give up *Pocahontas* until food should be sent. Her father was firm, and she remained a prisoner several months.

24. Meanwhile *John Rolfe*,[1] a well-born Englishman, fell in love with *Pocahontas,* and they wished to be married.

QUESTIONS.—20. What can you tell about the "starving time?" 21. What did the commissioners attempt to do, and what occurred? 22. What happy change occurred? 23. What remarkable event happened? What can you tell about Captain Argall? 24. What can you tell about the marriage of Pocahontas and its result?

[1] *ar'-gaul.* [2] *rolf.*

MARRIAGE OF POCAHONTAS.

Her father gave his consent, and they were married in the church at *Jamestown* in April, 1613. *Powhatan* was the friend of the *English* ever afterward. *Pocahontas* went to *England* with her husband, and there died.

25. Under a third charter, obtained in 1612, the *London Company* permitted the establishment of a **representative government** in *Virginia*. The colony was divided

QUESTIONS.—25. What good thing occurred under a third charter?

into counties. Each county was allowed two representatives, called burgesses, in a general assembly. In June, 1619, when *George Yeardly* was governor, the **first representative assembly** met at *Jamestown*. Then was laid the foundation of the **State of Virginia.**

26. We have considered in this section—

(1) The *nationalities of the discoverers* and the claims of the *English;* (2) the *divisions of Virginia* and the companies formed to colonize it ; (3) the companies of *settlers* sent there ; (4) the *progress* and *suffering* of the colony and the career of *Captain Smith;* (5) the services and marriage of *Pocahontas;* and (6) the establishment of *Representative Government.*

SECTION II.

SETTLERS AND SETTLEMENTS IN NEW YORK, MASSACHUSETTS AND NEW HAMPSHIRE.

1. We have observed that the discoveries of *Hudson* led to traffic, and the founding of a colony on the site of *New York.* One of the greatest of the *Dutch* seamen who came to the mouth of the *Hudson River* to trade was *Adrian Block,* who landed on the lower part of *Manhattan Island,* on which the city of *New York* now stands.

2. Late in 1613, *Block's* ship was burnt. During the following winter he and his men built another, and in it they sailed through *Long Island Sound,* discovering the *Con-*

QUESTIONS.—26. What have we considered in this section?

QUESTIONS.—1. What can you tell about a great Dutch seaman? 2. What can you tell about his ship and his explorations?

52   SETTLERS AND SETTLEMENTS.

New Netherland and Dutch West India Company.   Settlements.

necticut[1] *River* and other considerable streams, extending their explorations as far as the coasts of *Massachusetts.*

3. In 1614, the government of *Holland* granted exclusive permission to certain *Amsterdam* merchants to traffic on the *Hudson* and in the territory then included in *North Virginia.* This territory the *Dutch* or *Holland* people claimed as theirs, by right of discovery, and called the country **New Netherland.**[2]

DUTCHMAN [1620].

4. The vessels of these merchants went up the *Hudson* to the site of *Albany,* southward to the *Delaware,* and eastward to *Rhode*[3] *Island,* on trading voyages. These traders built a fort near the head of the tide-waters of the Hudson, and named it *Fort Orange.*

SEAL OF NEW NETHER-
LAND.

5. In 1621, these merchants and others formed the **Dutch West India Company.** They bought *Manhattan*[4] *Island,* at the mouth of the *Hudson,* from the Indians, for about twenty-five dollars; and *New Netherland* was made a province of *Holland.*

6. The **settlement of families** in *New Netherland* was desirable, and in 1623 about thirty families of *French Protestants,* who had lived in *Holland,* came over the sea to *Manhattan.* Some settled there; some founded a set-

---

QUESTIONS—**3.** What did the government of Holland do, and what was the result? **4.** What did Dutch vessels do? **5.** What can you tell about the Dutch West India Company and the island of Manhattan? **6.** What can you tell about colonizing New Netherland?

[1] *kon-net'-i-cut.*   [2] *neth'-er-land.*   [3] *rode.*   [4] *man-hat'-tan.*

SETTLERS AND SETTLEMENTS. 53

New England Explored. Permanent Settlements there. The Puritans.

tlement at *Fort Orange,* now *Albany,* and some young married couples located on the *Delaware River.*

7. Thus was established the colony of **New Netherland.** The city that grew on *Manhattan* was called **New Amsterdam.**[1] Both the province and city were afterward named **New York.**

8. We have observed that the *Plymouth Company* had made vain efforts to plant colonies in *North Virginia.* So early as 1614, Captain *John Smith* had explored the northeastern coasts of *America* from *Cape Cod* to the *Penobscot*[2] *River,* and made a map of the region, which he called **New England.**[3]

9. It was not until 1620 that a **permanent settlement** was made in *New England.* What the *Plymouth Company,* an association of rich speculators, failed to do, was done by a few humble Christian men and women. At that

A PURITAN.

time there was a large class of Protestants in *England,* who, because of the purity of their professions and lives, were called **Puritans.** These, as well as *Roman Catholics,* were persecuted by King *James* of *England* and the leaders in the church of *England.*

10. These *Puritans* were so annoyed, that many of them went to *Holland,* where they could worship *God* as they pleased. But they were obliged to go secretly. A

QUESTIONS.—7. What can you tell about the change of names? 8. What can you tell about explorations on the New England coasts? 9. Give an account of the Puritans, and how they were treated. 10. What did the Puritans do?

[1] *am'-ster-dam'.*   [2] *pe-nob'-scot.*   [3] *ing'-land.*

Attempted Embarkation for Holland.

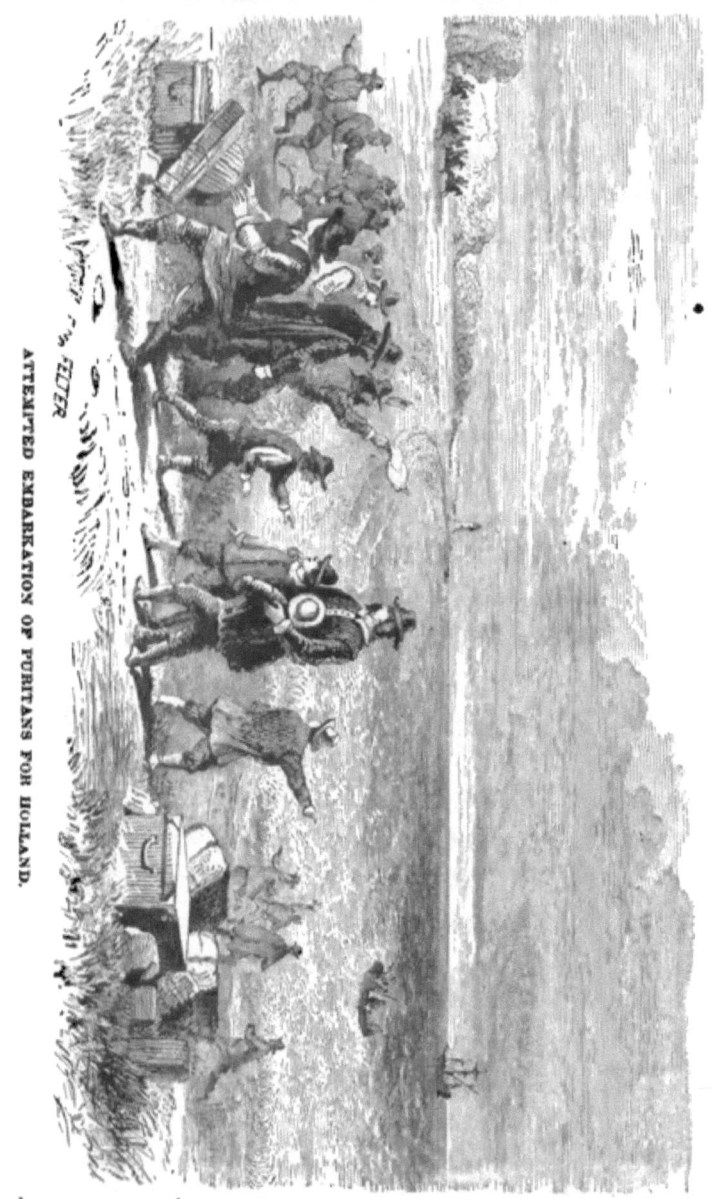

ATTEMPTED EMBARKATION OF PURITANS FOR HOLLAND.

whole congregation trying to get on board a *Dutch* vessel on the coast of *England*, were surprised by a party of horsemen sent to prevent their going. Some had embarked, and some, with women and children, were left on shore. But all got to *Holland* finally.

11. At *Leyden,*[1] in *Holland,* these Puritans formed a church, with *John Robinson* as their pastor. They concluded to plant a free colony in *America,* under the dominion of their native country. A bargain was made with the *Plymouth Company,* and a partnership was formed with

London merchants for planting a colony. In September, 1620, "the youngest and best" of the *Leyden* congregation, who went to *England,* left *Plymouth* in the *May-Flower,* in charge of *Elder Brewster.*

12. These "**Pilgrims,**" as they called themselves, one hun-

MAY-FLOWER.

dred and one in number, including women and children, arrived at *Cape Cod* in December, and landed on the shores of *Massachusetts* on the 22d of that month, at a place they called *Plymouth.* On the lid of Elder *Brewster's* chest, in the cabin of the *May-Flower,* they had signed an agreement for the government of the colony, and chose *John Carver* to be their governor. Thus they laid the basis of a **State.**

13. Log-huts were built in the snow. Here they passed a severe winter in extreme suffering. At one time only

QUESTIONS.—11. Give an account of the Puritans in Holland, and what they did. 12. Who were the "Pilgrims?" Tell about their coming to America. 13. Give an account of the sufferings of the "Pilgrims."

<hr />

[1] *li'-den.*

The Puritan Government in New England.

SIGNING THE COMPACT IN THE CABIN OF THE MAY-FLOWER.

seven persons were well enough to take care of the sick.
Before spring came one-half of the *Pilgrims* had died.

Governor *Carver* and his wife perished ; and *William Bradford* was chosen governor in his place.

GOV. CARVER'S CHAIR.

14. The survivors of that dreadful winter persevered. They built houses, planted grain, and were joined by other Puritans ; and so the foundations of the **State of Massachusetts**[1] were laid.

15. North of *Massachusetts* is *New Hampshire.*[2] It was, at first, part of a larger territory named *Maine.* In 1620, the *Plymouth Company* received a new charter, under the title of the "**Council of Plymouth**," with great powers ; and they put forth vigorous efforts to colonize *New England.*

16. In 1622, the Company granted to *John Mason*, its Secretary, and Sir *Ferdinando Gorges*,[3] its most active member, a tract of land "bounded by the *Merrimack*,[4] the *Kennebec*,[5] the *Ocean* and the *River of Canada*,"[6] or the *St. Lawrence.*

17. Fishermen employed by *Mason* and *Gorges* built log huts on the *Piscataqua*,[7] at *Portsmouth* and *Dover.* In 1629, Mr. *Wheelwright*, a clergyman, purchased from the *Indians* the territory between the *Merrimack* and *Piscataqua*, and founded *Exeter.*[8] The same year *Mason* and *Gorges* dissolved their partnership, when the former obtained a grant of the same territory, and called the domain **New Hampshire.**

QUESTIONS.—14. What did the surviving Pilgrims do, and what was the result? 15. What can you tell about New Hampshire and the Plymouth Company? 16. To whom did they grant a domain, and what were its boundaries? 17. How were the settlements begun in New Hampshire?

---

[1] *mas-sa-chu'-sets.* [2] *hamp'-sheer.* [3] *gor'-jes.* [4] *mer'-i-mak.* [5] *ken-e-bek'.* [6] *kan'-a-dah.* [7] *pis-cat'-a-kwah.* [8] *ex'-e-ter.*

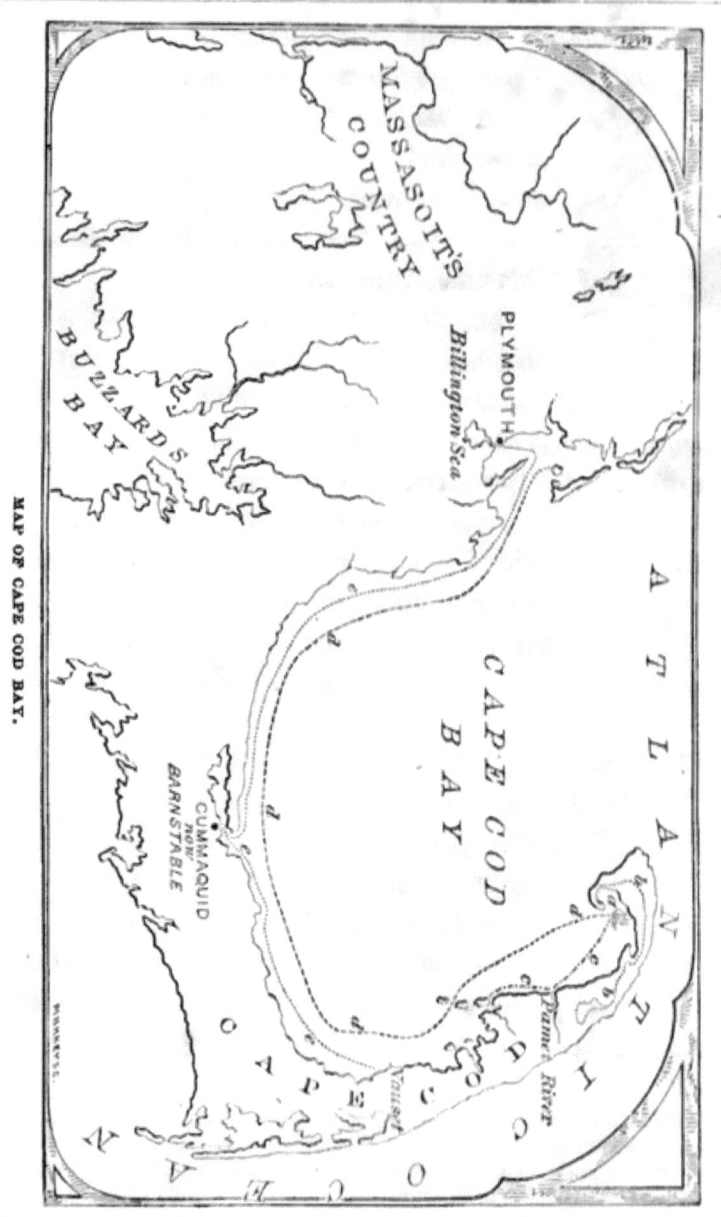

MAP OF CAPE COD BAY.

18. *Mason* had been governor of *Portsmouth,*[1] in

[1] *ports'-muth.*

SETTLERS AND SETTLEMENTS.   59

Founding of Portsmouth.   New Hampshire a Royal Province.

CLEARING THE LAND.

Hampshire, England. He built a house near the mouth of the *Piscataqua,* and named the place *Portsmouth.* Other feeble settlements were made further eastward. Those in *New Hampshire* were too scattered to form a government, and in 1641 that domain became a part of the colony of *Massachusetts.*

19. In 1679, *New Hampshire* was made a separate **royal province,** when its foundations as a commonwealth were laid. It was ruled by a governor appointed by the

QUESTIONS.—18. What did Mason do? What can you tell about the settlements? 19. How was the commonwealth of New Hampshire established and governed?

60 SETTLERS AND SETTLEMENTS.

King James and the Roman Catholics. Calvert, Lord Baltimore.

King and an assembly elected by the people. From 1641 to this date (1679) it had been for a large part of the time under the control of *Massachusetts*.

20. We have considered in this section—

(1) The *Dutch on Manhattan* and their explorations; (2) the *founding of New Netherland* by the *Dutch West India Company;* (3) the *colonizing* of New Netherland; (4) the *early explorations* in *New England;* (5) the *Puritans* and the *"Pilgrims";* and (6) the *settlements* in *Massachusetts* and *New Hampshire.*

SECTION III.

SETTLERS AND SETTLEMENTS IN MARYLAND, CONNECTICUT AND RHODE ISLAND.

1. *King James* persecuted the *Roman Catholics* as well as the *Puritans.* One of them, however, he esteemed and honored. That was *George Calvert,*[1] who was a zealous royalist. The King made him a Secretary of State and created him *Lord Baltimore.*[2]

2. *Baltimore* wished to find a place of refuge in *America* for his persecuted brethren. While he was seeking a place, the King died. His son and successor, *Charles the First,* granted to *Baltimore* a charter for a large terri-

---

QUESTIONS.—20. What have we considered in this section?

QUESTIONS.—1. What did King James do? What can you tell about George Calvert? 2. What did Lord Baltimore desire, and what did he obtain?

[1] *kaul'-vert.*   [2] *bawl'-ti-more.*

tory lying on each side of *Chesapeake Bay,* which was called **Maryland,** in honor of the King's wife, *Henrietta Mary.*

3. Before the charter was issued, *Lord Baltimore* died, and was succeeded by his son, *Cecil Calvert,* who received

CECIL, SECOND LORD BALTIMORE.

the grant in 1632. Late in 1633, a company of settlers, many of them *Roman Catholic* gentlemen, with their families and servants, sailed for the *Chesapeake,* with *Leonard Calvert* as their governor. This was the first **Roman Catholic colony** that came to *America* from *Great Britain.*

4. The colonists arrived in the spring of **1634.** The governor purchased an *Indian* village near the mouth of the *Potomac River,* named it *St. Marys,* and there founded the capital of the province. *William Clayborne,*[1] from *Virginia,* had established trading posts within the domain of *Maryland* as early as 1631, and he gave the colonists much trouble by his claims.

5. The charter of *Maryland* was a liberal one. It provided for a **representative government,** and left the people almost free in religious matters. The consequence was that persecuted persons flocked to *Maryland* from other places, and the colony flourished.

QUESTIONS.—3. What can you tell about Cecil Calvert and emigration to America? 4. What did the governor and colonists do? What can you tell about an earlier settler? 5. What have you to say about the charter of Maryland and the effects of its liberality?

---

[1] *kla'-born.*

6. The first legislature of *Maryland* met at *St. Marys*, to make laws, in March, 1635. It was a purely democratic assembly, for every freeman was allowed to vote. These freemen soon became so numerous that a representative government was established in 1639. Then the foundations of the commonwealth of **Maryland** were laid.

7. In the same year (1633) in which the *Roman Catholics* sailed for *Maryland, Puritans* from *Massachusetts* had **begun a settlement in the valley of the Connecticut River.** *Block's* discovery of that river, almost twenty years before, made the *Dutch* claim the territory as a part of *New Netherland.* They had already built a fort there near the site of *Hartford.*

8. In the fall of 1633, *Captain Holmes*,[1] with a number of *Puritans* from *Plymouth,* with materials for a house, went up the *Connecticut River* in a sloop. The *Dutch* at the fort ordered them to stop there, but they sailed by, and on the site of *Windsor,* above *Hartford,* they set up their house and began a settlement. Soldiers were sent from *Manhattan* (New York) to drive them away, but they were unable to do so.

9. Late in 1635, a company of men, women and children from the *Puritan* settlements in *Massachusetts,* went through the woods to the *Connecticut,* and on the site of *Hartford* they spent a severe winter. They suffered much from

FIRST MEETING-HOUSE.

QUESTIONS.—6. What can you tell about the government of Maryland? 7. What can you tell about the valley of the Connecticut? 8. Give an account of the first English settlers in Connecticut. 9. Give an account of a winter emigration to Connecticut.

[1] *homes.*

cold and hunger. They built log-huts and a small meeting-house, in which to worship *God* in common.

10. Many of the settlers at *Hartford* returned. In the following summer (1636) another company of *Puritans*, led from *Massachusetts* by the Rev. Mr. *Hooker,* went through the wilderness to *Hartford.* It was a pleasant journey. They arrived there on the 4th of July, and on the following Sabbath they worshipped in the little meeting-house. That was the **first permanent settlement made in the Connecticut Valley.**

11. The year before (1635), *John Winthrop* was sent to be governor of *Connecticut,* assisted by two others. They built a fort at the mouth of the river just in time to have it useful as a defence against the fierce *Pequod*[1] or *Pequot Indians,* who made war on the white people, kidnapped their children, and murdered their men in the woods and fields.

12. The *Pequods* were jealous because the *English* were the friends of the *Mohegans*[2] and *Narragansets,*[3] their enemies. They feared the white people would take their country away from them. They therefore determined to destroy the *English*.

13. In the spring of 1637, the *Massachusetts* colonies joined those of *Connecticut,* in fighting the *Pequods.* In May full five hundred *Englishmen* and *Narraganset Indians* marched into the country of these savages, between the *Mystic*[4] and *Thames*[5] rivers. They were led by Captain *Mason,* a famous *Indian* fighter.

QUESTIONS.—10. Give an account of a second emigration from Connecticut. 11. What did Winthrop and others do in Connecticut? 12. What can you tell about the Pequods? Why did the Pequods make war on the English? 13. What did the Massachusetts colonists do? Tell about their doings with Connecticut colonists.

[1] *pe'-quod.* [2] *mo-he'-g'ns.* [3] *nar-ra-gan'-sets.* [4] *mis'-tik.* [5] *tems.*

Dispersion of the Pequods.

MAP OF THE PEQUOD OR PEQUOT COUNTRY.

14. These allies attacked a strong fort of the *Pequods,* and by fire and weapons destroyed more than six hundred men, women and children. *Sassacus,*[1] their great sachem, fled westward, with a few followers, hotly pursued. Most of the *Pequods* were destroyed. *Sassacus* escaped to the *Mohawks.*[2] His nation had literally **perished in a day.** For forty years afterward, the white people of *Connecticut* were unmolested by the *Indians.*

QUESTIONS.—14. Give an account of the destruction of the Pequods as a nation.

---

[1] *sas'-sa-kus.*   [2] *mo'-hawks.*

SETTLERS AND SETTLEMENTS. 65

New Haven and Connecticut Colonies. Roger Williams Banished.

15. The *English* who chased the *Pequods* discovered the beautiful country that borders *Long Island Sound.* Its fame spread in *Massachusetts,* and in the spring of 1638, emigrants formed a settlement on the site of *New Haven.* They were led by Rev. *John Davenport,* who preached the first sermon there under a large oak tree. They formed a government after a pattern found in the Bible. It was called the **New Haven Colony.**

16. In 1639, the settlers in the *Connecticut Valley* met in convention at *Hartford,* and signed a written constitution. They formed a **representative government.** Provision was made for the annual election of a governor and legislature by the people. Allegiance to the new State, and not to the King, was required. It was called the **Connecticut Colony.** Thus were laid the foundations of the commonwealth of **Connecticut.**

17. At about the same time movements were in progress for the founding of a state between *Connecticut* and *New Plymouth.* The authorities in *Massachusetts,* in church and state, were such rigid disciplinarians, that a non-conformist to their rules could not be tolerated.

18. *Roger Williams,* a minister of the gospel at *Salem,* offended these authorities by his liberal and tolerant views, and late in 1635 they issued an order for his **banishment.** He left his home in the dead of winter (1636), and sought refuge among the savages of the wilderness near *Narraganset Bay.*

19. In the spring of 1636, *Williams* was joined by some

QUESTIONS.—15. What led to a settlement at New Haven? How was it accomplished? 16. What can you tell about the settlers in the Connecticut Valley, and the government which they formed? 17. What can you tell about movements for founding a new State? 18. What can you tell about Roger Williams?

66   *SETTLERS AND SETTLEMENTS.*

Providence Founded. Other Settlements in Rhode Island. Its Name.

friends, and at the head of *Narraganset Bay* they founded a settlement, which, in recognition of God's providential care, was named **Providence**. It is now the chief city of *Rhode Island.*

20. Men and women, persecuted by the authorities of *Massachusetts,* went to *Providence* to enjoy freedom of conscience. The settlement grew. The settlers established a purely **democratic government,** and the great chiefs of the *Narraganset Indians* were their fast friends. It was through the influence of *Roger Williams* that these *Indians* were induced to help the *English* against the *Pequods,* which **saved the New England settlements** from destruction.

21. Other persecuted men from *Boston* received from the *Narraganset* chief the island of *Aquiday,*[1] or *Aquitnet,*[2] the "Peaceable Isle." The *Dutch* called it *Roodt Eyland* —Red Island—which has been corrupted into **Rhode Island.** In 1638, the *English* settled at the upper end of it, and founded *Portsmouth* there.

22. The next year other immigrants from *Boston* settled toward the southern extremity of the island, and founded *Newport.* These settlers organized a democratic government after the model of that at *Providence,* and with the latter received the name of the **Providence and Rhode Island Plantations.** The seal bore the words, "*Amor vincit omnia*"—"Love is all-powerful."

23. In 1643, *Roger Williams* went to *England* to ob-

QUESTIONS.—19. Give an account of the settlement of Providence. 20. Give an account of the colony at Providence, its government, and the services of Roger Williams. 21. Give an account of the settlement of Portsmouth. 22. Give an account of the settlement of Newport and their government.

[1] *ah'-kwee-day.*   [2] *ah-kweet'-net.*

tain a charter for the creation of the settlements into a commonwealth. He succeeded, and in 1644, he returned with a charter, making the *Providence* and *Rhode Island* Plantations an **independent colony.** Thus were laid the foundations of the commonwealth of **Rhode Island.**

24. We have considered in this section—

(1) The *relations of King James to the Roman Catholics;* (2) the *creation of Lord Baltimore* and the *charter for Maryland;* (3) the *settlements of Maryland* and the *government* of the province ; (4) *settlements in the Valley of the Connecticut;* (5) the *war with the Pequods,* the *settlement at New Haven,* and the *founding of the commonwealth of Connecticut;* and (6) the *founding of the commonwealth of Rhode Island.*

SECTION IV.

SETTLERS AND SETTLEMENTS IN DELAWARE, NEW JERSEY AND PENNSYLVANIA.

1. In the year 1638, a small colony from *Sweden,* with *Peter Minuit*[1] as governor, sent by the **Swedish West India Company,** made the first permanent settlement on the present domain of *Delaware.* It was on the site of Newcastle. They built a fort and church on the site of *Wilmington,* and called the territory **New Sweden.**

QUESTIONS.—23. What can you tell about the charter of Rhode Island and the founding of the commonwealth? 24. What have we considered in this section?

QUESTIONS.—1. What can you tell about first permanent settlers in Delaware?

[1] *min'-wit.*

2. The *Dutch* claimed the territory as a part of *New Netherland,* and ordered the *Swedes* to leave. The *Swedes* stayed. The colony grew, and finally they laid the foundations of the capital of a Swedish province upon an island a little below *Philadelphia.*

3. The Dutch *West India Company* now resolved to subdue or expel the *Swedes.* Governor *Stuyvesant* [1] went to the *Delaware* from *Manhattan,* with ships and soldiers, in the summer of 1655, and within a month he **subjugated the Swedes** and destroyed their capital. *New Sweden* was no more. Its colonists remained faithful subjects of the *Dutch* and *English* ever afterward.

4. *New Jersey* was also a part of *New Netherland.* Just below the site of *Camden* the *Dutch* built a fort in 1623. Four young married couples came from *Manhattan* the same year, and began a settlement on the *Delaware,* near this fort. Some *Danes* had settled at *Bergen* [2] the year before.

5. In 1664, the *Duke of York,* to whom *New Netherland* had been granted by his brother, King *Charles,* took possession of the whole province by force of arms ; and the same year some *English* families of *Long Island* settled on the site of *Elizabeth,* in *New Jersey.*

6. The following year the Duke granted the territory between the *Hudson* and *Delaware* rivers to Lord *Berkeley* [3] and Sir *George Carteret.* The latter sent *Philip Car-*

QUESTIONS.—2. What did the Dutch do? What did the Swedes do? 3. What can you tell about the act of the Dutch West India Company and General Stuyvesant? 4. What can you tell about first settlements in New Jersey? 5. What did the Duke of York do? What people went to New Jersey? 6. What did the Duke of York do then? What did Carteret do?

[1] *stī'-ve-sant.*   [2] *bur·g'n.*   [3] *berk'-ly.*

teret [1] as governor, and steps were taken to promote emigration to that province.

7. The territory was called **New Jersey,** in honor of Sir *George,* who had been governor of *Jersey,* one of the *British* islands. A **representative government** was established in 1665, and then the foundations of the commonwealth of **New Jersey** were laid.

WILLIAM PENN.

8. Less than twenty years later, another colony was established beyond the *Delaware* by *William Penn,* son of the eminent *English* admiral of that name. He was of a sect who called themselves *"Friends,"* but who were named **Quakers** in derision. They were persecuted in *England,* and, like other leading non-conformists, *Penn* desired to find an asylum for his brethren where they might enjoy peace.

9. Already the *"Friends"* had possession of *West Jersey* by purchase, and had founded a settlement at a place which they called *Salem. Penn* sought and obtained a charter for the territory between *New Jersey* and *Maryland,* in 1681, to which the King gave the name of **Pennsylvania.** The land was given in payment of a debt which the King owed to *Penn's* father.

10. *Penn* sent a deputy to organize civil government on his domain. Emigrants followed ; and when *Penn* came

QUESTIONS —7. How came New Jersey to be so named? What can you tell about the government? 8. What can you tell about William Penn and the Friends or Quakers? 9. Give an account of the Friends in New Jersey and the charter given to Penn. 10. What did Penn do? Give an account of his coming to America and what was done.

[1] *kar'-te-ret.*

over the next year, and landed at *Newcastle,* he was met by a **thousand settlers.** He had purchased *Delaware* from the Duke of *York,* and, in the presence of the settlers, a formal surrender of the domain was made to *Penn.*

11. *Penn* made a wise and just **treaty with the Indians,** which remained inviolate so long as any of his family were proprietors of the province. He met the **first representative assembly** at *Chester,* and gave them a new and liberal charter ; and between the *Delaware* and *Schuylkill* he laid out a city, which he named **Philadelphia** [1]— City of Brotherly Love. Thus were laid the foundations of the commonwealth of **Pennsylvania.**

THE ASSEMBLY HOUSE AT CHESTER.

12. In this section we have considered—

(1) The *Swedish settlement on the Delaware ;* (2) the movements of the *Dutch in relation to them ;* (3) the *first settlements in New Jersey* and the *claims and acts of the Duke of York* and of the subsequent proprietor of *New Jersey ;* (4) *William Penn,* his *charter for Pennsylvania* and his *doings there ;* (5) his *treaty with the Indians,* his *meeting the first representative assembly* and his *founding of Philadelphia.*

QUESTIONS.—11. Give an account of Penn's treaty with the Indians, meeting the Assembly and laying out a city. 12. What have we considered in this section ?

[1] *fil-a-del'-fia.*

SECTION V.

SETTLERS AND SETTLEMENTS IN THE CAROLINAS AND GEORGIA.

1. We have noticed the unsuccessful attempts to make settlements on the coasts of *North* and *South Carolina.* The first persons who settled and remained in *North Carolina* went from *Jamestown,* between the years 1640 and 1650. They lived happily without any government for awhile.

2. Others followed these earlier emigrants, and in 1663, *William Drummond,* a Presbyterian preacher, was made their governor. The King had given the country to eight of his friends. One of these was the *Duke of Albemarle,*[1] and *Drummond's* province was called the **Albemarle County Colony.** In honor of the King (*Charles,* Latin **Carolus**), the country was named **Carolina.**

3. In 1665, some emigrants came from *Barbadoes*[2] with Sir *John Yeamans,* and made a settlement on the *Cape Fear River,* near *Wilmington.* A government was organized, with *Yeamans* as governor. In honor of *Lord Clarendon,* another of the proprietors, it was called the **Clarendon County Colony.**

4. These two colonies were within the limits of *North Carolina.* In 1668, a **popular legislative assembly** was convened at *Edenton,* in *Albemarle County Colony,* and then were laid the foundations of the commonwealth of **North Carolina.**

QUESTIONS.—1. What can you tell about settlers in North Carolina? 2. Give an account of permanent settlers there, with a governor. 3. Give an account of a settlement on the Cape Fear River. 4. What can you tell about government in North Carolina?

[1] *ahl'-be-marl.* [2] *bar-ba'-doze.*

5. Two years later (1670) some emigrants under *William Sayle* and *Joseph West* attempted to make a settlement on *Beaufort*[1] *Island.* They soon left that spot, sailed into the harbor of *Charleston,* and settled on the *Ashley River,* a few miles from its mouth. There they were joined by Sir *John Yeamans,* who brought fifty families from *Barbadoes* and two hundred **negro slaves.**

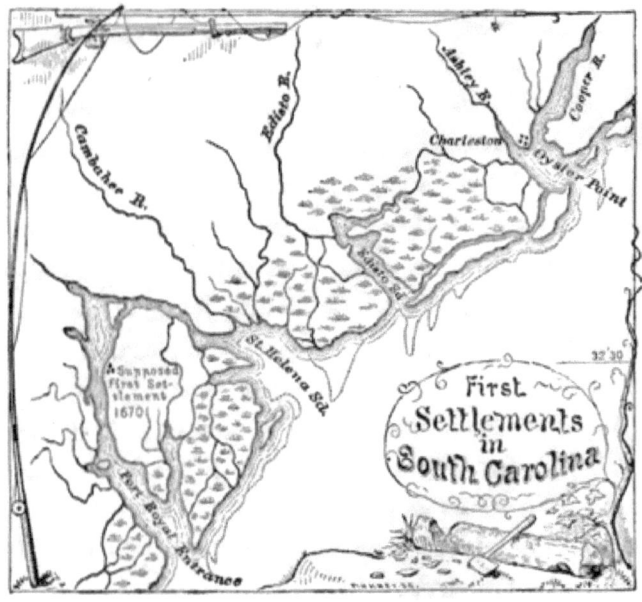

SETTLEMENTS IN SOUTH CAROLINA.

6. *Yeamans* was appointed governor of the settlers on the *Ashley,* and in honor of another proprietor, that settlement was called the **Carteret**[2] **County Colony.** That was in 1672.

QUESTIONS.—5. Give an account of settlements in South Carolina and the introduction of negro slaves. 6. What can you tell about the settlement on the Ashley River?

[1] *bo'-furt.*   [2] *kar'-te-ret.*

7. Eight years later (1680) *Charleston* was founded at the junction of the *Ashley* and *Cooper* rivers. Emigrants came and settlements spread. **Representative govern-**

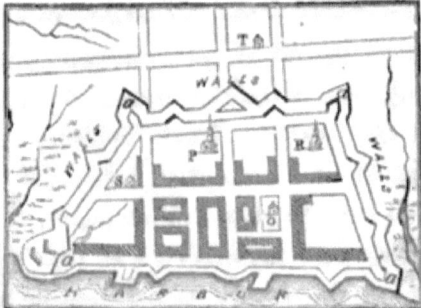

ment was established in 1682, and thus the commonwealth of **South Carolina** was founded.

8. The cruel laws of *England,* which caused many worthy people to be **imprisoned for debt,** caused General

CHARLESTON IN 1680.[1]

James Edward Oglethorpe,[2] a member of parliament, to assist in devising a scheme for their relief. He proposed to release all such prisoners on the condition that they should immediately emigrate to *America.*

9. A law to that effect was passed. The King granted a charter in 1732 for the **founding of a colony** in the country south of the *Savannah River.* A company

JAMES EDWARD OGLETHORPE.

was formed to act as trustees for twenty years. Late in the

QUESTIONS.—7. Give an account of the founding of Charleston and the spread of settlements. 8. What state of things in England caused Oglethorpe to propose emigration to America? What was his proposition? 9. What was done in the matter of emigration to Georgia?

[1] The above engraving illustrates the manner of fortifying towns, as a defence against foes. It exhibits the walls of Charleston in 1680, and the location of churches, in 1704. The points marked *a, a, a,* etc., are bastions for cannons. P, English church; Q, French church; R, Independent church; S, Anabaptist church; and T, Quaker meeting-house.

[2] *o-g'l-thorp'.*

autumn of 1732, one hundred and twenty emigrants—released prisoners for debt—sailed for the *Savannah* River, with *Oglethorpe* as their governor.

10. At the middle of February, 1733, *Oglethorpe* and his followers were on *Yamacraw Bluff*, the site of the city of *Savannah*. There they had a friendly interview with *To-mo-chi-chi*,[1] the great chief of the *Creek* confederacy, who showed warm friendliness, and presented *Oglethorpe* with a buffalo skin, on which was the figure of an eagle.

11. On that spot **Oglethorpe** built a fort and laid the foundations of the capital of the future State, which he called **Georgia**, in compliment to the reigning King, *George* the Second. Then and there the commonwealth of **Georgia** was founded.

12. In this section we have considered—

(1) The *beginning of settlements in the Carolinas;* (2) the causes which led to the *settlement of Georgia;* and (3) the *chief incidents* of that settlement.

13. In the chapter here ended we have considered the subject of the *settlers* and *settlements,* as the beginning of the *colonies* of *New England, New York, New Jersey, Pennsylvania, Delaware, Maryland, Virginia,* the *Carolinas* and *Georgia*. We will now consider the **history of these colonies,** until the period of the *French and Indian War,* when they assumed the form of a **national league.**

QUESTIONS.—10. Give an account of the emigration to Georgia. 11. What can you tell about the founding of Savannah and the name of the State? 12. What have we considered in this section? 13. What have we considered in the chapter here ended, and what shall we now consider?

---

[1] *to-mo-chi'-chi.*

OUTLINE OF IMPORTANT EVENTS FROM 1606 TO 1733.

1606, Plymouth and London Companies chartered.

1607. English emigrants land in Virginia, Captain Smith saves them from starvation. Smith saved by Pocahontas.

1608. Newport arrives at Jamestown with more emigrants. Smith explores Chesapeake Bay and its neighborhood. First English women seen in Virginia.

1609, London Company obtain a new charter. Many emigrants go to Virginia.

1610. Fatal sickness at Jamestown. Arrival of Governor Delaware.

1611, Better emigrants come to Virginia.

1611. Another charter given to the London Company.

1612. Pocahontas kidnapped. She marries John Rolfe.

1613, Block's ship burned at Manhattan.

1614. Block discovers the Connecticut River and other places on the New England coast. Holland charters a company to trade on the Hudson River. Captain Smith explores the New England coasts.

1620. English Puritans in Holland emigrate to America. They land on the shore of Massachusetts. Plymouth Company receives a new name and a new charter.

1621. Dutch West India Company chartered. They buy Manhattan island and establish the province of New Netherland. Plymouth Colony founded.

1622. Part of New England granted to Mason and Gorges. First settlement made in New Jersey.

1623. First settlement of families in New Netherland. First settlement on the Delaware, in New Jersey.

1629. Exeter, N. H., founded. New Hampshire granted to Mason

1631. Portsmouth, N. H., founded. Clayborne appears in Maryland.

1632. Charter for Maryland given to Lord Baltimore. First English settlers appear in the Valley of the Connecticut.

1634. Maryland settled.

1635. First legislature of Maryland meet at St. Marys. Second party of English emigrants in the Valley of the Connecticut.

1636. Third English emigrants to the Connecticut Valley. Roger Williams banished from Massachusetts, and founds Providence, R. I.

1637. War with the Pequods.

1638. Settlement at New Haven. First settlement on Rhode Island, Swedish colony settle on the Delaware.

1639. Newport founded. Representative government established in the Connecticut Valley and in Maryland.

1640, 1650. Settlements made in Upper North Carolina.

1641. New Hampshire annexed to Massachusetts.

1644. Royal charter for Rhode Island issued.

1655. Swedes on the Delaware subdued by the Dutch.

1664. New Netherland passes into the possession of the English. English families settle at Elizabeth, N. J.

1665. Territory of New Jersey granted to Lord Berkeley and Sir George Carteret. Emigrants from Barbadoes settle near the Cape Fear River.

1668. Representative government established in North Carolina.

1670. Emigrants settle on the Ashley River, in South Carolina. Negro slaves there first introduced into South Carolina from Barbadoes.

1672. Carteret County Colony founded in South Carolina.

1680. Charleston founded.

1681. William Penn receives a charter for Pennsylvania.

1682. Penn first visits America. He makes a treaty with the Indians. Meets the first legislative assembly of his province at Chester. Republican government established in South Carolina.

1733. Georgia founded by Oglethorpe.

CHAPTER III.

THE COLONIES.

SECTION I.

THE COLONY OF VIRGINIA.

SEAL OF VIRGINIA.

1. In the same order of time, and name, that we have considered the **English settlements in America,** out of which grew the **colonies,** we will now consider the **history of those colonies.** We will begin with **Virginia.**

2. We have seen that a representative government was established in *Virginia*—the first in *America*—in the sum-

QUESTIONS.—1, 2. What have we observed? and what was lacking in Virginia?

mer of 1619. But an important element in the structure of a state was wanting. There were **no white women** in the colony. That want was soon supplied.

3. In the year 1620, ninety young women, " pure and uncorrupt," were sent to Virginia to become **wives for the planters** or farmers there. The family relation and **homes** were thus established, and so the more solid foundations of a state were laid.

4. A year earlier a *Dutch* trader took twenty captives from *Africa* to Jamestown, and sold them for slaves. So **negro slavery** was first introduced into the *United States.*

5. Emigrants now flocked to *Virginia.* New settlements were formed. In 1621 Sir *Francis Wyatt* was appointed governor, and brought with him a written charter which gave the people the privilege of electing the members of the legislative assembly. He established regular **courts of justice** like those in *England.*

6. Trouble now fell upon the colonists. *Powhatan* was dead, and his brother, an enemy of the *English*, ruled the *Indian* empire. He planned the **destruction of the English** in *Virginia.* In April, 1622, his warriors fell upon the people of eighty plantations out of *Jamestown.*

7. Seventy-two of the plantations were desolated. Three hundred and fifty men, women, and children were **murdered.** The surviving *Englishmen* struck the *Indians* such a terrible blow in return that the dusky nation was almost destroyed.

QUESTIONS.—3. What can you tell about women and homes in Virginia ? 4. When and how were negro slaves first introduced into the United States? 5. What can you tell about emigration to, and a new government in, Virginia ? 6. What trouble befell the colony ? 7. Give an account of the massacre by the Indians.

8. Sickness followed the massacre, and of the four thousand settlers who were in *Virginia* in the spring, by midsummer not more than **twenty-five hundred** remained alive.

9. In 1624, King **James** took *Virginia* from the *London Company,* and it became a **royal province.** The governor and twelve councillors were appointed by the crown ; the members of the Assembly, or House of Burgesses, were chosen by the people.

10. As a rule, the people prospered under the royal governors. They lived well, and exported products of their soil. Tobacco became an important article of commerce, and a sort of **currency** for the colony, being rated at about seventy-five cents a pound.

11. After several changes in the governorship of *Virginia,* Sir *William Berkeley*[1] was appointed chief magistrate in 1641. He ruled the colony with wisdom, and held the people of *Virginia* loyal to the crown during the civil war in *England.* That war began in 1642, and ended in 1649, when the **Republicans** cut off the head of King *Charles* and made *Oliver Cromwell* ruler.

12. In 1644, the *Indians* again fell upon the *English* and murdered about three hundred of them. The savages were so terribly smitten in return by the *English* that they never again gave the colonists any trouble.

13. During *Cromwell's* rule, the *Virginians* remained

QUESTIONS.—8. What other misfortune fell upon the colony? 9. What can you tell about a change in the government of Virginia? 10. What can you tell about the life and industry of the people? 11. Who became governor of Virginia, and what did he do? What was a result of a civil war in England? 12. Tell about another massacre by the Indians. 13. How did the Virginians show their loyalty to the monarch?

[1] *burk'-ly.*

the firm friends of the dead King's family. They invited his son, *Charles,* to come to *Virginia* and **reign there as King.** He was placed on the throne of his father in 1660.

14. There were now many republicans in *Virginia,* for the new monarch became the oppressor of the colonists. These republicans opposed Governor *Berkeley,* for he was a proud *royalist,* and had become exacting and persecuting in matters of church and state. Disputes ran high, and led to **civil war** in 1676, in which the Republicans were led by *Nathaniel Bacon.*

15. *Berkeley* proclaimed *Bacon* to be a traitor. The majority of the people took sides with the **"rebel."** He drove the governor from *Jamestown.* When informed that royal troops were coming against him, he laid *Jamestown* in ashes. Everything was destroyed but the old church tower, which yet remains.

CHURCH TOWER.

16. *Bacon* died soon afterward, and the war, known as **"Bacon's Rebellion,"** ceased. At length King *James* the Second, who succeeded his brother, King *Charles* the Second, was driven from the throne, and in 1689 his son-in-law, *William* of Orange, with *Mary,* his daughter, became joint monarchs of *England.*

17. After that *England* had better rulers. *Virginia* and all the other colonies prospered wonderfully, until they joined in a common struggle for independence, in 1775.

QUESTIONS.—14. What can you tell about the governor and the cause of civil war in Virginia? 15. What did Berkeley and Bacon do? 16. How did the civil war end? what was it called? and what occurred in England? 17. What can you tell about the condition of England and the colonies after that?

18. In this section we have considered—

(1) The *state of society* in Virginia and its *improvement;* (2) the *introduction of negro slavery* into that colony ; (3) a change in the *government;* (4) the *sufferings* of the colonists ; (5) the effects of the *civil war* in *England;* (6) the *loyalty of the Virginians,* and (7) *" Bacon's Rebellion."*

SECTION II.

THE COLONY OF MASSACHUSETTS.

SEAL OF MASSACHUSETTS.

1. In the spring of 1621 *Indians* prowled around the settlement at **Plymouth.** One of them went among the huts, and in broken words said : " Welcome Englishmen ! "

QUESTIONS.—18. What have we considered in this section ?

QUESTIONS.—1. What can you tell about Indians at Plymouth ?

He was *Squanto,* who had been carried to *England* a captive, and had returned.

2. *Squanto* was the herald of *Massasoit,*[1] sachem of the *Wampanoags.* The latter came in stately pomp, with sixty warriors, to confer with Governor *Carver.* He tarried on a hill; and, when invited, he went into the village and made a **treaty of friendship** with the English, which was kept inviolate fifty years.

3. The colony, reduced by deaths, was reinforced by many new comers from *England* the following summer. The protection of *Massasoit's* friendship gave them peace. Prosperity and happiness followed industry and thrift, until society was disturbed by the arrival of some emigrants who had been sent by a discontented member of the Company to plant a new settlement.

4. Many of the new-comers were idle and vicious, and offended the *Indians* by their bad conduct. Fearing the savages, they called on Captain *Miles Standish* to protect them. After seeing several of the *Indians* slain by this fiery soldier, these worthless settlers returned to *England.*

5. The partnership between the *"Pilgrims"* and the *London* merchants was dissolved at the end of seven years, when the former became sole owners of the soil. Greater prosperity was the consequence of the change. Their democratic government con-

FIRST COLONY SEAL.

quence of the change. Their democratic government con-

QUESTIONS.—2. What did Squanto do? Give an account of an interview with Massasoit. 3. What can you tell about new emigrants, and the result of Massasoit's friendship? 4. Give an account of new comers and their conduct. 5. What can you tell about a change in ownership and in the government of Plymouth?

[1] *mas-sa-saw'-it.*

tinued in force until 1634, when a **representative system** was established, and a colonial seal was adopted.

6. The prosperity at *Plymouth* caused leading *Puritans* in *England* to form an association under the name of the **Massachusetts Bay Company,** to colonize other portions of *New England.* They purchased lands and sent out emigrants in 1628, with *John Endicot* as governor, who settled at *Salem* and built cabins at *Charlestown.*

7. The charter of the company was transferred to the colony in 1629, which gave the people self-government. The next year, three hundred more families came to *Salem,* and some of these settled on the peninsula where *Boston* now stands.

JOHN WINTHROP.

8. These settlements were soon united, with *John Winthrop* as governor. The foundations of the city of *Boston* were laid where this magistrate's cottage was built.

9. The **Plymouth** and **Massachusetts Bay** colonies existed separately until 1692, when they were united by *royal decree.* From that time until the **old war for independence,** the whole domain was known as *Massachusetts Bay.*

10. *Winthrop* was a wise man and ruled well. He made friends with the *Indians.* He held friendly intercourse with the *Dutch on Manhattan;* and ships came from *Virginia* to trade with the people of *Boston* and *Salem.* In this way the *Coast Trade* of this country was begun.

11. The colony prospered wonderfully. It comprised twenty settlements in 1636, when it was greatly agitated by **theological disputes.** Its government was carried on by a governor, deputy-governor, and magistrates called "assistants," who, with the members of the legislature, were all elected by the "freemen," who were church members.

12. The *Puritans* of *Massachusetts,* having escaped from the persecutions of **Churchmen,** regarded them as deadly foes, and kept them at a distance. Desiring to enjoy, without molestation, their peculiar religious doctrines and forms of worship, they could not tolerate any non-conformity, and so in turn became persecutors.

13. In 1635 the authorities of *Massachusetts* decreed the banishment of *Roger Williams,* a Puritan preacher, because he upheld the rights of conscience against the authority of magistrates, and advocated **toleration in matters of religion.** He went to *Narraganset Bay* and founded the colony of *Rhode Island.*

14. For a similar offence they first imprisoned and then banished an accomplished woman named *Anne Hutchinson,* with her family. She finally perished in the wilderness, at the hands of the *Indians,* near *New York.*

15. The civil war in *England* left the colonists free to act. Those of *New England,* excepting *Rhode Island,*

THE COLONIES. 85

New England Confederacy. Commerce and Coinage in Massachusetts.

formed a **political confederacy** in 1643, to oppose royal encroachments and hostile *Indians.*

16. At that time there were *fifty villages* and twenty thousand whites in *New England.* The Confederation promised good results. Each colony was represented in a .Congress which had general supervision of the affairs of the Union.

17. The **league** then formed lasted more. than forty years, when mutual jealousies caused it to be dissolved. It was the first important step toward the formation of a national **confederacy** in *America.*

18. Unlike the people of *Virginia,* those of *Massachusetts* took sides against the King during the Civil War. While *Cromwell* ruled they prospered wonderfully, and had almost absolute freedom. They built ships and traded with the *Spanish* colonies in the *West Indies.* Thus they began the **foreign commerce** of the *United States.*

19. The Massachusetts colonists also **coined** silver money. They issued six-pences and shillings, on which was the figure of a pine-tree. These were first issued in 1652. This was the first **coinage** in the *United States.*

FIRST MONEY COINED IN THE UNITED STATES.

20. The same year (1652) the jurisdiction of *Massachusetts* was extended over the territory of *Maine.* But while the *Puritans* were looking for a further extension of their domain, events occurred which produced lamentable scenes in *Boston.*

21. Two women of the sect called *Friends,* or *Quakers,* came to *Boston* in 1656. The authorities there had heard of the denunciations of magistrates by Friends in *England,* and they put these women in jail to stop their mouths.

22. Other Friends came. They were not, generally, true representatives of their sect. They were **fanatics**, and real disturbers of good order. They were driven away; and, finally, others who came, and seemed to court martyrdom, were imprisoned, whipped, and banished. They were threatened with death if they should return. Some did return and were hanged.

23. When persecution of these people ceased, the Friends were no longer disturbers of the peace. But another trouble came upon the people of *Massachusetts.* When *Charles the Second* came to the throne in 1660, he determined to punish the *New Englanders* for their friendship for *Cromwell* and Republicanism. He ordered them to pay taxes to the government in the shape of a certain amount of money for everything that was received from *England* in ships.

24. This act was in violation of their charter. The *Massachusetts* merchants **refused to pay the tax,** and the people upheld them in it. The King recalled his taxgatherers; and *Massachusetts* was ever afterward the leader in the march toward final independence.

25. A worse trouble now fell upon *New England.* Old *Massasoit* was dead. His brave son, *Metacomet*,[1] known as *King Philip,* did not respect the treaty made with the white people by his father. He suspected that they intended to seize all the lands of the *Indians,* and he determined to destroy them.

26. King *Philip* laid his plans secretly, and on Sunday,

KING PHILIP.

the 4th of July, 1675, he and his followers **attacked the inhabitants** of the village of *Swanzey,* thirty-five miles from *Plymouth,* when they were returning from public worship. Many were killed or made captives. Thus was begun the conflict known in history as

KING PHILIP'S WAR.

27. The white people of *New England* flew to arms, and *Philip* was closely pursued. Other tribes joined the *Wampanoags,* and **death** and **desolation** were spread over the settlements, even to the *Connecticut Valley.*

28. For several months the work of the savages was fearful. The white people palisaded their houses; but, for awhile, it seemed

PALISADED BUILDING.

as if the *English* would all be destroyed. In December,

QUESTIONS.—25. Give an account of the origin of trouble with the Indians. 26. What can you tell of King Philip and his attack on the white people? 27. What did the white people and the Indians then do? 28. What was done during several months in New England?

[1] *met-a-kom'-et.*

King Philip's Refuge in Rhode Island.

Philip's career was checked, and he took refuge with the *Narragansets*, who violated their treaties by giving him shelter.

29. In a swamp in *Rhode Island* the Indians had gathered their winter provisions. There, too, the *Narragansets*,

with *Philip* and his followers, took refuge from the white people. There were about three thousand *Indian* warriors there, with women and children.

QUESTIONS.—29. Give an account of the Indians and their stores in a swamp.

FELTER.

DEATH OF KING PHILIP.

30. Fifteen hundred *New Englanders* surrounded the swamp, and at the close of December, 1675, they destroyed by fire **five hundred wigwams** with provisions, and killed a **thousand warriors.** Hundreds of men, women, and children perished in the flames.

31. *Philip* escaped. He gathered new allies, and opened war vigorously in the spring of 1676. It spread over a space of **three hundred miles** along the coasts of *New England.* The white people fought the savages with equal vigor, killing many, and chasing *Philip* from one hiding-place to another.

32. At length *Philip's* family were made prisoners. He was shot in a swamp, and his **head** was cut off and carried into *Plymouth* on a pole. His body was quartered, and his little son was **sold for a slave** in *Bermuda.* So perished the last prince of the **Wampanoags,**[1] and the war was ended.

33. *King Charles the Second,* observing the power and independence of the *New England* people, determined to take away their charters and rule them himself. He died before he effected his purpose. His brother, *James* the Second, who succeeded him, attempted the same thing. He sent *Edmund Andros,* in 1686, to take away their charters and govern all *New England.* The people were about to send *Andros* back, when news came that *James* had been **driven from the throne** of *England* (1688) and had fled to *France.*

QUESTIONS.—30. What can you tell about an attack on the Indians in the swamp? 31. What did Philip and the white people then do? 32. Give an account of the fate of Philip and his family. 33. What did King Charles attempt to do? What did his successor do, and what occurred in England?

[1] *wam-pa-no'-ags.*

34. *William,* a Hollander, and his wife *Mary,* now (1689) sat on the throne of *England.* The King of *France* favored *James,* and the *French* and *English* made war upon each other. That war spread to the *French* and *English* colonies in *America,* and is known in history as

KING WILLIAM'S WAR.

35. During this conflict, which began in 1689, the *New Englanders* suffered dreadfully. The *French* had gained great influence over the *Indians* in *Canada* and in the *East,* and these savages joined them. Several *New England* villages were burned and the inhabitants were murdered.

36. In February, 1690, *French* and *Indians* went down from the *St. Lawrence,* and at midnight set fire to *Schenectady,* near *Albany,* in *New York,* and murdered many of the inhabitants. The people of *New York* joined those of *New England* in making war upon *Canada,* the home of these enemies.

37. A land force was sent by way of *Lake Champlain* to attack *Montreal,* and a naval force was sent up the *St. Lawrence* to capture *Quebec.*[1] Both expeditions failed. The war continued, and the *New Englanders* suffered much until it ended in 1697, by a treaty at *Ryswick.*

38. Meanwhile there was another change in the *govern-*

QUESTIONS.—34. Who succeeded King James? What caused "King William's War"? 35. What can you tell about the sufferings of New Englanders, and the French and Indian allies? 36. Tell about the destruction of Schenectady. What did New Yorkers and New Englanders do? 37. Give an account of expeditions against Canada. 38. What can you tell about changes in New England and the creation of a royal province?

[1] *ke-bek'.*

ment of New England. *Massachusetts* and *Plymouth* and the *Eastern settlements* were united under one government. A new charter was given in 1692, and the domain was made a **royal province,** under the name of **Massachusetts Bay Colony.**

39. A strange thing occurred in *Massachusetts* in 1692. There was a general belief in witches and witchcraft. At *Salem,* two young girls twitched and acted strangely. An old *Indian* servant woman was accused of bewitching them. Very soon all sorts of people acted as strangely, and many respectable persons—even the wife of Governor *Phipps*—were suspected of practising witchcraft.

40. The delusion spread, and lasted many months. Many persons, some of great respectability, were **punished as wizards and witches.** The jails were filled with the accused, and twenty suspected persons were **hanged.** The delusion ended as suddenly as it began, and the accusers were overwhelmed with shame.

41. The exiled King *James* died in 1701, and the *French* monarch acknowledged *James'* son to be the rightful sovereign of *England. William* and *Mary* were both dead, and *Mary's* sister *Anne* was on the throne. *England* declared war against *France.* The conflict that ensued is known in *American* history as

QUEEN ANNE'S WAR.

42. As before, the *English* and *French* colonies in *America* were involved in the **war.** The white people of

QUESTIONS.—39. Give an account of a delusion concerning witchcraft in Massachusetts. 40. What further can you tell about the delusion? 41. What caused war between England and France? Who then ruled England? 42. What have you to say about the effects of "Queen Anne's War"?

New England again suffered much from Indian cruelties. The frontiers were desolated by fire, and blood flowed in almost every valley. Among the victims at *Deerfield* was the Rev. *John Williams,* though his house escaped the flames.

WILLIAMS'S HOUSE.

43. A powerful confederation of Indians in the province of New York, known as the **Five Nations,** agreed not to fight for either party. This was a great blessing to the white people, for these nations stood as a wall between them and the fierce savages of *Canada.*

44. Some of the *New England* colonies united in fitting out a fleet and army to chastise the *French* in *Nova Scotia* or *Acadia.* Little was done until 1710, when an expedition from *Boston,* assisted by a fleet from England, captured *Port Royal,* in *Acadia.*

45. In August, 1711, seven thousand troops and a powerful *English* fleet, under Sir *Hovenden Walker,* sailed for *Quebec.* At the mouth of the *St. Lawrence,* eight of the ships were wrecked on the rocks, and a **thousand men** perished. The remainder returned. A land force of four thousand men, on their way toward *Montreal,* hearing of this disaster, returned to *Albany.*

46. The expedition against *Canada* was abandoned. In the spring of 1713, **peace** was secured by a treaty at *Utrecht.* The *Eastern Indians* sent chiefs to *Boston* to treat for peace the same year. For thirty years after-

QUESTIONS.—43. What can you tell about Indians in New York? 44. Give an account of expeditions fitted out against Nova Scotia. 45. Tell about an army and navy sent to capture Quebec. Also of a force sent toward Montreal. 46. What was done? What can you tell about treaties of peace and their result?

ward the New England colonies enjoyed quiet, and prospered.

47. *England* and *France* quarrelled again in 1744, and
commenced war. The *English* and *French* colonists were
involved in the contest. *George* the *Second* was then
monarch of *England,* and the conflict is known in *American* history as

KING GEORGE'S WAR.

48. Eastward of *Nova Scotia* is a large island called
Cape Breton.[1] On that island the *French* had a town
named *Louisburg,* and there they built a strong fort. This
gave them great strength in that region, and the people of
New England and *New York* determined to capture the
fort.

49. In April, 1745, a provincial army sailed from *Boston*
for *Cape Breton.* They were joined by *English* ships and
troops under Admiral *Warren,* which came from the *West
Indies,* and in May the land forces, four thousand in number, landed near *Louisburg.* The *French* garrison, alarmed
by such a force, made but little resistance. The fort and
town were **surrendered to the English** after a siege
of only a month.

50. The following year (1746) the Duke *D'Anville*[2] was
sent from *France* to recapture *Louisburg* and its fort. He

QUESTIONS.—47. What can you tell about the beginning of King George's War?
48. Give an account of Cape Breton and a French town and fort there. 49. What can
you tell about the capture of Louisburg by the English ? 50. Tell about an attempt
of the French to recapture Louisburg.

' *bre'-ton.*   ² *dan'-vill.*

had a powerful fleet and a large army. Terrible storms wrecked many of his vessels, and disease swept away many of his sol-diers and sailors. *D'Anville,* disheart-ened, returned to *France.*

51. A trea-ty of peace, made at *Aix-la-Chapelle* [1] in 1748, ended the war. There was peace for a

CAPTURE OF LOUISBURG IN 1745.

few years. Then mutual animosities growing out of these conflicts, and disputes concerning **territorial boundaries,** caused another long conflict between the three races. It is known in American history as the **French and Indian War.**

52. In this section we have considered—

(1) The *friendship of Massasoit* and his *people ;* (2) the coming of new *emigrants to Massachusetts* and their *character ;* (3) the changes in the *ownership* and *govern-ment of Massachusetts ;* (4) the *founding of Massa-chusetts Bay Colony ;* (5) the *government,* and the result of *theological disputes ;* (6) the *New England confed-eracy ;* (7) the *politics* of the *Massachusetts* people ;

QUESTIONS.—51. What can you tell about a treaty, and the causes which produced the French and Indian War ? 52. What have we considered in this section ?

[1] *äks-lah-shap'-el.*

(8) their *coinage of money;* (9) their treatment of the "*Quakers*"; (10) their defiance of the *King;* (11) King *Philip's* War; and (12) King *William's,* Queen *Anne's* and King *George's* Wars.

SECTION III.

THE COLONY OF NEW YORK.

SEAL OF NEW YORK.

1. We have observed that the colony of *New Nether-land* was established when families came from *Holland* and settled on *Manhattan Island* and elsewhere. That island was bought of the *Indians* for about twenty-five dollars, by *Peter Minuit,* who arrived there as governor in 1626.

2. Governor *Minuit* built a stockade at the lower end of the island, and called it **Fort Amsterdam.** The village

QUESTIONS.—1. What can you tell about the purchase of Manhattan Island? 2. What did Governor Minuit do?

that grew up near it—the germ of the city of *New York*—he called **New Amsterdam.** By kindness, *Minuit* made friends of the *Indians.* He had a friendly correspondence with the *Plymouth* people ; and *Dutch* traders trafficked with the *Indians* on the borders of *Narraganset Bay.*

3. To encourage emigration to *New Netherland,* the *Dutch West India Company* offered large tracts of land and many privileges to persons who would lead or send a certain number of persons to settle upon them. Several *Hollanders* accepted the conditions, and each received the title of **Patroon,** or patron.

4. *Wouter Van Twiller,* who came over to examine the country and select lands for *Van Rensselaer,* one of the Patroons, was appointed governor in 1633. He was a man of hasty temper, and involved the colony in trouble. He was followed by *William Kieft*[1] in 1638, who loved money, power, and strong drink.

5. *Kieft* quarrelled with everybody, and made the *English, Swedes* and *Indians* his bitter enemies. His conduct interfered with the prosperity of *New Amsterdam,* and the people raised a clamor against him because he made war upon neighboring *Indians,* and thereby lessened the fur trade.

6. The governor was afraid of the people. In 1641 he called some of the wisest men of *New Amsterdam* to confer with him on public affairs. This was the germ of **representative government** in *New Netherland.* These counsellors opposed the governor's projects, and talked

QUESTIONS.—3. What was done to encourage emigration ? 4. What can you tell about Governors Van Twiller and Kieft ? 5. Give an account of Kieft's conduct. What did the people do ? 6. What can you tell about the beginning of representative government in New Netherland ?

[1] *keeft.*

about the **rights of the people.** Alarmed by these indi-
cations of **democratic principles,** he dissolved them early
in 1642.

7. At length *Kieft* involved the colony in a terrible war
with the *Indians,* which, at one time, threatened its very
existence. Some " *River Indians,*" pursued by fierce *Mohawks,* took shelter at *Hoboken,*[1] opposite *New Amsterdam. Kieft* treacherously caused *Dutch* soldiers and some
Mohawks[2] to cross the river on a cold winter night, to
attack the sleeping fugitives. Before the dawn more than a
hundred helpless men, women and children were murdered,
or driven off the bank into the freezing waters.

8. This atrocious act kindled the fierce anger of the *Indians* all over the country. They killed every white person
whom they saw, and burned buildings and crops. The
savages were finally subdued. *Kieft* was recalled. On his

way to *Holland* with much ill-
gotten wealth, the ship in which
he sailed was wrecked, and his life
and property were lost.

9. *Peter Stuyvesant,*[3] a brave
soldier, became governor of *New
Netherland* in 1647. His kindness made friends of the *Indians,*
and his justice won for him the respect of the *English* in the East

PETER STUYVESANT.

and the *Swedes* in the West. He ruled with power, but
wisely and faithfully.

QUESTIONS.—7. What injurious things did Kieft do ? 8. What were the effects of
Kieft's bad conduct ? What was his fate ? 9. What have you to say about Governor
Stuyvesant ?

[1] *ho-bo'-ken.*   [2] *mo'-hawks.*   [3] *sti'-ve-sant.*

THE COLONIES. 99

The Swedes in the Delaware. Representative Government in New York.

10. As we have observed, the *Dutch* became jealous of the *Swedes* on the *Delaware*, who were clearly within the bounds of *New Netherland*. *Stuyvesant* was directed to bring them into subjection to the authorities at *Manhattan*. In 1651 he built a fort on the site of *Newcastle*, in *Delaware*, which territory the *Swedes* claimed as their own.

11. The *Swedes* attacked the *Dutch* fort ; *Stuyvesant* went there with an armed force and soon made them acknowledge his government as their own. With this conquest, the pacification of the *Indians,* and the settlement of a dispute with the *English* in *Connecticut, Stuyvesant* concluded that all causes for trouble were at an end.

12. For awhile everything was serene. But the people, who had tasted the sweets of **representative government** in *Kieft's* time, now yearned for more liberty. *Stuyvesant* never sought their counsel. Finally, in 1663, deputies, chosen by the people of each village in *New Netherland*, assembled at *New Amsterdam* without *Stuyvesant's* consent, to consult on public affairs.

13. This **representative assembly** proposed certain laws. *Stuyvesant* scolded, and violently opposed them. They refused to be **taxed without being consulted,** and told the governor plainly that they would prefer to bear *English rule* for the sake of enjoying **English liberty.**

14. It was not long before the *Dutch* in *New Netherland* had an opportunity to bear English rule. King *Charles,* who claimed the whole territory as *English* do-

QUESTIONS.—10. Tell about the Swedes on the Delaware and Governor Stuyvesant. 11. What did the Swedes and Dutch do? What good results followed? 12. What can you tell about another attempt to establish representative government? 13. What did a popular assembly and Governor Stuyvesant do?

main, and regarded the *Dutch* as intruders, gave it to his brother *James,* the *Duke of York,* in May, 1664. The Duke sent a land and naval force to take it from the *Dutch,* and early in September following, *Stuyvesant* was compelled to **surrender the fort and territory** to the *English.*

NEW YORK IN 1664.

15. The name of the territory and the city of *New Amsterdam* were changed to **New York,** in compliment to the Duke. The *Dutch* found that there was more **"rule"** than **"liberty"** under the *English.* Taxes were greater and **privileges** were less.

16. The *English* governor (*Nicolls*) said he would make the people think of nothing, except how to pay their taxes. They bore the burden impatiently about nine years, and when, in 1673, they were on the point of breaking out into open **rebellion,** a *Dutch* squadron appeared in *New York* harbor.

17. The *Dutch* and *English* governments were then at war. This squadron was looked upon with favor by the *Dutch* inhabitants of *New York;* and the fort and city were surrendered to the commander of the *Holland* navy. By a treaty of peace the city and province were restored to the *English* in 1674.

Questions.—14. Give an account of the passage of New Netherland from the possession of the Dutch to the English. 15. What can you tell about a change in names? 16. What can you tell about English rule and a Dutch squadron? 17. Tell about the Dutch and English at New York?

THE COLONIES. 101

Political Changes in New York. Execution of Leisler and Milborne.

18. *Edmund Andros*[1] was now made governor of *New York*. He was succeeded by *Thomas Dougan*[2] in 1683, when the Duke of York gave the people a constitution called a **Charter of Liberties**, which established a representative government in *New York*.

19. When Duke *James* became King in 1685, he withdrew the **Charter of Liberties** and refused to let the people make laws through representatives. They were on the point of rebellion when James was dethroned.

20. For awhile there was no royal governor in New York. The people chose *Jacob Leisler*,[3] a merchant and commander of militia, to govern the province until the new monarch should send them a ruler. Leisler managed well, but **royalists** were offended by this elevation of a **republican**. When Governor *Sloughter*[4] arrived they accused *Leisler* of treason, and urged the new magistrate to hang him.

21. *Sloughter* saw no reason for so harsh a measure. One day, while he was dining with one of *Leisler's* enemies, he became very drunk. In the absence of his reason he signed the **death-warrant**, and before he became sober *Leisler* and his son-in-law, *Milborne*,[5] were **hanged**. This was in 1691.

22. The death of *Leisler* created two violently antagonistic parties in the province of *New York*. Those who supported the royal governor were called **Aristocrats**, and those who favored the people were called **Democrats**. The latter regarded *Leisler* as a martyr.

QUESTIONS.—18. Who was appointed governor of New York? What did the Duke of York do? 19. What did the Duke do when he became King? 20. Give an account of Leisler's operations in New York, and their effects. 21. Tell about Governor Sloughter and the death of Leisler and Milborne. 22. What were the effects of Leisler's death?

[1] *an'-dros.* [2] *dou'-gan.* [3] *lise'-ler.* [4] *slaw'-ter.* [5] *mill'-born.*

23. The *Democrats,* having the advantage of a representative Assembly, held the royal governors in check. When, more than forty years after *Leisler's* death, one of them imprisoned the editor of a democratic newspaper (J. P. *Zenger*),[1] because of his criticism on the public conduct of the governor, the **liberty of the press** was nobly vindicated by a court and jury, who acquitted him.

24. So important was this vindication of the **freedom of the press** considered, that to Mr. *Hamilton* of *Philadelphia* (who was employed as *Zenger's* counsel), the authorities of the city of *New York* presented the " **freedom of the city** " in a gold box.

25. From that time until the beginning of the *French* and *Indian* war, the history of *New York* is made up chiefly of the stories of the quarrels of political partisans.

26. In this section we have considered—

(1) The establishment of the colony of *New Netherland;* (2) the management of successive *governors;* (3) the administrations of *Kieft* and *Stuyvesant;* (4) the attempts to establish *representative government* in *New Netherland;* (5) the surrender of *New Netherland* to the *English;* (6) affairs under *English rule;* (7) the martyrdom of *Leisler* and *Milborne,* and (8) the vindication of the *freedom of the press.*

QUESTIONS.—23. What did the Democrats do ? What can you tell about the vindication of the freedom of the press ? 24. What honors were paid to Hamilton, of Philadelphia ? 25. Of what was the later history of the province of New York made up ? 26. What have we considered in this section ?

[1] *zang'-er.*

THE COLONIES. 103

Birth of the Maryland Colony. Nature of its Government.

SECTION IV.

THE COLONY OF MARYLAND.

SEAL OF MARYLAND.

1. In 1635 a legislative Assembly of all the freemen in *Maryland* met at *St. Marys* and formed that colony. It began its vigorous growth when, in 1639, the more convenient form of **representative government** was established.

2. The freemen chose as many representatives as they pleased, and so did the proprietor. These, with the governor and secretary, formed the government. At their first session they adopted a **Declaration of Rights**; defined the powers of the governor, and guaranteed to the people the privileges of *English* subjects.

QUESTIONS.—1. At what time do you date the birth of Maryland, and the beginning of its growth, and why? 2. What was the nature of the government?

3. *William Clayborne* has been mentioned as a disturber of the peace. He claimed to have a better right to the soil of *Maryland* than *Lord Baltimore*. It is believed that he did much to excite the *Indians* against the white people, and to urge them to the hostilities which broke out in 1642. In 1645 he stirred up dissensions among the people, and kindled the flames of **civil war.** *Clayborne's* faction was defeated in 1646.

4. In 1649 an important law called the **Toleration Act** was passed by the Assembly. It gave freedom of opinion and action to nearly all men in religious matters. It fostered democratic ideas, and when royalty was **abolished** in *England* the same year, a large portion of the people of *Maryland* were republicans.

5. The Toleration Act caused persecuted Protestants in other colonies to flock to Roman Catholic *Maryland*. In 1654 the Protestants outnumbered the *Roman Catholics*. They bore rule in the Assembly, which changed the laws so as to deprive *Roman Catholics* of rights. This led to a **civil war** which lasted two years.

6. The legislature took all power from Lord *Baltimore* early in 1660, and gave it to the people. There was confusion and great trouble in the province for several years. Later, in 1660, the **restoration of monarchy** in *England* caused the old order of things in *Maryland* to be restored. For almost thirty years afterward the colony was peaceful and prosperous.

7. *Charles Calvert* became proprietor of *Maryland*, on

QUESTIONS.—3. Give an account of Clayborne's doings. 4. What can you tell about a generous law and its effects? 5. How did the Toleration Act affect the growth of the province? What did the Protestants do? 6. What did the legislature do? What have you to say about confusion and a restoration of order?

the death of his father, in 1684, as the fourth Lord *Balti-more*. In 1689, when news of the revolution in *England* which dethroned King *James,* reached *Maryland,* a turbulent man, named *Coode,*[1] stirred up the people to rebellion by false stories concerning the intentions of the governor, who was slow to acknowledge *William* and *Mary* as his sovereigns. King James was a *Roman Catholic,* and so was the governor. This fact gave ready belief to *Coode's* stories.

8. The *Protestants* flew to arms. Led by *Coode,* they took possession of the public records, deposed Lord *Baltimore* as proprietor, and declared that the province belonged to the inhabitants of *Maryland.*

9. In 1691, *William* and *Mary* made a **royal province** of *Maryland*. The Church of *England* was made the **established church** of the province. The proprietor's rights were restored in 1715, when Lord *Baltimore* was dead and his eldest son was an infant. The child's rights were protected, and he and his family owned the province and appointed governors to rule it until it became an **independent State** in 1776.

10. The growth of Maryland was rapid after the Revolution of 1688. *Annapolis* was made the capital in 1699. The province then contained 30,000 inhabitants. **Tobacco** was one of its staple productions, and much of the labor was done by **negro slaves.** The population of *Maryland* in 1776 was 120,000.

QUESTIONS —7. Who became the fourth Lord Baltimore, and when? Give an account of a disturbance caused by Coode. 8. What did the Protestants do? 9. What did William and Mary do? What can you tell about the proprietor's rights, and the fifth Lord Baltimore? 10. What can you tell of the progress of Maryland?

[1] *kood.*

11. We have considered in this section—

(1) The *birth* of the *colony of Maryland* and the beginning of its *permanent growth;* (2) the *forms* of its *government;* (3) the *disturbances* raised by *Clayborne*-and *Coode;* (4) the *Toleration Act* and its effects; (5) the ungenerous *conduct* of the *Protestants;* (6) the *changes in the proprietorship,* and its *general condition* down to 1776.

SECTION V.

THE COLONY OF CONNECTICUT.

SEAL OF CONNECTICUT.

1. We have observed how the foundations of the *colony* of *Connecticut* were laid in 1639. The example of the set-

QUESTIONS.—11. What have we considered in this section?

QUESTIONS.—1. What can you tell about the foundations of the Connecticut colony?

tlers in the Valley was followed, the same year, by those at *New Haven.* The government of each was similar, being founded upon a pattern taken from the *Bible.*

2. Many of the *New Haven* settlers were merchants, and they tried to found a commercial colony. Disasters at sea caused them to abandon the project, and to become tillers of the soil. They and the settlers in the valley joined the **New England Confederacy** in 1643 ; and in 1650 all disputes between *Connecticut* and *New Netherland,* concerning territorial claims, were settled.

3. On the **restoration of monarchy** in *England* in 1660, *Winthrop,* governor of *Connecticut,* made application to *Charles the Second* for a charter for the Valley settlers. The King had been informed of their republicanism, and refused. *Winthrop* gave to the monarch a ring which the King's father had given to *Winthrop's* grandfather. The heart of the King was touched, and he **granted a charter.**

4. That charter, given in *May,* 1662, included a portion of *Rhode Island,* and the whole of the *New Haven* colony, and westward to the *Pacific Ocean.* *Rhode Island,* which had a charter of its own, refused to be joined to *Connecticut,* but the *New Haven* colony consented to the union in 1665, and so the real **colony of Connecticut** was formed. *Rhode Island* and *Connecticut* disputed about boundary lines for sixty years afterward.

5. When, in 1674, *Andros* was made governor of *New*

York, he claimed jurisdiction over the valley of the *Connecticut*, and went to the mouth of that river to assert it. He was driven away. Twelve years later, when he was gov-

ANDROS AND THE CHARTER OF CONNECTICUT.

ernor of all *New England*, he demanded the **surrender of all the colonial charters.** *Connecticut*, alone, refused to comply with his demand.

Andros attempts to seize the Connecticut Charter.

6. In the autumn of 1686 *Andros* went to *Hartford* with sixty armed men, to demand the charter of *Connecticut* in person. The Assembly was in session. They knew his errand, and treated him very civilly. He went into the Assembly chamber and told them to bring the charter to him.

7. Debates in the Assembly were purposely kept up until the candles were lighted, when the box containing the charter was brought in and laid upon the table. Just as *Andros* stepped forward to take it, the **lights** were all put out, and the **charter was carried away.**

8. A plan had been laid for the preservation of the charter, and was successfully carried out. Captain *Wadsworth* had seized the charter in the dark, carried it to a field, and hid it in the hollow of an old oak tree, where it remained until *Andros* was driven away from *New England* in 1689. Then it was brought out, and a **new Assembly** was held under it at *Hartford*.

9. That venerable and venerated tree was ever afterward called the "**Charter Oak.**" It was blown down in a gale in August, 1856.

THE CHARTER OAK.

10. Four years after the **restoration of government** under the charter, the people of *Connecticut* again showed their bravery and love of freedom. Governor *Fletcher* of *New York* claimed the right to rule the

QUESTIONS.—6. Give an account of the visit of Andros to Hartford. 7. How was the charter kept from the hands of Andros? 8. What plan had been laid and how was it carried out? 9. What was the fate of the Charter Oak? 10. How were the people of Connecticut again tried? What did Governor Fletcher claim and do?

Connecticut **militia.** The people refused to acknowledge his authority, and defied him.

11. In 1693 *Fletcher* went to *Hartford* to enforce his authority. He called out the militia, who were commanded by the same Captain *Wadsworth* who hid the charter. The governor commenced reading to them a royal commission which gave him command of them.

12. *Wadsworth* then ordered the drums to be beaten. "Silence!" said the governor, angrily. The drummers stopped, and the governor began to read. "Play," said *Wadsworth* to the drummers. "Silence!" again shouted the governor. *Wadsworth* then stepped in front of *Fletcher*, and said, firmly: "Sir, if they are interrupted again, I'll make daylight shine through you in a moment!" The frightened governor then put the paper into his pocket and returned to New York.

13. From that time until the beginning of the *French* and *Indian* war, when her people numbered one hundred thousand, *Connecticut* went hand in hand with her sister colonies in promoting the growth of an independent **American nationality.**

14. In this section we have considered—

(1) The *foundations* of the colony of *Connecticut;* (2) the *colonial charter,* and the refusal of *Rhode Island* to be joined to *Connecticut;* (3) the *efforts* and *failure* of Governor *Andros* to get possession of the *charter* of *Connecticut,* and (4) the *efforts* and *failure* of Governor *Fletcher* to get control of the *Connecticut militia.*

QUESTIONS.—11 and 12. Give an account of Governor Fletcher's visit to Hartford. 13. What have you to say about Connecticut from that time? 14. What have we considered in this section?

SECTION VI.

THE COLONY OF RHODE ISLAND.

SEAL OF RHODE ISLAND.

1. *Massachusetts* claimed jurisdiction over *Rhode Island,* notwithstanding *Roger Williams* had obtained a **charter** from the *English* government in 1644.

2. *Massachusetts* denied the validity of that charter. *Williams* went to *England* again in 1652 to seek its confirmation. It was first confirmed by the *Parliament,* and then by *Cromwell* in May, 1655.

3. The question of jurisdiction was settled, but disputes concerning the *boundary* between the colonies were not adjusted until 1741.

QUESTIONS.—1. What can you tell about a claim of jurisdiction by Massachusetts? 2 What have you to say about the confirmation of the Rhode Island charter? 3. What about disputes concerning boundary?

4. In 1653 *Roger Williams* was chosen the *first president* of *Rhode Island,* and the colony prospered. Ten years afterward *Charles the Second* gave the colony a new charter, similar in character to that which he gave to *Connecticut. Benedict Arnold* was the first governor chosen under this royal charter.

5. *Andros* took the royal charter from *Rhode Island* in 1687. When he was driven from *New England* two years afterward, the people resumed their **independent government.** The seal of the colony bore the figure of an anchor, and the motto was **Hope.**

6. Under that charter *Rhode Island* continued to be governed until 1842, when the people adopted a **constitution.** From King *William's* war until the Revolution in 1775, *Rhode Island* showed active sympathy with its sister colonies.

7. In this section we have considered—

(1) The *claims* of *Massachusetts* to *jurisdiction* over *Rhode Island;* (2) the *confirmation* of the *charter* of *Rhode Island,* and (3) the *granting* of a *royal charter* to *Rhode Island.*

QUESTIONS.—4. Who was chosen the first President of Rhode Island? What can you tell about a royal charter and another governor? 5. What can you tell about Andros, the government, and a seal? 6. What did Rhode Island do? 7. What have we considered in this section?

SECTION VII.

THE COLONY OF NEW JERSEY.

SEAL OF NEW JERSEY.

1. The colony of *New Jersey* was **permanently founded**, when families from *Long Island* settled on the site of *Elizabethtown* in 1664.

2. According to an agreement, the *settlers* were to be exempted from rents for their lands for five years. When, at the end of that time, the owners asked for a rent of only a halfpenny an acre, the people complained and refused to pay it.

3. For two years the settlers resisted the demand for rent, and then **openly rebelled.** They drove Governor *Carteret* out of the province and elected an unworthy man to fill his place. The owners were about to take steps to com-

QUESTIONS.—1. When was New Jersey permanently settled, and by whom? 2. What can you tell about the rent of the land in New Jersey? 3. Give an account of a rebellion and the change that followed.

pel the tenants to pay, when the *Dutch* became possessors
of *New Netherland* again.

4. When *New Netherland* was restored to the *English*
in 1674, the western half of *New Jersey* was sold to Friends,
or Quakers ; and in 1676 the province was divided into
West and **East Jersey.**

5. The next year (1677) more than four hundred Friends
came from *England* and settled in *West Jersey;* and in
1681 the first **legislative Assembly** in that province met
at *Salem.*

6. *East Jersey* was sold to the Friends in 1682, and
Thomas Barclay, a leader among them, was chosen governor.   Everything was doing well in the *Jerseys* until the Duke
of *York* became King, when he **took away their charters.**

7. For several years there was great confusion in the *Jerseys,* the people denying the rights of the owners.   Finally,
in the spring of 1702, Queen *Anne* made of them one
royal province, under the control of the governor of
New York.

8. *New Jersey* was allowed to have an independent Assembly.   It remained in that political condition until 1738,
when *Lewis Morris* was appointed its first **royal governor.**   It so remained until 1776.

9. In this section we have considered—

(1) The *disputes* between the *people* and the *proprietors*
of New Jersey ; (2) its *division* into *West* and *East Jersey;* (3) their *possession by Friends,* and (4) their erection into a *royal province.*

QUESTIONS.—4. What can you tell about the sale and division of New Jersey? 5.
What can you tell about settlers and government in West Jersey? 6. What can you
tell about East Jersey? 7. Give an account of affairs in both, and their being made
a royal province. 8. What was the government of New Jersey? 9. What have we
considered in this section?

SECTION VIII.

THE COLONY OF PENNSYLVANIA.

SEAL OF PENNSYLVANIA.

1. *Delaware* had been annexed to *Penn's* domain, and the city of *Philadelphia* was laid out in 1682. The colonial career of *Pennsylvania* was then fairly begun. Settlers came from *England* in great numbers. Just dealings with the *Indians* made it a peaceful province to live in.

PENN'S HOUSE.

2. In 1683, *Penn*, then living in a small house in *Philadelphia*, gave the people a liberal government, under the title of **The Charter of Liberties.** The inhabitants were allowed self-government

QUESTIONS.—1. What can you tell about the beginning of the colonial career of Pennsylvania? 2. Where did Penn live and what did he do for the people? What can you tell about the prosperity of Pennsylvania?

and great personal freedom. When *Penn* returned to *England* in 1684, there were **twenty settled townships** and seven thousand inhabitants in *Pennsylvania.*

3. Because *Penn* and King *James* were personal friends, the former was suspected of disloyalty to *William* and *Mary.* In 1692 *Penn* was imprisoned and deprived of his domain in *America.* It was then made a **royal province,** under the governor of *New York.*

4. *Penn's* chartered rights were restored to him in 1694. In 1699 he sailed for *America,* and in 1701 he gave to the people of *Pennsylvania* a *new charter.* He allowed the inhabitants of *Delaware* to have a **separate legislature,** but they remained under the governor of *Pennsylvania* until 1776.

5. Soon after completing these arrangements, *Penn* returned to *England,* and never saw *America* again. His family owned and governed the province until the war for independence broke out. It was sold to the commonwealth of *Pennsylvania* for $580,000.

6. There were long and sometimes bitter disputes about the boundary between *Pennsylvania* and *Maryland.* These were settled in 1761 by a careful resurvey made by *Mason* and *Dixon.* That boundary was known as **Mason and Dixon's Line.**

7. We have considered in this section—

(1) The *time* when the colony of *Pennsylvania* was *founded;* (2) the *government* and *population* of the province ; (3) the *relations* of Penn to the *English gov-*

THE COLONIES.   117

Government for the Carolinas.   A Rebellion.   A Bad Governor.

ernment; (4) the *restoration* of his *chartered rights* and final *disposition* of the province ; and (5) *boundary disputes.*

SECTION IX.

THE COLONIES OF NORTH AND SOUTH CAROLINA.

1. The proprietors of the *Carolinas* wished to establish a grand empire in *America,* with orders of nobility such as then existed in *England,* They employed the Earl of *Shaftesbury* and the famous *John Locke* to prepare a form of government for the purpose.

2. That form of government, which was called the **Fundamental Constitutions**, was completed in the spring of 1669. The plan was totally unfitted for the country and the people of the *Carolinas,* and was rejected by the inhabitants.

3. An attempt to force the people into submission to this government and its **scheme of taxation** caused an open rebellion in the northern colony. The inhabitants drove the governor and other officers from the province in 1677. They called a new Assembly, and for two years maintained an **independent government.**

4. In 1683, *Seth Sothel,* a dishonest member of the company, was sent to govern the northern or *Albemarle County Colony.* He was a rapacious swindler. The people endured his rule about six years, and then drove him away. He took refuge in the southern colony.

QUESTIONS.—1. What did the owners of the Carolinas wish and do? 2. What have you to say about the form of government proposed? 3. What can you tell about the attempt to force the people into submission to the government? 4. Tell about Seth Sothel.

118   *THE COLONIES.*

Good Government in the Carolinas. Later Settlers in North Carolina.

5. Other and better governors came to the northern colony, but no one was so acceptable as *John Archdale,* a Friend, who was sent in 1695 to govern both of the sections of the *Carolinas.* There was repose and happiness during his administration.

6. From the close of *Archdale's* administration in 1698, the two portions of the *Carolinas* worked separately, until 1729, when they were formally divided into *distinct provinces* under the titles of **North and South Carolina.**

NORTH CAROLINA.

SEAL OF NORTH CAROLINA.

7. At the beginning of the year 1700, settlers were cultivating lands in *North Carolina* from the sea to the *Yadkin.* In 1707, a large number of **Huguenots** settled on the River *Trent,* and in 1710 a body of *German Lutherans* formed settlements at *New Berne* and other places.

8. The people were enjoying repose and happiness, when

QUESTIONS.—5. What can you tell about other governors in North Carolina? 6. What have you to say about the two Carolinas? 7. Tell about various settlers in North Carolina.

suddenly, in 1711, the *Indians* commenced a **war of extermination** upon the *German* settlements. They plundered and destroyed their property, and murdered one hundred and thirty *Germans.*

9. The *South Carolinians* helped their brethren in the north. In 1713, eight hundred of the *Tuscarora*[1] *Indians* —the leaders in the massacre—were made prisoners. The remainder fled and joined their brethren in *New York,* so completing the **Iroquois Confederacy of Six Nations.**

SOUTH CAROLINA

SEAL OF SOUTH CAROLINA.

10. The *South Carolinians* had trouble with the **Spaniards** in *Florida* in 1702. The *Spaniards* excited the *Indians* against the *English.* The governor of *South Carolina* led twelve hundred white men and friendly *Indians* to attack *St. Augustine* and punish the offenders.

QUESTIONS.—8. What can you tell about an Indian massacre? 9. What did the South Carolinians do? What was the fate of the Tuscaroras? 10. Tell about trouble with the Spaniards in Florida.

[1] *tus'-ka-ro'-ra.*

The expedition was a failure, and its cost was so great that the colony was compelled to **issue paper money** with which to pay expenses.

11. The next year (1703) the *South Carolinians* marched against the Indians in *Georgia* and *Florida,* who were the allies of the *Spaniards.* They captured several hundred of the *savages,* dispersed the rest, and desolated their country.

12. An attempt was now made to **establish the Church of England** as the state church in *South Carolina.* Those who did not conform to it were deprived of precious privileges, such as having a voice in the government. The Parliament interfered, and relieved the people of the grievous burden.

13. In 1706, a land and naval force, composed of *Frenchmen* and *Spaniards,* entered *Charleston Harbor,* to attack the town. Eight hundred *Spanish* soldiers were landed. The *South Carolinians* captured one of their vessels and drove the rest of the force away. The invaders sustained a severe loss in the conflict.

14. A **confederation of the Southern Indian tribes** was formed in 1715, for the extermination of the white people. These dusky allies numbered about six thousand warriors. They fell suddenly upon the back settlements, and murdered a hundred people before the news of hostility reached *Charleston.*

15. The governor (*Craven*) of *South Carolina* immediately marched against the *Indians* with twelve hundred men.

QUESTIONS.—11. Tell about an expedition against the Indians. 12. Give an account of an attempt to establish the Church of England in South Carolina. 13. Tell about an expedition against Charleston. 14. What can you tell about an Indian confederation ? 15. What did the South Carolinians do, and what was the effect ?

After several hard fights, the savages were driven back with much slaughter. The frightened *Indians,* impressed with the belief that the *South Carolinians* were mighty warriors, let them alone after that.

16. The proprietors of the *Carolinas* not only refused to bear any of the expense of these wars, made for the protection of their domain, but **taxed** the people heavily. In 1719, the people **rebelled,** and elected a governor to suit themselves. Finally, becoming wearied by **unjust treatment** from the owners, the people asked King *George the Second* to take them and the province under his protection.

17. The King gratified the discontented people by purchasing the two provinces of the proprietors in 1729. The two *Carolinas* were then legally separated, and over each a **royal governor** was placed.

18. These royal governors were no better than the proprietary governors. From 1729, the history of *North* and *South Carolina* is made up largely of a record of *disputes* between the people and the governors. The people endured the affliction until 1776, when the two provinces became **independent States.**

19. In this section we have considered—

(1) The *grand scheme of government* formed for the *Carolinas;* (2) the *opposition to it;* (3) the *character* and *career* of several *governors;* (4) the history of *North* and *South Carolina* separately ; (5) the *settlements* and *wars* in each ; (6) the *complaints of the people* in each ; and (7) the *final establishment of royal rule* in each province.

QUESTIONS.—16. How did the proprietors of the Carolinas act ? What did the people do ? 17. What did the King do, and what was the result ? 18. What have you to say about the royal governors and the people ? 19. What have we considered in this section ?

SECTION X.

THE COLONY OF GEORGIA.

SEAL OF GEORGIA.

1. Within eight years after the interview between *Ogle-thorpe* and *To-mo-chi-chi*, on the site of *Savannah*, in 1733, full twenty-five hundred *Europeans* were in *Georgia.* In addition to the debtors from the prisons were *German* and *Swiss* families, attracted by the liberal grants of land.

2. *John* and *Charles Wesley,* the founders of the Metho-dist denomination, were among the early immigrants, who came to labor for the good of the souls of the settlers. Afterward came the celebrated *George Whitefield* for the same purpose. They found the settlers indifferent to re-ligion.

3. Many of the *English settlers* had been unaccustomed

QUESTIONS.—1. What can you tell about the earlier settlers in Georgia? 2. What have you to say about the Wesleys and Whitefield? 3. What was the character of the settlers?

to manual labor, and did not thrive. The *Germans* and *Swiss* were industrious and thrifty. The colony increased rapidly for awhile.

4. The *Spaniards* in *Florida* claimed jurisdiction as far north as *Port Royal* in *South Carolina.* Oglethorpe expected they would be jealous of his intrusion, and prepared to resist their hostility. Being in *England* in 1736, he persuaded three hundred tall *Scotch Highland* soldiers to go with him to *Georgia.* With these he felt strong.

5. The *Spaniards* soon began to show signs of hostility. *Oglethorpe* built forts in the lower parts of *Georgia* and adjacent Islands. This act made the *Spaniards* angry, and they sent word to the governor that he and his followers must leave the country below the *Savannah,* or they would be driven out by force.

6. *Oglethorpe* went back to *England,* and in the autumn of 1737 he returned with six hundred troops and the commission of general. For two years the soldiers were not much needed.

7. When, in 1739, war broke out between **England** and **Spain,** *Oglethorpe* did not wait for an attack. He marched into *Florida* in May, 1740, with two thousand white men and *Indians.* He captured two forts and **besieged St. Augustine,** when lack of artillery, exhaustion of food, and sickness in his camp, compelled him to abandon the siege and return to *Savannah.*

8. In 1742 the *Spaniards* prepared to retaliate. With a large fleet three thousand troops were borne to the confines

QUESTIONS.—4. What did Oglethorpe expect, and what did he do? 5. What did the Spaniards and Oglethorpe do? 6. What can you tell about Oglethorpe's second visit to England? 7. What event occurred in 1739? Give an account of an expedition against St. Augustine.

THE COAST OF FLORIDA.

of *Georgia.* They landed and built a strong fort. *Oglethorpe* was wide awake. With a smaller force he prepared to attack the invaders. His plans were defeated by the treachery of a *Frenchman* who deserted.

9. By a clever trick *Oglethorpe* made the enemy believe that a *British* fleet was near *St. Augustine.* The alarmed *Spaniards* at once marched to attack one of *Oglethorpe's* forts, with the intention of returning immediately thereafter to *St. Augustine.*

10. In a dark swamp the *Spaniards* were **surprised** by *Oglethorpe,* and they suffered severely in a fight that ensued. So many *Spaniards* were killed that the place is still known as **Bloody Marsh.** The invaders hastened to their ships and sailed for *St. Augustine.* So *Georgia* was **saved.**

11. *Oglethorpe* left the colony in 1743 and never returned. That year the Trustees established a sort of **local government** in *Georgia.* The colony now grew very slowly. The people were not allowed to traffic with the *West Indies,* nor with the *Indians* around them. They did not own the land which they cultivated, nor were they permitted to employ **slave labor.**

12. These prohibitions bore heavily upon the prosperity of the colony. People preferred to settle in *South Carolina,* where no such prohibitions existed. Finally, in 1752, the King took possession of *Georgia,* made it a **royal province,** and removed all prohibitions. From that time until the war for independence *Georgia* prospered.

QUESTIONS.—8. Give an account of an expedition of the Spaniards against Georgia. 9 and 10. Continue your account of that expedition. 11. What more have you to say about Oglethorpe? What about the condition of the inhabitants of Georgia? 12. What were the effects of prohibitions, and how were they remedied?

13. We have now traced, in sharp outline, the **fortunes of the thirteen English-American** colonies from the planting of the seeds of settlement until the period when they were joined in a **national Union.**

14. In this section we have considered—

(1) The *early colonists* of *Georgia;* (2) the *jealousy* of the *Spaniards* in *Florida* and preparations to meet its *consequences;* (3) the *hostilities* between the *Georgians* and the *Spaniards,* and (4) the *peculiar condition* of the people of *Georgia* until it was made a *royal province.*

SECTION XI.

A RETROSPECT.

1. During a period of about two hundred and sixty years fifteen colonies were planted, thirteen of which were commenced within the space of about sixty-six years [1607 to 1673]. By the union of *Plymouth* and *Massachusetts,* and also of *Connecticut* and *New Haven,* the number of colonies was reduced to thirteen, and it was these which went into the Revolutionary contest in 1775.

2. Several *European* nations contributed men and women for the founding of these colonies. They were distinguished by differences in language, tastes, habits, and religious faith. *England* furnished far the greater number, and the settle-

---

QUESTIONS.—13. What have we now traced? 14. What have we considered in this section?

QUESTIONS.—1. What can you say about the establishment of colonies in America? 2. What materials composed the colonists? What position did England hold? Did unity mark the colonists, and how?

ments came to be known as *Anglo-American* colonies, governed by *English* laws. Very soon, common interests produced a unity, and the people, of whatever nation, joined heartily in maintaining the integrity of the *British* realm when it was assailed. They were still more united in opposing *British* aggressions upon their rights.

3. There were differences in the character of the people of the several colonies. The *Virginians* and their southern neighbors were mostly from a class of *English* society in which restraints were not very rigid ; and the warm climate produced a tendency toward indolence and ease. Hence slave labor, relieving the white man from toil, was regarded as a great blessing.

4. The *New Englanders* were chiefly from another class of *English* society, and included many religious enthusiasts, who sometimes possessed more zeal than wisdom. They were rigid disciplinarians in church and state, and their early legislation exhibits some curious laws respecting the minute details of social and domestic life. Their sterile soil made industry a necessity, and the climate inclined them to activity. Their habits and their dwellings were simple ; and their influence in the creation of our Republic was most salutary.

EARLY N. E. HOUSE.[1]

5. The industry, thrift, honesty, and aversion to change,

QUESTIONS.—3. What can you say about the Virginians and their southern neighbors ? 4. What can you say about the New England people—their laws and habits ?

[1] This is a picture of one of the oldest houses in New England, and is a favorable specimen of the best class of frame dwellings at that time. It is yet [1874] standing, I believe, near Medfield, in Massachusetts.

128   *THE COLONIES.*

Chief Pursuits of the Colonists.   Commerce and General Industry.

peculiar to the *Dutch,* prevailed in *New York* and *New Jersey,* and portions of *Pennsylvania,* for almost a century after the first settlements were made. The *Swedes* were similar; while the Friends or *Quakers* were marked by a refined simplicity and equanimity which won the esteem of all. Their lives were governed by a religious sentiment without fanaticism, which formed a powerful safeguard against vice and immorality. The people of *Maryland* exhibited some of the traits of all.

6. Agriculture was everywhere the chief pursuit, yet commerce and navigation were not wholly neglected, notwithstanding the restrictions of the navigation laws. The people were compelled, by necessity, to be self-reliant, and what they were unable to purchase from the workshops of *England,* such as apparel, furniture, and implements of agriculture, they rudely manufactured, and were content.

7. *Commerce* had a feeble infancy. Until their separation from *England,* in 1776, their interchange of commodities with the rest of the world might not, with propriety, be dignified with the name of *commerce. English* jealousy of the prosperity and independence of the colonies led to the imposition of many unwise restrictions upon their industry and enterprise; and these were the principal causes which finally led to the great revolt in 1775, and the separation of the colonies from the "mother country," as *England* was called.

8. Education was early fostered among the people, particularly in *New England,* where the **common school,** the chief glory of our Republic, was early established and tenderly nurtured. Provision was made for the education of all. The rigid laws which discouraged all frivolous amusements, were productive of a habit of reading. The books were devoted chiefly to history and religion, and large numbers were sold. A traveler, as early as 1686, asserts that several booksellers in *Boston* had "made fortunes by their business." Newspapers, the great educators of the people in our day, were very few and of little worth before the era of the Revolution.

9. Such were the people, and such their political and social condition, at the commencement of the great struggle between the *French* and *English* for supreme dominion in *America,* which we are now to consider.

SECTION XII.

THE STRIFE FOR POWER; THE FRENCH AND INDIAN WAR.

1. We have briefly noticed the **wars in America** between the *English* and the *French* and *Indians.* The causes of these wars often concerned Europeans more than Americans. The **strife** we are now about to consider began in a **quarrel about boundaries** between the *French* and *English,* in *America.*

QUESTIONS.—8. What can you say about education in the colonies? What encouraged reading? What kind of books were read? What have you to say about books and newspapers?

QUESTIONS.—1. What have we noticed? What have you to say about the causes of strife?

2. The French traded with the Indians in the country west of the *Alleghany*[1] *Mountains*, from *Lake Erie* to the *Mississippi* and *New Orleans*. They built forts in those regions, and thus made the *English* jealous.

3. In 1749, some *Englishmen* and *Americans* formed the **Ohio Company.** The King granted them a large tract of land on the upper waters of the *Ohio River.* The *French* claimed this region as their own. An old *Indian* who heard the quarrel said, "You *English* claim all on one side of the river, and you *French* all on the other side ; where does the **Indian's land** lay ?" They could not answer.

4. The Ohio Company sent men to survey these lands in 1753. *French* soldiers siezed and imprisoned these surveyors, and built forts in the country between the head-waters of the *Ohio* and *Lake Erie.*

5. The governor of *Virginia* sent young *George Washington* with a letter to the *French* commander, inquiring what was meant by such conduct. After a fatiguing journey of four hundred miles, *Washington* returned early in 1754 with an answer in writing. The *French* commander told the governor that **the land belonged to his King**, and that he and his soldiers should stay there as long as they' pleased.

6. The governor (*Dinwiddie*[2]) made *Washington* a major, and placed him in command of *Virginia* troops

---

QUESTIONS.—2. What did the French do westward of the Alleghany Mountains? 3. Tell about the Ohio Company and the claims to the lands on the Ohio. 4. What did the Ohio Company do? What did the French do? 5. What did the Governor of Virginia do? Give an account of Washington's mission. 6. What did Governor Dinwiddie then do?

[1] *al-le gā'-ne.*   [2] *din-wid'-de.*

that were to be sent against the *French.* These were joined by troops from *New York* and *South Carolina.* The whole were commanded by Colonel *Fry.*

FORT DU QUESNE.

7. Meanwhile the *English* had begun to build a fort on the site of the city of *Pittsburgh.* The *French* **drove them away,** finished the work, and called it *Fort Du Quesne,*[1] the name of the governor of *Canada.*

8. *Washington,* with his *Virginians,* pressed forward to retake the fort. He met the *French* coming to oppose his march, and in a skirmish at the *Great Meadows* the **first blood was spilled** (May 28, 1754) in the long war that ensued. The commander of the *French* party was killed.

9. Colonel *Fry* died two days after this skirmish, and *Washington* was made chief leader of the troops. With these he pressed forward. Hearing of the approach of a large party of *French* and *Indians,* he fell back to the *Great Meadows,* and built a stockade, which he called *Fort Necessity.*

10. Early in July the *French* attacked *Fort Necessity.* After a fight for ten hours (July 4), *Washington* was compelled to surrender. The *French* commander generously allowed all of his prisoners to return to their homes.

11. During the same summer (1754) representatives from several colonies met at *Albany,* in *New York,* to consider

QUESTIONS.—7. Tell about a fort on the site of Pittsburgh. 8. What did Washington and Virginia troops do? Tell about a skirmish. 9. How came Washington to be chief commander of troops? What did he do? 10. Tell about a battle. 11. What can you tell about a plan for the union of the colonies?

¹ *du-kane'.*

plans for **united action** against the *French* and *Indians.* They made a covenant of peace with the *Six Nations,* and then agreed upon a plan of **Union** proposed by Dr. *Franklin.*

12. The plan was not favored by the King nor the colonies, and it was abandoned. Soon after the Congress adjourned, the *Indians,* incited by the *French,* commenced plundering and murdering the *English* of the frontier settlements.

13. The endangered colonists, with a promise of assistance from the *English* government, prepared for war. That government sent *Edward Braddock* (an *Irish* officer) to *America* early in 1755, with troops, as commander-in-chief of all the *British* forces in *America.* He met the governors of several colonies at *Alexandria,* in *Virginia,* in April, when they arranged

GENERAL BRADDOCK.

THE CAMPAIGN OF 1755.

14. Three separate armies were to be mustered. One was to march against *Fort Du Quesne ;* a second against forts near each end of *Lake Ontario,* and a third against forts on *Lake Champlain.*

15. An expedition against the *French* in *Acadia* [1] had already been arranged. In May three thousand men, under General *Shirley,* sailed from *Boston,* landed at the head of

QUESTIONS.—12. What was the fate of the plan of Union ? What did the Indians do ? 13. What did the colonists do ? What did the British government do ? What can you tell about General Braddock ? 14. What was the plan of the campaign of 1755 ? 15 What can you tell about an expedition against Acadia ?

[1] *a-ka'-de-a.*

the *Bay of Fundy,* and captured the *French* forts in that vicinity. Fort *Beausejour*[1] was taken on the 15th of June, and Fort *Gaspereau*[2] on the 17th. They desolated *Acadia* and cruelly drove the innocent inhabitants to the woods or carried them away in ships.

16. In June *Braddock* marched from the *Potomac River,* with two thousand men, against *Fort Du Quesne.* On the 9th of July, when they were near the *Monongahela*[3] *River,* the *English* were assailed by *Indians* concealed in ambush.

17. A severe battle ensued. *Washington* was *Braddock's* aid. He knew how to fight *Indians,* and ventured

QUESTIONS.—16. Tell about the expedition of Braddock against Fort Du Quesne.

[1] *bo-seh'-yure.*　[2] *gah-speh-ro'.*　[3] *mo-non'-ga-he-lah.*

Braddock's Defeat, Death, and Burial.

to offer *Braddock* some advice. That general would not listen to him. The *French* and their *Indian* allies fought

BURIAL OF BRADDOCK.

bravely. *Braddock* was defeated, and he and several of his officers were mortally wounded.

18. *Washington* was the only officer not injured. He

QUESTIONS.—17. Tell about a battle near the Monongahela. What did Washington do, and what occurred?

took the command, and skillfully conducting a retreat, saved the remainder of the army. *Braddock* died, and was buried by torch-light, Colonel *Washington* reading the burial service of the *English* church at the grave.

19. Governor *Shirley*[1] led the troops destined to attack the forts on *Lake Ontario.* Storms and sickness prevented his going farther than *Oswego.* He commenced a fort there, left a small garrison, and returned to *Albany.*

WILLIAM JOHNSON.

20. *William Johnson,* an *Indian* agent in the *Mohawk* country, led troops against the forts on *Lake Champlain.* In July, 1755, **six thousand** of these were collected, under General *Lyman,* at *Fort Edward,* from which place *Johnson* led nearly all of them to the head of *Lake George.*

21. Informed that the Baron *Dieskau*[2] was leading a force of *French* and *Indians* against him, *Johnson* sent out a thousand men, under Colonel *Williams,* to attack them. *Williams* was **defeated** (September 8, 1755), and *Dieskau* hurried on to attack *Johnson*

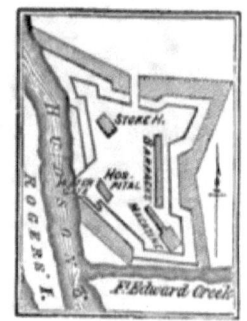

FORT EDWARD.

in his camp. The *French* and *Indians* were driven off, and *Dieskau* was *mortally wounded.*

QUESTIONS.—18. What have you to say about Washington and the army, and the death of Braddock? 19. What did Governor Shirley do? What was the result? 20. What can you tell about William Johnson and troops in Northern New York? 21. Give an account of fighting near Lake George.

[1] *shur'-le.*   [2] *dee-es-ko'.*

22. Believing the forts on *Lake Champlain* to be too strong for his force, *Johnson* remained where he was and built Fort *William Henry*. Leaving some troops there and at *Fort Edward,* he marched the remainder of his army back to *Albany,* and so closed the campaign of 1755.

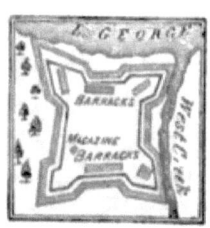

FORT WILLIAM HENRY.

CAMPAIGN OF 1756.

23. *England* declared war against France in 1756. Lord *Loudon,*[1] a very indolent man, had been appointed commander-in-chief in *America,* but did not arrive until late in the summer. General *Abercrombie,*[2] a good soldier, came in his place in June.

ABERCROMBIE.

24. The plan of the campaign was similar to the one formed the previous year. *Abercrombie* found seven thousand troops ready for action at *Albany.* Foolish contentions about rank delayed their march until August. Then *Montcalm,*[3] *Dieskau's* successor, was well prepared to meet the *English.*

25. Early in August *Montcalm,* with **five thousand** *French, Canadians,* and *Indians,* went up the *St. Law-*

QUESTIONS.—22. What did General Johnson do? 23. What can you tell about a declaration of war, and the English commanders in America? 24. What was the plan of the campaign for 1756? Tell about the movements of Abercrombie, and the consequence of delay. 25. What did Montcalm do? What occurred at Oswego?

loo'-dun. [2] *ab-er-krom'-be.* [3] *mont-kam'.*

138   *FRENCH AND INDIAN WAR.*

Oswego Taken by the French.   General Alarm.   Indians Humbled.

rence and *Lake Ontario* to *Oswego,*[1] and on the 14th **cap-**

tured an *English* fort there.   The spoils of victory were many cannon, vessels in the harbor, and fourteen hundred men.

FORTS AT OSWEGO.

26. This event so frightened the indolent *Loudon,* who had arrived and taken the general command, that he ordered all the other expeditions **to be abandoned.**   There was general alarm.   The *Indians* desolated the frontiers, and killed or carried away almost a **thousand white people.**

27. The *English* strengthened their forts and block-houses.   A heavy blow was given to the *Indians* at *Kittanning,*[2] in *Pennsylvania,* by troops under Colonel *Armstrong,* on the 8th of September, which made the savages quiet, and so ended the campaign of 1756.

BLOCK-HOUSE.

CAMPAIGN OF 1757.

28. Lord *Loudon's* laziness ruined everything in which he was concerned.   It allowed the *French* to take *Louisburg;* and at a council held in *Boston,* he proposed to confine the campaign of 1757 to the recapture of that town and fortress.   The disappointed colonists yielded to him.

QUESTIONS.—26. What effect did the capture of Oswego have on Loudon? Tell about the Indians. 27. What did the English do? What event made the Indians quiet? 28. What have you to say about Lord Loudon's laziness? What did he propose, and what did the colonists do?

[1] *os-we'-go.*   [2] *kit-tan'-ning.*

29. Lord *Loudon* was at *Halifax* at the close of June, with a large land and naval force, wherewith to attack *Louisburg.* There he was informed that the *French* at *Louisburg* were stronger in soldiers and ships than he, and after some delay he thought it prudent to **leave them alone.** He returned to *New York* in August.

30. As a consequence of *Loudon's* ignorance and inefficiency, *Montcalm* had won victories in northern *New York.* With seven thousand white men and two thousand *Indians,* he left *Ticonderoga* late in July, and compelled the garrison at *Fort William Henry* to **surrender** early in August.

31. *Montcalm* promised to protect the prisoners from the savages. He was unable to do so, and a large number of them were **cruelly murdered** when they marched out to go to *Fort Edward. Fort William Henry* was destroyed. This sad event ended the campaign of 1757. With it was ended the leadership of Lord *Loudon* in *America.*

32. *William Pitt* was now made prime minister of England. He was a man of energy and wisdom ; and he made grand preparations for the

CAMPAIGN OF 1758.

33. General *Abercrombie* was placed in chief command of the troops in *America.* Admiral *Boscawen*[1] was put in charge of a large number of ships for service in *American*

QUESTIONS.—29. Tell about Loudon's expedition against Louisburg, and what did he finally do? 30. What can you tell about the consequences of Loudon's delay and Montcalm's operations? 31. What did Montcalm promise, and what occurred? 32. What have you to say about William Pitt? 33. What can you tell about a land and naval force in 1758? What did the colonists do?

[1] *bos-kaw'-en.*

140　　　　*FRENCH AND INDIAN WAR.*

Louisburg Taken by the English.　English Defeated at Ticonderoga.

waters. The colonists were encouraged, and cheerfully answered all calls for **men and supplies.**

34. It was decided to attack *Louisburg, Ticonderoga,*

LORD HOWE.

and *Fort Du Quesne.* Twelve thousand men under Generals *Amherst* and *Wolfe,* went from *Halifax* in *Boscawen's* fleet of forty vessels, and on the 8th of June landed near *Louisburg.* After a siege of about fifty days, **the French surrendered** (July 20) the fort and five thousand soldiers.

35. Meanwhile *Abercrombie* and young Lord **Howe** were leading sixteen thousand men and a heavy train of artillery, against *Ticonderoga.* They went over *Lake George* early in *July,* and in an encounter near *Ticonderoga,* on the 6th, Lord *Howe* was killed.

TICONDEROGA.

36. The *English* pressed on through the woods, and without waiting for the artillery to come up, attacked *Ticonderoga* on the 8th. *Montcalm* was there with four thousand men. The *English* were defeated with a loss of two thousand men.

37. *Abercrombie* retreated to the head of *Lake George,* and then sent Colonel *Bradstreet,*[1] with *three thousand* men, to attack Fort *Frontenac,* at the foot of *Lake On-*

QUESTIONS.—34. What was it decided to do? What can you tell about an expedition against Louisburg? 35. What can you tell about an expedition against Ticonderoga, and the death of a leader? 36. Give an account of the attack on Fort Ticonderoga. 37. What did Abercrombie do? Tell about an expedition against Fort Frontenac.

[1] *brad'-street.*

tario. It was on the site of *Kingston,* in *Canada.* The fort was taken on the 27th of August.

38. In July, General *Forbes* [1] commenced a march against *Fort Du Quesne,* with nine thousand men. He moved so slowly that he did not get over the *Alleghany Mountains* until November, when his troops were attacked and defeated in a battle on the 21st. Then *Washington,* with his *Virginians,* moved rapidly forward. Hearing of his approach, the *French* **set fire to Fort Du Quesne** (Nov. 24), and fled down the *Ohio River* in boats.

RUINS OF TICONDEROGA IN 1858.

39. In honor of the great statesman, the name of *Fort Pitt* was given to the ruin, and there the city of *Pittsburgh* now stands. This event ended the campaign of 1758. Its results were **favorable to the English.** They had captured Forts *Louisburg, Frontenac,* and *Du Quesne,* with very little loss to themselves, and so **alarmed the Indians,** that they agreed, in council, not to fight the *English* any more.

QUESTIONS.—38. Give an account of an expedition against Fort Du Quesne and the result. 39. What new name was given to the fort? What were the results of the campaign of 1758?

[1] *forbz.*

Military Operations in New England and Canada.

CAMPAIGN OF 1759.

LORD AMHERST.

40. *Pitt* now resolved to take *Canada* and crush the **dominion of the French in America.** General *Amherst*[1] was made commander-in-chief in *America;* and in the spring of 1759, he found twenty thousand Provincial troops ready to march against *Canada.*

41. A land and naval force was sent over from *England,* and early in the summer **three** expeditions were in motion. One went up the *St. Lawrence* to attack *Quebec;* another went to drive the *French* from *Lake Champlain* and force them into *Canada,* and a third was destined to attack the fort on the *Niagara River.*

LAKE GEORGE AND VICINITY.

42. *Amherst* appeared before *Ticonderoga* late in July with eleven thousand men. The *French* commander had just heard of the arrival of *Wolfe* before

FORT AT CROWN POINT.

Quebec. He fled in haste to *Crown Point.* *Amherst* pursued the *French,* who went down the lake into *Canada.* They never came back. *Amherst* then built the strong fort, now in ruins, at *Crown Point.*

QUESTIONS.—40. What did Pitt resolve to do? What have you to say about General Amherst? 41. What can you tell about preparations for the campaign of 1759 and the movements of troops? 42. Tell about the expedition of Amherst against Ticonderoga and the flight of the French. What did Amherst do?

[1] *am'-erst.*

43. General *Prideaux*[1] led the expedition against *Fort Niagara.* He sailed from *Oswego* in July, with Sir *William Johnson* as his lieutenant. On the 17th he commenced a **siege of Niagara,** where he was soon killed by the bursting of a gun. *Johnson* continued the siege, and on the 25th the fort surrendered to the English.

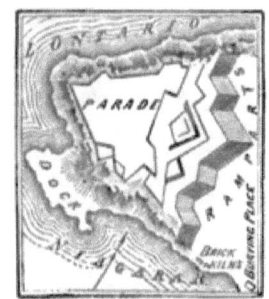

FORT NIAGARA.

44. General *Wolfe,* who went up the *St. Lawrence* with eight thousand troops and many battle-ships, under Admirals *Holmes* and *Saunders,* was now near *Quebec.* It was a strong, walled town, under the command of General *Montcalm,* whose army lay along the *St. Lawrence,* from the city to the *Montmorenci*[2] *River.*

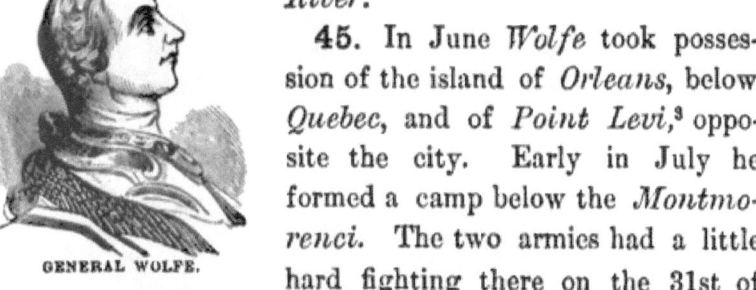

GENERAL WOLFE.

45. In June *Wolfe* took possession of the island of *Orleans,* below *Quebec,* and of *Point Levi,*[3] opposite the city. Early in July he formed a camp below the *Montmorenci.* The two armies had a little hard fighting there on the 31st of July, but the **grand assault** was deferred until September.

46. *Wolfe* waited in vain for *Amherst* to come to his aid. Prostrated by fever at the close of summer, he held a **council of war** at his bedside. It was determined to

QUESTIONS.—43. Tell about the expedition against Fort Niagara, and the result. 44 What can you tell about an expedition under General Wolfe? What have you to say about Quebec and an army under Montcalm? 45. What position did Wolfe take near Quebec? 46. What did Wolfe do, and what was determined upon in council?

[1] *pre-doz'.*   [2] *mont-mo-ren'-ci.*   [3] *lee'-vi.*

LANDING UNDER THE CLIFF.

scale the rocky heights above the town, ascend to the *Plains of Abraham,* and there attack *Quebec* on its weakest side.

47. Feeble as he was, *Wolfe* determined to lead his troops. These were conveyed silently, in boats rowed with muffled oars, to a cave at the mouth of a winding ravine. They were all landed at midnight, unobserved by the *French* sentinels.

48. *Montcalm* was ignorant of this movement until he

was **surprised** at sunrise on the morning of the 13th of September by the glow of British uniforms on the high plain. He immediately marched his whole army

MILITARY OPERATIONS AT QUEBEC.

across the *St. Charles River* and attacked the enemy.

49. A very **severe battle** was fought. Wolfe was three times wounded, the last time mortally, by a bullet which pierced his breast. He was taken to the rear, faint from the loss of blood. He heard a shout, "They run! They run!" "Who runs?" feebly asked the dying leader. "The *French*," was the reply. "Then I die **content**," he said, and expired.

50. *Montcalm* was killed at about the time *Wolfe* expired, and now one tall monument stands in *Quebec,* erected to the memory of the two heroes. Five days after the battle *Quebec* was **given to the English**. But *Canada* was not yet conquered.

CAMPAIGN OF 1760.

51. The *French* tried to retake *Quebec* in the spring of 1760. A very severe battle was fought at *Sillery*, three miles above *Quebec,* on the 28th of April, when the *British* were driven into the city and a **siege commenced.** Rumors of an approaching *British* fleet alarmed the *French*

MONUMENT TO WOLFE AND MONTCALM.

and they fled to *Montreal,* then the last stronghold left of the **French empire in America.**

52. The whole summer was consumed by *Amherst* in preparations to attack the *French* in *Montreal.* He went down the *St. Lawrence* with ten thousand white men and a thousand *Indian* warriors, and arrived before *Montreal* on the 6th of September.

53. General *Murray,* with four thousand troops from *Quebec,* joined *Amherst* the same day. On the next day Colonel *Haviland*[1] came with three thousand troops from *Crown Point.*

54. The *French* commander saw that resistance would be useless, and on the 8th he **surrendered the post** to the *English.* General *Gage* was appointed governor. Thus was completed the **conquest of Canada**; and the power

QUESTIONS.—51. What did the French try to do, and what did they do? 52. What did Amherst do? 53. What can you tell about the English before Montreal? 54. What did the French commander see, and what did he do? What have you to say about the conquest of Canada and the French power?

[1] *hav'-i-land.*

of the *French* in *America* was broken.   The **French and Indian War** was essentially ended from this time.

55. *French* emissaries, however, continued to excite the *Indians* against the *English.*   A bloody warfare was kept up along the frontiers of *Virginia* and the *Carolinas* by the savages for more than a year.

56. These troubles in the *South* had scarcely ended when *Pontiac,*[1] an *Ottawa*[2] chief, induced several of the northwestern tribes to join in trying to drive the white people from the country.

57. *Pontiac* was one of the greatest of the *Indian* chiefs known to *Europeans.*   In the summer of 1763, he **kindled a fierce war.**   It was terrible for awhile, but the Confederacy was subdued and destroyed.   *Pontiac* fled to the country of the *Illinois,* where he was murdered in 1769.

58. The last act in the *French* and *Indian War* was a **treaty of peace,** which was concluded at *Paris* in 1763, by which *France* was shorn of the best part of her **dominions in America.**   This struggle with the *French* revealed to the colonists their inherent strength in **Union,** and prepared them for the greater struggle for **independence,** in which they were engaged soon afterward.

59. We have considered in this section—
(1) The *causes* which brought the *French* and *English* into conflict in the *Ohio* country ; (2) the *beginning* of hostilities between the *three races in America* in 1754 ; (3) the *preliminary steps* toward a *union of the colonies;*

QUESTIONS.—55. What can you tell about the Indians on the Southern borders ? 56. What can you tell about Pontiac and Indians in the northwest? 57. What have you to say about Pontiac, his doings and his fate? 58. What was the last act in the French and Indian War? What was the more remote result of the struggle? 59. What have we considered in this section ?

[1] *pon-ti-ak'..*   [2] *ot-taw'-wah.*

(4) the *declaration of war* between *France* and *England;* (5) the several *campaigns* from 1755 to 1760, which ended in the *conquests of Canada,* and (6) *Indian hostilities* and a final *treaty of peace.*

OUTLINE OF IMPORTANT EVENTS FROM 1619 TO 1763.*

1619. Representative government established in Virginia. Slaves introduced into Virginia.

1620. Young women sent to Virginia for wives.

1621. Indians appear at Plymouth.

1622. Massacre by Indians in Virginia.

1624. Virginia made a royal province.

1626. First governor of New Netherland arrives.

1628. Salem and Charlestown settled.

1629. Charter of Massachusetts transferred to the colony.

1635. Roger Williams banished from Massachusetts.

1639. Representative government established in Maryland.

1643. New England confederacy formed.

1644. Massacre by Indians in Virginia. Charter for Rhode Island granted.

1647. Governor Stuyvesant arrives at New Amsterdam.

1649. Toleration Act passed in Maryland.

1650. Disputes between Connecticut and New Netherland settled.

1651. Dutch build a fort on the Delaware.

1652. Silver money first coined in Massachusetts.

1653. Roger Williams elected first president of Rhode Island.

1654. Protestants disfranchise Roman Catholics in Maryland.

1655. Rhode Island charter confirmed by Cromwell.

1656. Quakers first appear in Boston.

1660. Charles the Second enthroned. Colonies subjected to import duties.

1662. Charter given to Connecticut.

1663. First representative Assembly in New Netherland.

1664. New Netherland surrendered to the English. New Jersey founded.

1665. New Haven and Connecticut colonies united.

1669. Grand scheme of government for the Carolinas perfected.

1673. New York retaken by the Dutch.

1674. New York given back to the English.

* See foot-note on page 32.

1675. King Philip's war breaks out.

1676. Civil war breaks out in Virginia.

1676. New Jersey divided into East and West Jersey.

1681. First legislative Assembly in New Jersey.

1682. City of Philadelphia laid out.

1683. Charter of Liberties given to New York. Charter of Liberties given to Pennsylvania.

1685. Charter of Liberties withdrawn from New York.

1686. Andros sent to take away the New England charters.

1687. Andros attempts to seize the Connecticut charter. Takes the Rhode Island charter.

1689. Accession of William and Mary. King William's War breaks out. Coode's Rebellion in Maryland. Connecticut resumes her charter.

1690. Schenectady burned by the French and Indians.

1691. Execution of Leisler and Milborne. Maryland made a royal province.

1692. Massachusetts and Plymouth united. The witchcraft delusion at Salem. Pennsylvania made a royal province.

1693. Governor Fletcher attempts to control the militia of Connecticut.

1694. Penn's charter rights restored.

1695. Archdale made governor of both Carolinas.

1699. Annapolis made the capital of Maryland.

1701. Queen Anne's War breaks out. Penn gives a new charter to Pennsylvania.

1702. The Jerseys made a royal province under the governor of New York. South Carolinians go to attack St. Augustine.

1703. South Carolinians subdue hostile Indians.

1706. Expedition of Spaniards against South Carolina.

1707. Huguenots settle in North Carolina.

1710. Port Royal, in Acadia, captured by the English. Germans settle in North Carolina.

1711. Unsuccessful expedition against Quebec. Massacre by Indians in North Carolina.

1713. Peace with French and Indians secured by treaty. North Carolina Indians subdued.

1715. Confederation of Southern Indians formed. South Carolinians subdue the Indians.

1716. Rights of Lord Baltimore restored.

1720. North and South Carolina made separate royal provinces.

1736. Scotch Highland soldiers go to Georgia.

1737. Six hundred other soldiers go to Georgia.

1738. First royal governor in New Jersey.

Outline of Important Events.

1740. Georgians make war on the Spaniards in Florida.

1742. Spaniards threaten Georgia. Fight at Bloody Marsh.

1743. Local government first established in Georgia.

1744. King George's War breaks out.

1745. Louisburg captured by the English.

1746. D'Anville's fleet dispersed.

1748. King George's War ended by treaty.

1749. Ohio Company formed.

1752. Georgia made a royal province.

1753. French soldiers imprison English surveyors.

1754. Young Washington's delicate mission to the French. Fort Du Quesne built. First blood shed in the French and Indian War. Colonial Congress at Albany.

1755. Braddock comes to America with troops. Defeated and killed near the Monongahela River. Battles near Lake George, and Fort William Henry built. Acadia desolated.

1756. England declares war against France. Montcalm captures Oswego. Indians defeated at Kittanning.

1757. Montcalm captures Fort William Henry. Pitt made Prime Minister.

1758. Louisburg captured by the English. The English repulsed at Ticonderoga. Forts Frontenac and Du Quesne taken by the English.

1759. Forts Ticonderoga and Niagara, and the city of Quebec taken by the English.

1760. The conquest of Canada by the English completed.

1761. Troubles with the Southern Indians.

1763. War with Pontiac. Treaties of Peace concluded at Paris.

A LIST OF BATTLES IN THE FRENCH AND INDIAN WAR.

NAME.	DATE.	NAME.	DATE.
1754.		**1758.**	
Great Meadows	May 28	Near Ticonderoga	July 6
Fort Necessity	July 4	Ticonderoga	July 8
1755.		Louisburg	July 26
Fort Beausejour	June 16	Fort Frontenac	Aug. 27
Fort Gasperau	June 17	Alleghany Mountains	Sept. 21
Monongahela	July 9		
Near Lake George	Sept. 8	**1759.**	
Head of Lake George	Sept. 8	Fort Niagara	July 25
1756.		Montmorenci	July 31
Oswego	Aug. 14	Plains of Abraham	Sept. 13
1757.		**1760.**	
Fort William Henry	Aug. 9	Sillery	April 28

CHAPTER IV.

THE STRIFE FOR FREEDOM, OR THE REVOLUTION.

SECTION I.

THE PRELIMINARY EVENTS.

1. The love of liberty of thought and action, which caused a greater portion of the settlers in *America* to leave home and make an abode in the **wilderness**, was increased by its indulgence here. They loved **father-land** much, but **freedom** more.

2. There was a tendency toward **national indepen-dence** from the first planting of the colonies. The people, however, gloried in being subjects of *Great Britain,* so long as the imperial government treated them justly. When it ceased to do so, they asserted their **independence,** and fought to secure it.

3. The natural tendency toward independence ; the neg-lect of the parent country ; the misrule of many royal governors ; the exactions of proprietors, and the peculiar conditions of society in *America,* were the chief causes which made the struggle for independence a sort of necessity.

QUESTIONS.—1. What induced persons to settle in America ? 2. What was the ten-dency of the colonists ? What did the people glory in, and what did they do ? 3. What were the chief causes that led to the struggle for independence ?

4. The immediate occasion of that struggle may be found in the persistence of the *British* ministry in **taxing the colonies,** while, at the same time, they denied them a **representation in the parliament.** The *Americans* said, " **Taxation without representation is tyranny.**" Under the circumstances their principles made rebellion a necessity.

5. *George the Third* took his seat on the throne of *England* at the close of the *French* and *Indian* war. That war had cost England much money, and her treasury was empty. The King asked how it should be filled, and bad advisers said, **Tax the Americans**; they are rich, and willing to pay freely.

6. The colonists were called upon to pay to the government certain sums of money for everything which they might receive in ships. This is called an **impost duty.** Officers were sent to *America* to collect this duty, or **tax.** Leading men in *Massachusetts,* among them the eloquent *James Otis,* advised the people not to pay the tax, and they refused to do so.

JAMES OTIS.

7. Then a law was passed, that no paper for certain business or social purposes should be used, unless it should bear a stamp issued by the *British* government, for which certain sums of money were charged.

QUESTIONS.—4. What was the immediate occasion of that struggle? How did the colonies express their chief grievance? 5. What can you tell about George the Third and the public treasury? What advice was given him? 6. What can you tell about taxing the colonists? What were they advised to do? 7. What can you tell about stamped paper?

8. These stamps were made on bits of paper—some white and many blue—bearing royal emblems and the money value of the stamp. This law, known as the **Stamp Act,** made the *Americans* indignant, for it was a new and indirect mode of taxation. Delegates were appointed in the different colonies, to meet in *New York* in the autumn of 1765, to agree upon a plan of action in the matter.

A STAMP.

9. This **"Stamp Act Congress,"** as it was called, sent strong petitions to Parliament asking for justice ; also an able address to the King, and a declaration of their rights as British subjects.

10. Encouraged by the tone of these papers, the people rejected the stamps. Merchants agreed not to buy any more goods in *England* until justice was done to the American colonies. The great *William Pitt* advised Parliament to **repeal** the act, and it was done in the spring of 1776.

WILLIAM PITT.

11. Among the most earnest opposers of *British* oppression at that day was *Patrick Henry.* When, in the *Virginia* legislature, he was one day speaking of the dangers that threatened a monarch who oppressed his people, he said, " *Cæsar* had his

Brutus, Charles the First his *Cromwell,* and *George the Third* "— He was interrupted at this point by cries of " **Treason! Treason !** " *Henry* concluded by saying— " may profit by their example ; if that be treason, make the most of it."

PATRICK HENRY IN THE VIRGINIA ASSEMBLY.

12. The *British* government tried other measures to get money from the *Americans.* Parliament laid an impost duty on goods wanted by them. The Colonial Assemblies declared that Parliament had no right to so **tax the colonists,** and merchants agreed to buy nothing from *England* until the government should be just.

13. The tax-gatherers came in 1768. They were treated

with contempt. Soldiers, under General *Gage,* were sent to Boston from *Halifax* to assist the tax-gatherers in enforcing the law.

14. The royal governors, seeing the determination of their government, became more proud and insolent. They treated the people as **rebels,** and irritated them beyond endurance. Even the common soldiers treated citizens with disrespect.

15. Finally, in March, 1770, the soldiers and citizens in *Boston* had a quarrel, which resulted in the killing of three persons and the wounding of several others by the soldiers.

16. The citizens resolved not to endure **military rule** any longer. They demanded the instant removal of the soldiers to a military post on an island in *Boston Harbor.* The frightened governor removed them, and quiet was restored. But the **"Boston Massacre,"** as it was called, was long remembered.

LORD NORTH.

17. The *British* ministry, with Lord *North* at their head, now concluded to lay an impost tax upon **tea** alone. They taxed a single article only to **assert their right to tax the Americans.** The colonists refused to pay it, and agreed not to buy any tea.

QUESTIONS.—13. What occurred in Boston in 1768? 14. What have you to say about the royal governors and the soldiers? 15. Give an account of disturbances in Boston. 16. What did the citizens do? 17. What did the British ministry do, and why? What did the colonists do?

156 *THE REVOLUTION.*

The "Regulators." Burning of the Gaspé. Stupidity of Ministers.

18. In 1771, the home taxes in *North Carolina* were burdensome, owing to the **extravagance of the royal governor.** The people formed associations for the regulation of public affairs. These were called **Regulators.**

19. The royal governor led soldiers into a district to assist the tax-gatherer in collecting the taxes. The Regulators met him. A battle ensued. The Regulators were defeated, and several of them were hanged. **Hatred of royal rule** there was intense ever afterwards.

20. In 1772, a *British* vessel was in *Narraganset Bay* to enforce the collection of taxes. Her commander irritated the people, and on a stormy night in June, about sixty men, led by Captain *Whipple,* went in a boat and burned the vessel.

21. Three years afterward, Sir *James Wallace,* in command of a *British* vessel in the same waters, wrote a note to Captain *Whipple,* saying: "You, *Abraham Whipple,* on the 17th of June, 1772, burned his Majesty's vessel, the *Gaspé,* and I will hang you to the yard-arm." *Whipple* instantly replied: "Sir,—Always *catch* a man before you *hang* him."

22. The *English* merchants, suffering a great **loss of trade** because the *Americans* refused to buy of them, asked their government to take off the obnoxious duties. Lord *North,* the *British* prime minister, persisted in retaining the tax on **tea,** but devised a plan which, he thought, would please the *Americans.*

QUESTIONS.—18. What can you tell about disturbances in North Carolina? 19. What can you tell about the royal governor and the Regulators in North Carolina? 20. Tell about the burning of a vessel in Narraganset Bay. 21. Give an account of a correspondence on the subject. 22. Tell about the action of English merchants. What did Lord North do?

BURNING OF THE GASPE.

23. The *East India Company* then brought all the tea from *China. North* made arrangements with them to sell their tea to the *Americans* at a sum less than the market price, which would be equal to the small impost tax.

24. It was **principle,** not **money,** that the *Americans* were contending for. The tax was retained, and they refused to buy tea. They resolved not to allow a pound of it to be landed on their shores.

25. Cargoes came to *Boston harbor* and remained there in defiance of public feeling. An immense concourse of people assembled at *Faneuil Hall* in December,

FANEUIL HALL.

1773, when it was resolved that the tea should be sent back. The ships remained. Disguised men went on board of them in the evening, **broke open the tea-chests,** and poured their contents into the waters of *Boston* harbor.

26. The ministry proceeded to punish the people of Boston. All public offices were removed from the city, and the harbor was **closed against commerce.** On the first of June, 1774, General *Gage* appeared with soldiers to enforce the decrees of his government.

27. The whole country sympathized with the *Bostonians.* The leading patriots took energetic measures. At the suggestion of *Samuel Adams,* the *Massachusetts* patriots in

QUESTIONS.—23. What arrangement was made with the East India Company? 24. What did the Americans contend for, and what did they do? 25. Give an account of tea-ships in Boston harbor. 26. What did ministers do to the inhabitants of Boston? 27. What was the effect of these acts on the Americans? What did Samuel Adams propose?

council resolved to invite all the other colonies to choose

SAMUEL ADAMS.

men to meet in a **general congress** to consult upon public affairs.

28. The idea of **Union** now took strong hold of the public mind in *America*. The newspapers printed a device of a disjointed snake, each part representing a separate colony, with the words: **" Unite or Die "**— that is, the colonists must form a Union or become slaves.

29. At the beginning of September, 1774, delegates from all the colonies but *Georgia* assembled in Carpenter's Hall, in *Philadelphia*. That assembly is known as the **First Continental Congress.**

SNAKE DEVICE.

30. *Peyton Randolph* of *Virginia* was chosen President, and *Charles Thomson* of *Pennsylvania,* Secretary of the Congress. This was the first important step toward the formation of the **United States of America.**

CARPENTER'S HALL.

31. For fifty days that Congress was in session. Their wisdom and firmness astonished the statesmen of *Europe.* Their addresses to the King and Parliament

QUESTIONS.—28. What can you tell about the idea of Union? 29. Give an account of a Continental Congress. 30. Who were the officers of the Congress, and what was it the first step towards? 31. What have you to say about the session and the work of the Congress? What did they resolve to do?

form remarkable **State papers.** When they separated, they resolved to meet again the next spring, unless the grievances of the *Americans* should be redressed.

32. The grievances were not re-dressed, but were aggravated. The **second Continental Congress** assembled in Carpenter's Hall, in *Philadelphia,* on the 10th of May, 1775. Meanwhile a great Revolution had begun. *British* troops had

CHARLES THOMSON.

forced the armed patriots into the **war for indepen-dence,** the history of which we will now consider.

33. In this section we have considered—

(1) the *tendency* toward *independence;* (2) the *chief grievance* of which the colonists complained ; (3) the em-ployment of *soldiers to enforce the laws;* (4) the relations *between the citizens and soldiers ;* (5) various *schemes of taxation ;* (6) the *acts* and *punishment* of the *inhabi-tants of Boston,* and (7) the *assembling of a Continen-tal Congress.*

QUESTIONS.—32. What was done the next spring, and what was then begun ? 33. What have we considered in this section ?

SECTION II.

FIRST YEAR OF THE WAR FOR INDEPENDENCE.

[1775.]

1. During the summer of **1774**, the *Americans* prepared for **war** by military drilling and collecting supplies of arms and ammunition. A large body of men were enrolled, who were to be ready to go to the field at a minute's warning. These were called **minute-men.**

2. These hostile measures, and the assertion, of the newspapers and the pulpit, that the people had a right to **resist oppression**, alarmed General *Gage*, who was governor of *Massachusetts*. He built fortifications across *Boston Neck* to prevent an attack from the patriots, and placed sentinels and cannon there.

3. The *Massachusetts* patriots formed a Provincial Congress at *Salem* early in October. They took all political power into their own hands, and vigorously **prepared for war.** This was the first really **independent government ever formed in America.**

4. The King and his advisers were amazed by these proceedings. The attention of Parliament was called to the subject early in 1775. Dr. *Franklin,* then in *England,* said to the King's ministers : "Be just to the *Americans* and they will be loyal." *Pitt* proposed conciliatory measures. But the **blinded ministers** refused to act on good advice.

QUESTIONS.—1. What can you tell about preparations for war? 2. What can you tell about the effect of these preparations ? 3. What did Massachusetts patriots do? 4. What have you to say about the King and ministers and Dr. Franklin ?

5. There were three thousand *British* soldiers in *Boston* in the spring of 1775. With these *Gage* felt strong. Hearing that the patriots were gathering ammunition and stores at *Concord,* a few miles from *Boston,* he sent out troops at midnight on the 18th of April to seize them.

6. These troops, eight hundred in number, reached *Lexington* at daybreak on the 19th. There they found a body of **minute-men** to oppose them. A sharp skirmish followed, when eight patriots were killed and the rest were dispersed.

7. The *British* pushed on to *Concord,* where they had another fight. Seeing the minute-men coming from all quarters, they hastily destroyed the stores and **retreated toward Boston.** They were assailed by the bullets of minute-men on the way, fired from behind fences and buildings. The *British* lost two hundred and seventy-three men killed and wounded.

8. The news that **blood had been shed by British troops** aroused the *Americans* everywhere. Hundreds of people, armed and unarmed, started for *Boston.* Before the end of May twenty thousand patriots, chiefly from *New England,* were there, building fortifications to keep the *British* in *Boston.*

9. In other colonies equally bold measures were taken. Arms and ammunition were seized by the people. Royal governors were plainly told that their services were not needed. **Provincial governments were established** by the people, who had resolved to fight for their rights.

QUESTIONS.—5. Give an account of affairs at Boston and vicinity in the spring of 1775. 6. Give an account of the skirmish at Lexington. 7. Tell about a skirmish at Concord and retreat of the British. 8. What were the effects of these skirmishes? 9. What was done in other colonies?

10. On the day when the second Continental Congress met (May 10) *New Englanders,* led by *Ethan Allen* and *Benedict Arnold,* captured Fort *Ticonderoga,* on *Lake Champlain.* "By what authority do you demand the surrender of this fort?" asked the commandant. "By that of the *great Jehovah* and the Continental Congress," *Allen* replied.

11. Meanwhile the Provincial Congress of *Massachusetts* had placed all authority for conducting the war in the hands of a **Committee of Safety.** They appointed *Artemas Ward* commander-in-chief; and important commands were given to *Putnam, Starke,* and other veterans of past wars.

12. By the first of June *British* war-ships and soldiers had arrived at *Boston,* with eminent generals. There were then twelve thousand British troops in that city. *Gage* determined to **attack the Americans,** who were gathered chiefly at *Cambridge.*

13. Expecting an attack, a thousand men were sent in the night from Cambridge to **fortify Bunker's Hill.** By mistake they went to *Breed's Hill,* not far off, and there, before morning, they had cast up a redoubt.

14. The *British,* amazed by the appearance of that redoubt at dawn on the 17th of June, fired upon it from the city and their ships. At noon three thousand troops, under General *Howe,* crossed over in boats to attack the redoubt.

15. Twice, in a severe battle, the *British* were repulsed. At length the powder of the *Americans* was used up, when they were **driven from the redoubt,** and General *Joseph Warren* was killed. Supposing the eminence to be on *Bunker's Hill,* the battle was called by that name. The **Bunker Hill Monument** stands on the site of the redoubt.

JOSEPH WARREN.

16. The *Americans* fled to *Cambridge* across *Charleston Neck,* gallantly covered by *Putnam* and a few brave men. All the *American* soldiers at *Cambridge* were soon afterward formed into a **Continental Army,** under a single general.

17. While these events were occurring in *New England,* the Revolution was rapidly progressing

BUNKER'S HILL BATTLE.   MONUMENT.

QUESTIONS.—16. What did the Americans do? 17. What can you tell about the Revolution in Virginia and the doings of Patrick Henry?

elsewhere. As in Stamp Act times, so now, *Patrick Henry* was the leader of the *Virginia* patriots. At the head of minute-men, he compelled the royal governor (*Dunmore*) to give up *gunpowder* belonging to the people, which he had seized.

18. In the back country of *North Carolina* the patriots, in convention, had declared themselves **independent of Great Britain.** In *South Carolina* and *Georgia* they took the government into their own hands, and drove away the royal governors.

19. At the beginning of this excitement the second Continental Congress met (May 10) at *Philadelphia.* They were united in saying to the King : " Be just and we will **lay down our arms.** We have counted the **cost of war,** and find it not so dreadful as **slavery.** Be just, or we will **fight your fleets and armies** until we are a **free people."**

20. The Congress did not wait for the King's answer, but prepared for war. They voted to raise an army of twenty thousand men, and authorized the issue of $2,000,000 in **paper money.** On the 15th of June they appointed *George Washington* **commander-in-chief of all the armies,** with able assistant generals. On the 3d of July Washington went to *Cambridge,* and there, under the shadow of a great elm, he took command of the *army.*

21. The *Congress* resolved to send an army to take possession of *Canada.* General *Philip Schuyler*[1] was placed

[1] *ski'-ler.*

in command of it, and late in August went down *Lake Champlain* and attempted to capture *St. John's,* on the *Sorel,*[1] but failed.

22. Falling back to *Isle aux Noix,*[2] in the *Sorel,* the Northern army lay there some time. General *Schuyler* becoming sick, General *Richard Montgomery,* his lieutenant, took the chief command. He besieged *St. John's,* and captured it on the 3d of November.

GENERAL SCHUYLER.

23. Meanwhile a detachment of *Americans* under Colonel *Bedel,*[3] and Major *Livingston* captured *Fort Chamblee,*[4] at the foot of the *Sorel* rapids. At about the same time Colonel *Ethan Allen,* with a few men, attempted to capture *Montreal;*[5] he and his followers were defeated and made prisoners. *Allen* was sent to *England in irons.*

GENERAL MONTGOMERY.

24. From *St. John's, Montgomery* pushed on to *Montreal,* and captured the city on the 13th of November. Then he hastened toward *Quebec* to meet Colonel *Benedict Arnold,* who, he was informed, was approaching the city from the wilderness.

25. That **march of Arnold** was a marvellous exploit.

QUESTIONS.—22. What did the patriot army do? 23. What can you tell about Fort Chamblee and an attempt to take Montreal? 24. What did Montgomery do? 25. Give an account of Arnold's march through the wilderness.

¹ *sor-el'.* ² *eel-ñ-noo'ah.* ³ *be-del'.* ⁴ *sham'-blâ.* ⁵ *mont-re-awl'.*

He crossed the wilderness by way of the *Kennebec*[1] and *Chaudiere*[2] rivers, with about a thousand men. They traversed dark forests and tangled morasses filled with snow and ice. They suffered dreadfully from cold, hunger and fatigue, and appeared at *Point Levi,* opposite *Quebec,* on the 9th of November.

26. *Arnold* crossed the river, ascended to the *Plains of Abraham,* and demanded the surrender of the city to him. The demand was refused. He could not enforce it. Marching up the *St. Lawrence* about twenty miles, he there met *Montgomery* on the 1st of December.

27. The united troops now marched directly for *Quebec.* For three weeks they **besieged the city,** in the midst of fearful snow-storms. At length *Montgomery* determined to force his way into the town through one of the gates.

28. *Montgomery* divided his army. He led a part of them on the *St. Lawrence* side of the town, and *Arnold* led

another division on the *St. Charles* side. They were to meet, and force *Prescott* gate. While pressing forward at the head of his men, to attack a battery, at dawn on the 31st of December, *Montgomery* was killed.

29. *Arnold* was wounded. After a combat of several hours, and the capture of many of his troops, *Arnold,* who was now

WALLS OF QUEBEC.

chief in command, withdrew, and with the little army re-

QUESTIONS.—26. What did Arnold do at Quebec? 27. What can you tell about beginning the siege of Quebec? 28. Tell about an attempt to force an entrance into Quebec. 29. What can you tell about Arnold and the army at Quebec?

[1] *ken-ne-bek'.* [2] *sho-de-ehr'.*

mained near *Quebec,* behind ramparts of snow, all winter. He was relieved by General *Wooster* in the spring.

30. The *British* at *Quebec* were strongly reinforced in the spring of 1776, and the patriots were all **driven out of Canada** before the middle of June.

31. In *Virginia* the patriots were more successful. After Governor *Dunmore* had been driven to the shelter of *British* war-ships, he collected a motley force of royalists, and began to **desolate** *Southwestern Virginia.*

32. The minute-men gathered in large numbers to oppose him. At the *Great Bridge,* near the *Dismal Swamp,* they fought a severe battle on the 9th of December. *Dunmore* was defeated and **driven to his ships** at *Norfolk.* In revenge he **burnt that city** on the 1st of January, 1776.

33. The minute-men of *Culpepper County* had a flag with a snake device different from the one in the newspapers. It was the picture of a rattlesnake coiled, ready to bite. Under it were the significant words : **"Don't tread on me!"** It meant to say, "I have dangerous fangs." It also bore the words of Patrick Henry : **"Liberty or Death."**

CULPEPPER FLAG.

34. Circumstances now drew a strong line of distinction between the friends and the opponents of the *British* government. The loyalists were called **Tories**; the patriots were called **Whigs.**

35. In this section we have considered—

(1) The *preparations* of the *Americans* for *war;* (2)

the *effect* of these preparations ; (3) the *skirmish at Lexington* ; (4) the *gathering of patriots* near *Boston* ; (5) *revolutionary* movements in the *Carolinas* and *Georgia* ; (6) the *capture of Ticonderoga* and the *Battle of Bunker's Hill* ; (7) the formation of a *continental army* ; (8) the appointment of *Washington* to the *chief command* ; and (9) *military operations* in *Canada* and *Virginia.*

SECTION III.

SECOND YEAR OF THE WAR FOR INDEPENDENCE.

[1776.]

A BILL OF CREDIT, OR CONTINENTAL MONEY.

1. We have observed that the Continental Congress authorized the issuing of **bills of credit,** or paper money.

QUESTIONS.—35. What have we considered in this section?
QUESTIONS.—1. What have you to say about bills of credit?

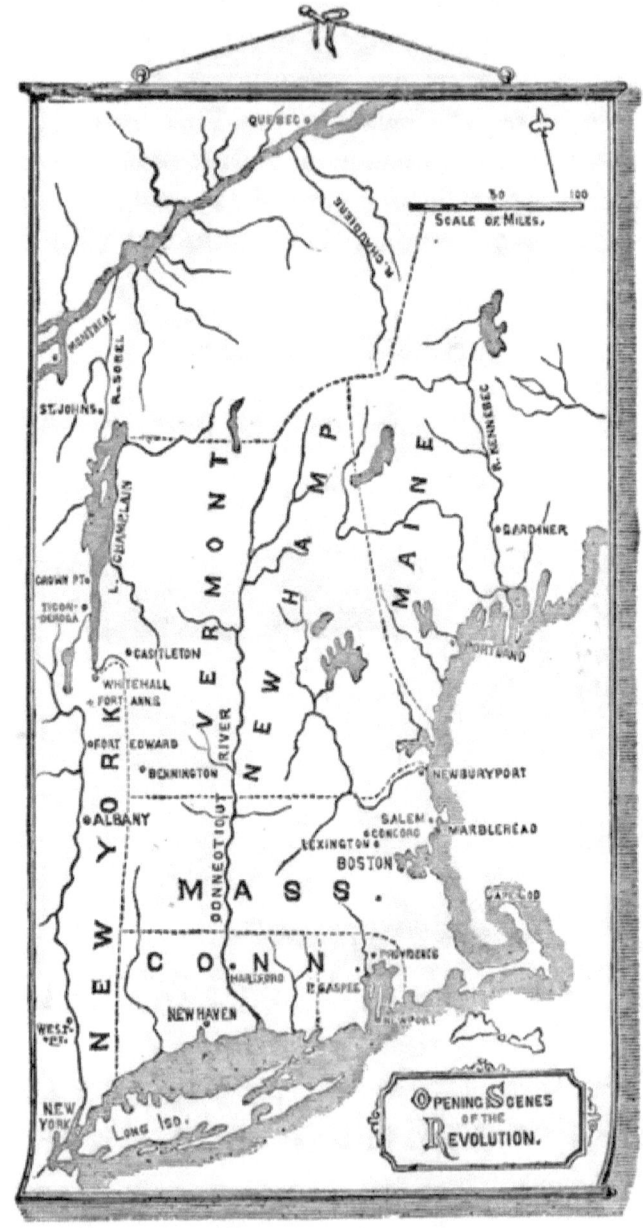

Opening Scenes of the Revolution.

These bills were very rude in appearance when compared with our present paper money.

2. The people received these bills freely at first, for they promised the holder **gold** or **silver** in exchange for them. That promise could not be met, and in time the **bills became worthless.** They answered a good purpose at the time, in helping the colonists to gain their independence.

3. In the autumn of 1775 the *British* Parliament declared the *American* patriots to be **rebels,** and prepared a heavy force of ships and soldiers to make war on them. They also hired several thousand *German* soldiers to **fight the Americans,** and these were sent over the *Atlantic* in the spring of 1776.

4. The *Americans* prepared to meet their foes. The Congress authorized the **building of vessels of war,** and also **privateering,** and very soon there were many armed vessels on the ocean committing depredations on *British* commerce.

5. *Washington* felt the necessity of **striking an effectual blow** for the liberties of his country at once. So did the Congress. Both worked for the expulsion of the *British* from *Boston.*

6. As *Washington* could not leave the army, Mrs. *Washington* joined him at *Cambridge* in December. She arrived there, with her son, Mr. *Custis,* and his wife, on the 11th of December, and passed the winter there.

7. At the beginning of 1776, *Washington* had fourteen thousand men. With these he prosecuted the **siege of**

QUESTIONS.—2. What can you tell about the people receiving bills of credit and their use? 3. Tell about the British making preparations for war. 4. What did the Americans do? 5. What have you to say about Washington and the Congress? 6. What can you tell about Mrs. Washington? 7. What can you tell about the American army, and the British proposing to leave Boston?

ARRIVAL OF MRS. WASHINGTON IN CAMP.

Encampment on Boston Common.

ENCAMPMENT ON BOSTON COMMON.

Boston with vigor. General *Howe,* in command of the *British* there, perceiving his danger, proposed to leave the

174   *THE REVOLUTION.*

The British leave Boston. Lee Foils Clinton. Washington at New York.

city and harbor, with his ships and troops, if *Washington* would allow him to do so quietly.

8. *Washington* consented, and on Sunday, the 17th of March, the **British army,** with many **Tories,** sailed from *Boston* for *Halifax,* in *Nova Scotia.* Congress caused a gold medal to be presented to *Washington* in commemoration of the evacuation of *Boston.*

9. One of *Howe's* best lieutenants was General Sir

GENERAL CHARLES LEE.

Henry Clinton. He left *Boston* several weeks before the evacuation, with ships and troops. *Washington* suspected that he was going to attack the city of *New York,* and sent General *Charles Lee,* a fiery soldier, to raise troops in *Connecticut,* and hasten to the defence of the menaced city.

10. *Lee* worked vigorously, and six weeks before the evacuation of *Boston,* he was encamped, with twelve hundred men, near *New York,* watching for *Clinton.* That general had heard of *Lee's* movement, and sailed southward to attack *Charleston, South Carolina.*

11. Suspecting that *Howe,* also, had sailed for New York, *Washington* led his army to that city, leaving a sufficient number of troops at *Boston* to prevent the return of the *British.* At *New York* the *American* army was increased, and *Washington* built fortifications there and on the *Hudson River.*

QUESTIONS.—8. Tell about the evacuation of Boston. 9. What can you tell about the movements of Generals Clinton and Lee? 10. What more can you tell about Clinton and Lee? 11. What did Washington suspect and do?

12. On the coast of *North Carolina, Clinton* was joined by a fleet under Sir *Peter Parker,* and early in June the combined forces appeared at the entrance of *Charleston Harbor.* On *Sullivan's* island, within that harbor, the patriots had a nearly completed **fort,** garrisoned by five hundred men, under Colonel *William Moultrie.*[1]

13. The patriots hastened to arm their fort well with cannon, and when *Clinton* landed his troops on *Long Island,* which is separated from *Sullivan's* by a shallow strait, they were ready to receive him. *Lee* arrived at *Charleston* on the same day on which *Clinton* landed.

GENERAL MOULTRIE.

14. While *Clinton's* troops were trying in vain to reach the fort from *Long Island, Parker* sailed into the harbor and opened a heavy fire upon the patriots on the 28th of June. The storm of cannon-balls was terrible, but did not do much harm, for the fort was built of soft palmetto logs.

15. The garrison answered the assault so vigorously that, after a conflict of ten hours, the *British* ships were **dreadfully shattered.** They were compelled to withdraw. *Clinton* placed his troops on some of them, and they all **sailed for New York.**

16. The work so gallantly defended was named **Fort**

[1] *mool-tre'.*

Moultrie. During the battle the flag-staff was shot away, and the flag fell outside of the fort. A sergeant named *Jasper* climbed down while the balls were flying thickly, picked up the flag, and placed it on a temporary staff. It was kept flying during the rest of the battle.

17. The Continental Congress, sitting in the State House  at *Philadelphia,* now took an important step. On the 7th of June, 1776, *Richard Henry Lee,* of *Virginia,* offered a resolution that the colonies were, and ought to be, **free and independent States.**

STATE HOUSE.

18. For almost a month the Congress had this subject under consideration. On the 2d of July the resolution was **adopted,** and on the 4th of July a **Declaration of Independence** was made.

19. This Declaration was at that time signed by only *John Hancock,* the President of Congress. In the course of a few months it received the signatures of **fifty-two** other members of that body. This laid the foundation of our republic, with the title, **The United States of America.**

JOHN HANCOCK.

20. There were great rejoicings throughout the country when this Declaration was proclaimed. In the city of *New*

QUESTIONS.—17. What was done in the Continental Congress? 18. What can you tell about a resolution for and declaration of Independence? 19. What can you tell about the signing of the Declaration? 20. What can you tell about rejoicings and the destruction of a statue and royal arms?

York, citizens and soldiers **pulled down the leaden statue of King George.** It was broken in pieces and cast into bullets. In various places the royal arms were taken from public buildings and burned.

21. At about the time the Declaration of Independence was being considered, General *Howe* was making his way toward *New York* with a large body of troops. These were landed on *Staten Island* on the 2d of July.

22. *Howe* was joined by *Clinton,* who came from the South on the 11th, and by his brother, Lord *Howe,* with a fleet, on the 12th. Very soon afterward a large number of the hired *German* troops joined the *British.* They were chiefly from *Hesse-Cassel,*[1] and were called **Hessians.**[2]

23. The British were now threatening *New York* with thirty thousand veteran troops. *Washington* had, for its defence, only seventeen thousand, mostly militia. General *Sullivan* was in a fortified camp at *Brooklyn* with a few troops.

24. On the 26th of August, ten thousand *British* troops and forty pieces of cannon were landed on the western end of *Long Island,* and moved toward *Brooklyn.* *Wash-*

GENERAL PUTNAM.

ington sent General *Putnam* with some troops to reinforce Sullivan and take the chief command.

25. There were now about five thousand *American* sol-

QUESTIONS.—21. Give an account of the arrival of British troops near New York. 22. By whom was General Howe joined? 23. What can you tell about British troops and General Sullivan? 24. What did the British do? What did Washington do?

[1] *hess-cas'-sel.*   [2] *hes'-she-ans.*

178 THE REVOLUTION.

Battle on Long Island. Battle on Harlem Plains and on White Plains.

diers on *Long Island*. The *British* pressed forward, and on the 27th of August a **very severe battle** was fought near *Brooklyn*. The *Americans* were defeated with heavy loss.

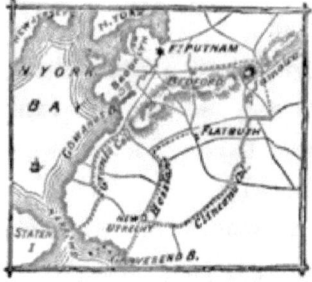
BATTLE OF LONG ISLAND.

26. Early on the morning of the 30th of August, the *American* troops on *Long Island*, under the cover of a thick fog, **passed over to New York** unobserved by the enemy. The *British* prepared to follow, when *Washington* left *New York* and took a strong position upon *Harlem Heights,* near the northern end of *Manhattan Island*.

27. The British crossed over and **took possession of the city of New York.** They proceeded to attack the *Americans* in their new position, and were defeated in a sharp battle on **Harlem Plains,** on the 16th of September.

28. *Howe* now determined to get in the rear of *Washington*. He went up the *East River* and landed his troops in *Westchester County*. The *Americans* also went into *Westchester County,* leaving a garrison in *Fort Washington,* a strong work on the highest hill near *Harlem Heights*.

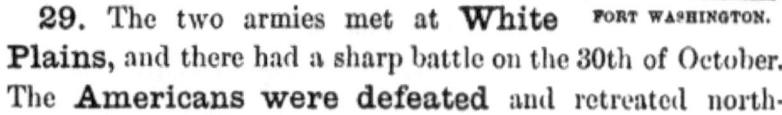
FORT WASHINGTON.

29. The two armies met at **White Plains,** and there had a sharp battle on the 30th of October. The **Americans were defeated** and retreated north-

BATTLE FIELDS
of the
REVOLUTION
IN THE
Northern
AND
EASTERN STATES

SCALE OF MILES
50   100   150   200

180   *THE REVOLUTION.*

Capture of Fort Washington.   Washington Chased by Cornwallis.

ward.   On the 4th of November, *Washington* crossed the *Hudson River* into *New Jersey* with the greater portion of his army, and joined General *Greene* at *Fort Lee,* opposite *Fort Washington.*

30. *Hessians,* under General *Knyphausen,*[1] and some *English* troops now crossed the *Harlem River,* and after a severe conflict on the 16th of November, **captured Fort Washington.**   Two thousand *Americans* were made prisoners. They suffered much, and many died, in the **prisons** in *New York,* and **prison ships** near *Brooklyn.*

THE JERSEY PRISON-SHIP.

31. Lord *Cornwallis,* one of *Howe's* best generals, followed *Washington* across the *Hudson,* and chased him to *Trenton,* on the *Delaware River.*   *Washington* crossed that river on the 8th of December, with less than three thousand men.

32. This was a dark hour in the history of our country. But *Washington* was hopeful. Believing that *Cornwallis* intended to seize *Philadelphia,* the Congress, sitting in that city, fled to *Baltimore,* in alarm, leaving a Committee to deal immediately with the army.

33. *Cornwallis* did not cross the *Delaware.*   He placed the army in **winter quarters** on its borders, and returned to *New York.*   The *Hessians* were at *Trenton.*   *Wash-*

QUESTIONS.—30. Give an account of the capture of Fort Washington and the prisons. 31. What can you tell about Cornwallis and Washington? 32. What have you to say about the time, and Washington and Congress? 33. What did Cornwallis do?

[1] *nip-haw'-zen.*

THE REVOLUTION.   181

Battle at Trenton.   Washington a Dictator,   Cornwallis at Princeton.

ington, having received reinforcements, resolved to attack them there.

34. On Christmas night *Washington* crossed the river in boats, among floating ice, a few miles above *Trenton.* At dawn the next morning (Dec. 26) he **attacked the Hessians at Trenton.** They were defeated. Their commander was killed, and a thousand of them were made prisoners. *Washington* then re-crossed the river.

BATTLE AT TRENTON.

35. This victory encouraged the people. The Congress gave the powers of a **Dictator** to Washington to do as he pleased for six months. His army was strengthened and he resolved to **drive the British out of New Jersey.** So he crossed the Delaware again and formed a camp at *Trenton.* *Cornwallis* had hastened back to his army, and brought with him *German* and *British* soldiers, and formed a camp at *Princeton,* ten miles from the *Delaware.*

36. In this section we have considered—

(1) The issue of *Bills of Credit;* (2) the *preparations for war* on both sides of the *Atlantic;* (3) the *evacuation of Boston;* (4) the *care for New York;* (5) the *repulse* of the *British* at *Charleston;* (6) the *Declaration of Independence;* (7) the *possession* of *New York* and its vicinity by the *British;* (8) the *flight of Washington* to the *Delaware* and of the *Congress to Baltimore,* and (9) the *victory at Trenton.*

SECTION IV.

THIRD YEAR OF THE WAR FOR INDEPENDENCE.

[1777.]

1. The *British* ministry and the parliament did not seem to comprehend the character of the *Americans*. They seemed to think that thirty thousand troops would frighten them into submission. They were amazed at the obstinate courage of the "rebels." Feeling sure that a few more troops would **crush the rebellion,** they prepared to send them.

2. The Congress comprehended the power and the weakness of *Great Britain*. They knew that her **haughty pride** had offended other nations, and that *France* longed for an opportunity to humble her.

3. So the Congress sent Commissioners to ask the King of **France to help the Americans** in their struggle for independence. *Silas Deane* was first sent. He was joined at *Paris* by Dr. *Franklin* and *Arthur Lee*. The King

SILAS DEANE.

was made to see in this war an opportunity of depriving the *British* realm of more domain in *America* than the *English* had won from *France*. He therefore consented to help the patriots secretly.

QUESTIONS.—1. What have you to say about the British ministry and parliament? 2. What about the knowledge of the Congress? 3. What did the Congress do? Who were sent as commissioners to France, and what was the nature and effect of their mission?

4. Meanwhile the subject of a **permanent national government** had engaged the attention of the Congress. Dr. *Franklin* had submitted a plan of government as early as 1775. Early in 1777 a more perfected plan for a **National league** was laid before the Congress. It was finally adopted. It was, however, several years before the scheme of government known as **The Articles of Confederation** was adopted by the several colonies.

DR. FRANKLIN.

5. We left the *American* and *British* armies in *New Jersey,* near each other. *Washington* had five thousand men at *Trenton* on the first of January, 1777. *Cornwallis* marched from *Princeton* on the 2d, with a larger force to attack him.

6. *Washington* saw his peril. He lighted his camp-fires, and at midnight he **stole away** silently with his troops and cannon, and marched rapidly to *Princeton.*

7. *Cornwallis* was persuaded that he might easily capture *Washington* and his army in the morning. He was astonished and mortified when he found they had **escaped.** He heard the firing of cannon, and mistook the noise for thunder. "Thunder in a clear winter sky!" exclaimed one of his officers. "**Washington has outgeneralled us!** You hear his cannon at *Princeton!*"

8. *Washington* had attacked a strong guard at *Prince-*

QUESTIONS.—4. What have you to say about a national government? 5. What can you tell about the American and British armies in New Jersey? 6. What did Washington do? 7. What have you to say about Cornwallis?

¹ *corn-wal'-lis.*

ton at sunrise, and in a severe battle had **gained a victory**. But he lost the brave General *Mercer*. *Cornwallis* hastened toward *Princeton*. When he arrived, *Washington* and his men were far on their way toward **Morristown**, in East Jersey.

9. From this hill-country, where he recruited his army, *Washington* sent out parties to attack the *British* and armed *Tories*, and very soon they were driven out of *New Jersey*, excepting at two places. The Congress now returned to *Philadelphia*.

BATTLE AT PRINCETON.[1]

10. It was almost June before the campaign of 1777 was really begun. Neither party had been idle, meanwhile. In March and April *British* and *Hessian* troops had **destroyed American stores** at *Peekskill*, on the *Hudson*, and **burned Danbury**, in *Connecticut*.

11. General *Tryon*, who had been governor of *New York*, led the troops to *Danbury* from vessels in which they went up *Long Island Sound*. The *Connecticut* people were *aroused*. Led by Generals *Arnold*, *Wooster*, and *Silliman*, they **fought the marauders** near *Ridgefield*, on the 27th of April.

12. In that engagement General *Wooster* was killed.

QUESTIONS.—8. Tell about the battle at Princeton. 9. What did Washington do in the hill-country of New Jersey? 10. What have you to say about the beginning of the campaign? What did the British do? 11. What can you tell about Tryon's expedition into Connecticut?

[1] The little building in the corner of this map is a view of the house in which General Mercer died.

Tryon was defeated and driven back to his ships with a loss of almost three hundred men.

13. The *Americans* retaliated. Toward the close of May a party under Colonel *Meigs* crossed *Long Island Sound* to *Sag Harbor*, and **burned a dozen British vessels** there, and carried off ninety prisoners.

14. The *British* had held possession of *Rhode Island* for several months. General *Prescott*, their commander, was a tyrant, and the people were much irritated by his conduct. On a warm night in July, Colonel *Barton*, of *Providence*, and some others, went across the Bay to *Prescott's* quarters, seized him in his bed, and carried him away a prisoner.

15. The *British* ministry had formed a plan for **separating New England from the rest of the colonies**, by taking military possession of the *Hudson Valley* and *Lake Champlain.* They tried to effect it in 1777.

16. For that purpose, a large force under General *Burgoyne*,[1] then in *Canada*, assembled at *St. Johns*, preparatory to a movement up *Lake Champlain* and so into the *Valley of the Hudson.* General *Howe* was to send a force up the *Hudson River* to co-operate with *Burgoyne*.

17. For a long time *Washington* (who had about **ten thousand** men under him at *Middlebrook* in *New Jersey*), was uncertain as to the intention of Howe. The latter, with a large army at *New Brunswick,* tried to draw *Washington*

[1] *bur-goin'.*

186 *THE REVOLUTION.*

Movements of Burgoyne and Howe.   Washington at Philadelphia.

into battle. Then he suddenly withdrew his troops from *New Jersey,* and encamped them on *Staten Island.*

18. *Burgoyne*[1] went up *Lake Champlain.*[2] Early in July he took possession of *Crown Point* and *Ticonderoga,* and spread terror over *northern New York* and *New England.* At the same time *Howe* embarked eighteen thousand troops in *British* ships which were in *New York* harbor, and seemed to be preparing to ascend the Hudson.

GENERAL LAFAYETTE.

19. Suddenly the *British* fleet sailed southward. *Washington* was satisfied that the troops were destined to attack *Philadelphia.* With the greater portion of his army he hastened to that city, where he was met by young *Lafayette,*[3] who had come from *France* to fight for the Americans.

20. *Lafayette* was a *French* nobleman who had just married a beautiful girl. He had heard of the **struggle for freedom** in *America,* and he determined to help the patriots. His friends tried to keep him at home, but his wife, generous as he, consented to his departure. He was commissioned a general, and served our cause faithfully.

21. The *Americans* had built forts on the *Delaware River,* below *Philadelphia,* and put obstructions called *chevaux-de-frise*[4] in the stream. *Howe* could not safely pass up that river, so he went around to *Chesapeake Bay,* and landed his troops at the head of it, near *Elkton,* on the 25th of August.

QUESTIONS.—18. What did Burgoyne and Howe do? 19. What can you tell about a British fleet and the movements of Washington? What about Lafayette? 20. Give an account of Lafayette. 21. What can you tell about forts on the Delaware and the movements of Howe?

[1] *bur-goin'.*   [2] *sham-plane'.*   [3] *lah-fā-et'.*   [4] *shev'-o-de-frees'.*

22. *Washington* had marched from *Philadelphia* to meet General *Howe.* On the *Brandywine Creek,* several miles above *Wilmington,* the *American* and *British*

BATTLE AT THE BRANDYWINE.

armies had a severe battle on the 11th of September. The **British were victorious.** The *Americans* lost, in killed, wounded and prisoners, about twelve hundred men. The *British* loss was about eight hundred.

23. *Washington* and his thinned ranks **retreated to Philadelphia.** After his soldiers had rested a little, he recrossed the *Schuylkill*[1] to meet the approaching *British* army and to protect his stores at Reading. On the 16th of September the two armies met and skirmished twenty miles west of *Philadelphia.*

QUESTIONS.—22. What did Washington do? Tell about a battle. 23. What did Washington and his troops do? What then occurred?

[1] *skool'-kil.*

24. General *Wayne* was hanging on the rear of the *British,* with a considerable force. On the night of the 20th he was surprised by a **fierce attack** near the *Paoli* [1] tavern, and lost about three hundred men. Three days afterward *Howe* crossed the *Schuylkill,* at *Norristown,* and marched toward *Philadelphia.*

25. On the 18th, when the *British* were approaching *Philadelphia,* the Congress adjourned. They reassembled at *Lancaster* on the 27th, and on the same day adjourned to *York,* on the other side of the *Susquehanna River*—a place of greater safety, as they thought. There they remained several months.

26. *Howe* encamped at *Germantown,* four miles from *Philadelphia,* and prepared to make that city his **winter quarters.** It was important for the *British* to possess the forts and remove the obstructions below *Philadelphia,* that they might receive supplies by water.

27. One of these works, on an island, was called *Fort Mifflin.* The other, on the *New Jersey* shore, was called *Fort Mercer.* They were attacked late in September, and were finally **captured** early in November, when the obstructions were removed, and *British* ships went up to *Philadelphia.*

28. When *Washington* heard that *Howe* had sent a part of his army against the Delaware forts, he attacked him at *Germantown* on the 4th of October. After a severe conflict for several hours, the **patriots were beaten,**

[1] *pah-o'-lee.*

with heavy loss, and retreated to *White Marsh*. Later in

the season they marched to *Valley Forge*, where they encamped until spring, suffering dreadfully from cold and hunger.

29. While these events were occurring in *Pennsylvania*, more important ones were taking place in Northern *New York*. *Burgoyne*

BATTLE AT GERMANTOWN.

and his well-armed force caused General *St. Clair*, who commanded *Ticonderoga*, to **retreat from that post** on the night of the 5th of July.

30. The *Americans* fled toward *Fort Edward*, through *Vermont*, closely pursued by *British* and *Hessian* soldiers. They were overtaken at *Hubbardton* on the 8th, when a sharp battle occurred. The **Americans were beaten and dispersed,** and in remnants made their way to *Fort Edward*.

31. At the same time the stores which *St. Clair* had sent up the *lake* in boats to *Skenesborough* (now *Whitehall*) were overtaken by another pursuing party and destroyed.

32. General *Schuyler* was then

GENERAL ST. CLAIR.

in command of the Northern Department. His force was small, and was composed chiefly of **raw militia.** In the

---

QUESTIONS.—29. Give an account of events in Northern New York. 30. What did the Americans and British do? Give an account of a battle. 31. What have you to say about the destruction of stores? 32. What have you to say about General Schuyler and his army?

loss of *Ticonderoga* he had been deprived of **two hundred pieces of cannon** and much provision.

33. *Schuyler's* army was too weak to warrant him in giving battle to *Burgoyne.* He could only **impede his march** toward the *Hudson.* For this purpose parties were sent out to *destroy bridges* and *fell trees* across the roads on the line of *Burgoyne's* march. In this way he was prevented from reaching *Fort Edward* until the close of July.

34. Meanwhile *Schuyler* retreated slowly down the Valley of the *Hudson* to the mouth of the *Mohawk River,* followed as slowly by *Burgoyne.* When the latter had almost reached *Saratoga,* his provisions were nearly exhausted, and he sent a force into *Vermont* to seize some stores belonging to the *Americans* at *Bennington.* There the invaders were attacked by a force under General *Starke,* on the 16th of August, and after a sharp battle the **British were defeated.**

35. In this battle the invaders lost a thousand men. It was a severe blow for *Burgoyne.* It encouraged the *Americans,* who now began to flock to *Schuyler's* camp. At this point in the campaign, when the tide was turning in favor of the patriots, General *Gates* succeeded *Schuyler* in the **command of the Northern Army.**

36. While *Burgoyne* was pressing slowly down the *Hudson Valley,* Colonel *St. Leger,*[1] a *British* soldier, whom he had sent for the purpose, was making his way from *Oswego* to the *Mohawk Valley,* with orders to meet *Bur-*

QUESTIONS.—33. What did General Schuyler do and effect? 34. What can you tell about a march down the Hudson Valley and an expedition to Bennington? 35. What was the result of the battle at Bennington? What change in command was made? 36. What can you tell about an invasion of the Mohawk Valley?

[1] *leh-sha'.*

THE REVOLUTION. 191

Battle of Oriskany. Siege of Fort Schuyler. Americans at Stillwater.

goyne at *Albany.* The militia of the valley gathered under General *Herkimer*[1] to defend it.

37. *St. Leger* led a motley host of **Tories** and **Indians.**

The latter were led by *Brant,* the great *Mohawk* chief. At *Oriskany,*[2] on the *Mohawk,* they encountered *Herkimer,* and a severe battle was fought on the 6th of August. *Herkimer* was mortally wounded, and his followers were beaten.

38. At the same time *St. Leger* was **besieging Fort Schuyler,** on the site of *Rome.* When General *Schuyler* heard of this siege, he sent

JOSEPH BRANT.

some volunteers under General *Arnold* to relieve the garrison. Hearing of his approach, *St. Leger* and his savages fled back to *Oswego.*

39. This failure was another sore disappointment to *Burgoyne.* He could not retreat ; to advance would be perilous. He cautiously crossed the Hudson at *Saratoga,* and formed a fortified camp on the hills there.

40. *Gates* was now with his army at *Stillwater,* where he caused his camp to be fortified under the direction of *Kosciuszko,*[3] a brave *Polander,* who, like *Lafayette,* had come over the sea to **help the Americans.**

41. *Burgoyne* moved forward, and on the morning of the 19th of September the belligerents met in battle on

QUESTIONS.—37. What have you to say about St. Leger's force and a battle ? 38. What can you tell about a siege and the driving away of the besiegers ? 39. What have you to say about Burgoyne and his movements ? 40. Where was General Gates and his army ? Who fortified his camp ?

[1] *her'-ki-mer.* [2] *o-risk'-a-ne.* [3] *koh-zooz'-ko.*

192   THE REVOLUTION.

Capture of Forts in the Hudson Highlands.   A Marauding Expedition.

Bemis' Heights, and fought all day. Both parties claimed a victory. *Burgoyne* fell back to his camp, where he resolved to wait for a *British* force, under General Sir *Henry Clinton,* which he expected would be sent up the *Hudson.*

KOSCIUSZKO.

42. *Clinton* tried to fulfill the promise. He went with ships and soldiers to the *Hudson Highlands,* and there captured Forts *Clinton* and *Montgomery* on the 6th of October.

43. Then a large party of soldiers went up the river in

BEMIS' HEIGHTS.

ships to desolate the country with fire and sword, with the hope that troops might be drawn from the army of *Gates* to defend it, and so give *Burgoyne* a better chance for success. These marauders **burned Kingston,** and extended their raid to **Livingston's Manor,** where they heard of such disasters above, that they hastened back to *New York.*

44. *Burgoyne* again ventured to advance toward *Bemis' Heights* early in October. In a hard conflict that ensued on the 7th of October he was beaten, and on the 17th of the

same month he **surrendered his whole army,** almost six thousand in number, into the hands of the *Americans.*

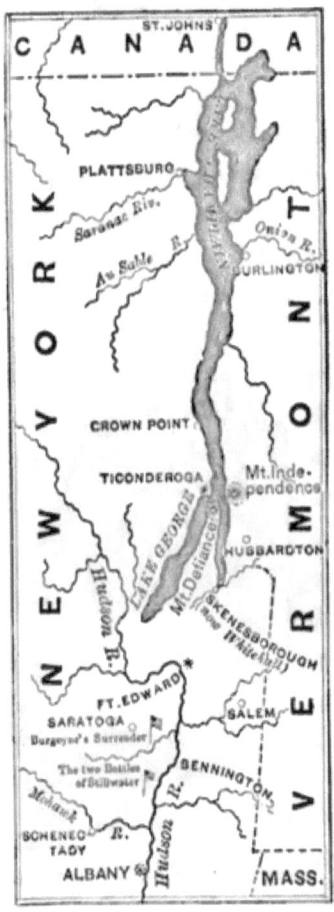

BEGINNING OF BURGOYNE'S INVASION.

45. This was a most **important victory** for the patriots. It made the *Americans* very hopeful. *European* governments, satisfied that the *Americans* would secure the independence of their country, were now willing to help them.

GENERAL BURGOYNE.

The King of *France* resolved to **aid them openly.**

46. In this section we have considered—

(1) The *opinions* of the contending parties of each other's *strength* and *weakness;* (2) the appeal of the *Americans* for *foreign aid;* (3) the attempts to form a *national government;* (4) the *military operations* in *New Jersey, Pennsylvania* and *Northern New York* in 1777; and (5) the *effects of the capture of Burgoyne and his army.*

QUESTIONS.—45. What have you to say about the victory and its effects ? 46. What have we considered in this section ?

SECTION V.   •

FOURTH YEAR OF THE WAR FOR INDEPENDENCE.

[1778.]

1. Twenty miles northwest from *Philadelphia* is a little valley that opens upon a wide plain, through which flows the *Schuylkill* river. On a little stream in that valley, more than a hundred years ago, was a forge. It was called the valley forge, and after awhile the region was called *Valley Forge.*

2. To that valley *Washington* led his troops from his encampment at *Whitemarsh,* through the snows of December, and there placed them in log-huts for the winter. The soldiers suffered dreadfully on their march and in their huts, for want of food and clothing. Many of them were *bare-footed ;* and their footprints on that march were **marked by blood** from their wounded feet.

ENCAMPMENT AT VALLEY FORGE.

3. In the spring news reached that suffering army that **French ships and soldiers** were coming to help the *Americans.* This news created great joy. The *Americans* had asked the *French* to help them. They did so, secretly. When the capture of *Burgoyne* showed the world that the Americans could help themselves, the *French* openly made a **treaty** with the Congress of the United States, by which both nations agreed to help each other in time of war.

4. News also came that messengers of peace and reconciliation were coming from *England*. When they came they were kindly received. They would not acknowledge the **independence of the Americans**, and the latter would not confer with them without such acknowledgment. So their errand was fruitless.

5. In the month of May, 1778, General *Howe* left the

British army in *Philadelphia* in charge of General Sir *Henry Clinton,* and returned to *England*. When the news reached the *British* commanders that a *French* fleet under Admiral *D'Estaing*[1] was coming, they prepared to leave *Philadelphia*. Admiral *Howe* sailed out of the *Delaware*

GENERAL CLINTON.

River and went to *Amboy Bay*. Sir *Henry* crossed into *New Jersey* with his whole army, and hastened toward the fleet. This was at about the middle of June.

6. *Washington* immediately left *Valley Forge,* and pursued the *British* army with his own. He overtook them near **Monmouth Court-House**, in West Jersey. There, on Sunday, the 28th of June, the two armies fought a severe

QUESTIONS.—4. What can you tell about messengers of peace and reconciliation ? 5. What did the British forces at Philadelphia do in the spring of 1778 ? 6. What did Washington then do ? What occurred in New Jersey ?

[1] *dehs-tang'.*

battle. The *Americans* would have won but for the bad conduct of General *Lee.* It was a very hot day. Fifty *American* soldiers died of thirst.

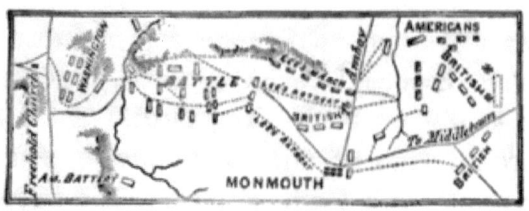

BATTLE OF MONMOUTH.

7. Both armies rested on the battle-field that night. *Washington* intended to renew the fight in the morning, but Sir *Henry* **stole away** with his broken army under cover of the darkness, and **escaped to the fleet.** *Washington* then marched his troops slowly to the *Hudson* River, crossed it, and encamped near *White Plains,* in *Westchester County.* Late in autumn he made his winter quarters at *Middlebrook,* on the *Raritan,* in *New Jersey.*

COUNT D'ESTAING.

8. *D'Estaing* could not reach the British vessels in shallow *Amboy Bay,* with his great ships. At the request of *Washington,* he sailed eastward with his ships and five thousand troops to assist the *Americans* under Generals *Sullivan* and *Lafayette,* in their efforts to **drive the British from Rhode Island.**

9. In August, when the *French* fleet lay in *Narragan-*

set Bay, the *British* fleet appeared in sight. The *French* vessels went out to attack them, taking the troops with them. A violent storm which arose suddenly **shattered both fleets.** *D'Estaing* went to *Boston* to get his ships repaired, leaving the *Americans* to help themselves.

10. *Sullivan,* who had marched almost to *Newport,* now retreated. The British pursued. On *Quaker Hill,* near the northern end of the Island, the two armies fought. The **British were repulsed** in the battle, but the *Americans* were **compelled to leave the island.**

11. The *Six Nations* of *Indians* in the State of *New York* took sides with the *British.* They joined the *Tories,* or friends of the King, and made sad havoc among the settlements in *New York* and *Pennsylvania,* in the summer and autumn of 1778. In the *Mohawk, Schoharie,* and *Cherry Valleys,* they murdered men, women, and children, and burned their houses.

12. Early in July, a leader named *John Butler,* with a band of *Tories* and *Indians,* broke into the *Wyoming Valley.* Most of the strong men were away in the army. Old men and boys, under *Zebulon Butler,* fought the invaders, but were overpowered. The savages swept through the valley, **murdering and plundering the inhabitants** and **burning their houses.** Some of the people escaped from the valley and suffered in the wilderness on its borders.

13. Meanwhile *Brant,* the *Mohawk* chief, with a son of Sir *William Johnson,* were desolating the *Mohawk* Valley and its neighborhood with fire, sword, musket, and tomahawk.

QUESTIONS.—10. What did the Americans do on Rhode Island? 11. What can you tell about the doings of the Six Nations and their allies? 12. Give an account of events in the Wyoming Valley. 13. What have you to say about Brant and Johnson?

So dreadful were the events there during three or four years that the region was called **"the dark and bloody ground."**

14. Late in the autumn of 1778, the seat of actual war was transferred to *Georgia.* In November, *D'Estaing* sailed to the *West Indies* to attack the *British* possessions there, and the *British* fleet hastened to protect them. Being deprived of a naval power, *Clinton* could not do much in the populous north, so he sent Colonel *Campbell* with two thousand troops to invade *Georgia.*

15. General *Robert Howe* commanded the few *American* troops then in *Savannah.* He was driven up the *Savannah River,* and took shelter in *South Carolina.* *Savannah* then became the head-quarters of the British in the South, and they held it almost four years.

BARON STEUBEN.

16. During the fourth year of the war the *British* gained almost nothing, while the *Americans* had found a powerful ally in *France,* with the *Baron de Steuben* as Inspector-General, and had gained strength by military experience. Their **finances,** however, were in a wretched condition. They had **a hundred million dollars of paper money afloat,** which was rapidly depreciating in value; and the public credit was daily sinking. Yet the *Americans* were hopeful.

QUESTIONS.—14. What can you tell about a change in the seat of war ? 15. Give an account of the American troops in Georgia, and the possession of that State by the British. 16. What was the relative condition of the British and Americans at the close of the fourth year of the war ?

17. In this section we have considered—
(1) The *Americans* at *Valley Forge;* (2) the alliance
with *France,* and the advent of *English commissioners;*
(3) the *flight of the British* from *Philadelphia* and the
pursuit by Washington; (4) *operations* on and near
Rhode Island; (5) the distressing warfare of *Indians* and
Tories; (6) the invasion of *Georgia,* and (7) the relative
position of the *contending parties.*

SECTION VI.

FIFTH YEAR OF THE WAR FOR INDEPENDENCE.

[1779.]

1. The *Americans* determined to **act on the defensive** during the campaign of 1779, excepting in chastis-
ing the hostile Indians.   The *British* were to be confined to the sea-board.   A wild scheme for the conquest
of *Canada* was abandoned.   The safer and less expensive
mode of warfare was applauded by the
people.

2. *Campbell* opened the campaign
at *Savannah,* where he was joined
by General *Prevost,*[1] from *Florida.*
Prevost took the chief command, and
prepared to penetrate the State.   General *Lincoln* was sent to take command of the *Americans* in the

GENERAL LINCOLN.

South.   He made his headquarters at *Purysburg,* about

QUESTIONS.—17. What have we considered in this section?
QUESTIONS.—1. Give an account of the plan of the campaign for 1779 by the Americans. 2. What can you tell about operations on the banks of the Savannah River?

[1] *pre-vost'.*

twenty miles above *Savannah,* where, with the broken
army of *Howe,* he had collected a considerable force at the
close of January.

3. *Campbell,* meanwhile, marched up the *Georgia* side
of the *Savannah River,* and **took possession of Augusta.** · This enabled the *British* to communicate with
their friends, the *Creek Indians,* in *Alabama.* At the
same time a band of *Tories* were **desolating the Carolina frontier.** They were defeated, however, in a battle
on *Kettle Creek* on the 14th of February (1779).

4. *Lincoln* sent Colonel *Ashe* with some troops to drive
Campbell from *Augusta.* He did so, and then pursued the
enemy forty miles down the *Savannah,* where he encamped
on *Brier Creek.* There he was surprised and attacked by
Prevost on the 3d of March (1779), and **lost nearly the
whole** of his two thousand troops.

5. By this disaster *Lincoln* was deprived of a **quarter
of his army.** Yet he was not discouraged. *Prevost,*
feeling strong, crossed the *Savannah River,* with a large
force of *British,* Tories and Indians, and marched on the
capital of South Carolina. *Lincoln* followed him with a
larger force, to prevent his capturing that city.

6. *Prevost* appeared before *Charleston* early in May, and
demanded the surrender of the city. It was promptly refused. The inhabitants expected an immediate attack, and
slept but little the ensuing night. To their surprise, no
enemy was visible in the morning. *Prevost* had heard of
the near approach of *Lincoln,* and had **fled at midnight,** along the sea islands, toward *Savannah.*

QUESTIONS.—3. Tell about Campbell's movements and their effects, and a battle
with Tories. 4. What can you tell about Colonel Ashe and his defeat? 5. What
have you to say about the armies of Lincoln and Prevost? 6. What did Prevost do?

British Marauding Parties in Various Places.

7. *Prevost* lingered among the islands. On the 20th of June a fight occurred between a detachment of his army and the *Americans* at *Stono Ferry,* below *Charleston.* The latter were defeated. But the capital was saved.

8. Sir *Henry Clinton* contented himself with sending out *marauding parties* to plunder and destroy towns. Governor *Tryon,* whom the patriots had driven from *New York,* was a willing leader in these expeditions. First he scattered some *American* troops, under General *Putnam,* at *Greenwich,* in *Connecticut.* Later in the season he landed on the shores of *Connecticut* with two thousand troops. He plundered *New Haven,* and laid *East Haven, Fairfield* and *Norwalk* in ashes.

9. Meanwhile some *British* vessels, commanded by Sir *George Collier,*[1] bore troops to *Hampton Roads, Virginia.* They **plundered the country** in the vicinity. The same ships, at the end of May, went up the *Hudson River* with troops, and captured *Stony* and *Verplanck's Points,* below the *Highlands.* At the beginning of July these vessels bore *Tryon* and twenty-five hundred men to *Connecticut.*

10. The bold and dashing General *Wayne* struck the British a retaliating blow about the middle of July. He marched some troops secretly to the vicinity of *Stony Point* on a warm evening. At midnight he surprised and attacked the fort ; and at two o'clock in the morning of the 16th, though badly wounded in the hand, he wrote to *Wash-*

QUESTIONS.—7. What more have you to say about Prevost and a battle? 8. What can you tell about British marauding expeditions? 9. What can you tell about the doings of British ships and troops? 10. Tell about a brave exploit of General Wayne.

[1] *kol'·yer.*

ington: "**The fort and garrison, with Colonel Johnson, are ours.**" The *British* lost in killed, wounded and prisoners six hundred men.

11. A few weeks later (August 19) Major *Henry Lee* captured a *British* post at *Paulus's Hook* (now *Jersey City*), killing thirty-six of the garrison and making one hundred and sixty men prisoners. The Congress voted to *Wayne* and *Lee* each a silver medal.

GENERAL WAYNE.

In September, forty vessels, sent from *Massachusetts,* with soldiers, to seize *Castin,* at the mouth of the *Penobscot River,* were captured or destroyed, and the soldiers were driven into the wilderness.

STONY POINT.

12. The war had now extended into the wilderness beyond the *Allegha-*

DANIEL BOONE.

ny Mountains, where *Daniel Boone,* the great hunter and pioneer, had made settlements. They had there been fighting the *Indians* for several years. Further north, in the present State of *Illinois,*[1] the *British* had forts, and the

---

QUESTIONS.—11. What did Major Lee do? What happened on the Eastern coast? 12 and 13. What can you tell about the war beyond the Alleghany Mountains?

[1] *Il-le-nois'.*

THE REVOLUTION. 203

Events in the Illinois Country.   Indians in New York Scourged.

soldiers there were continually urging the *Indians* to fight the *Americans.*

13. In January, 1779, Major *George Rogers Clarke* led an expedition from *Kentucky* against these posts. After great hardships in the wilderness, they **captured the forts,** drove away the *British,* and formed peaceable rela-' tions with the *Indians.*

14. In the summer of 1779, General *Sullivan* was sent

with a military force to chastise the Six Nations in *New York,* who had been engaged in the horrid cruelties the previous year. He collected an army in the *Wyoming Valley,* and marched up the *Susquehanna River* into the country of the *Senecas.* In the course of a few weeks he **destroyed forty Indian villages** and a vast amount of corn, fruit and

GENERAL SULLIVAN.

garden vegetables.   This chastisement was long remembered by the *Indians* with bitter hatred.

15. Early in September (1779) *D'Estaing* appeared off the coast of *Georgia* with a powerful *French* fleet, to assist *Lincoln* in an attempt to drive the *British* from *Savannah.*   *D'Es-*

SIEGE OF SAVANNAH. 1779.

taing landed troops and siege-guns; and for more than a fortnight the town was bombarded.

QUESTIONS.—14. What can you tell about Sullivan's campaign against the Indians? 15. Give an account of operations against Savannah.

16. On the 9th of October an attempt was made to take the town by a close and furious assault. After a **desperate fight of five hours,** there was a truce to bury the dead. Many brave men had been killed. Among them was Count *Pulaski*,[1] who, like *Kosciuszko,* came from *Poland* to help the *Americans* in their struggle for freedom.

COUNT PULASKI.

17. *D'Estaing* now suddenly proposed to **abandon the siege.** *Lincoln* believed that the *British* would soon surrender; but he was compelled to submit to *D'Estaing's* determination, and a few days afterward the *French* fleet was at sea and the *Americans* were in full retreat toward *Charleston.* This was the second time *D'Estaing* had **abandoned the Americans** when a speedy victory seemed certain.

18. During the summer of 1779 *Lafayette* was in *France,* and persuaded the King to send another fleet and thousands of soldiers to help the *Americans.* The *British* were alarmed when they heard this news, and their troops in *Rhode Island* were ordered to *New York,* so that the army should not be too much scattered.

19. Other dangers now threatened *England. Spain* declared war against her, and a *French* and *Spanish* armament attempted an **invasion of England** in August, 1779. In the autumn, *French* and *American* cruisers

QUESTIONS.—16. What further can you tell about the siege of Savannah? 17. What did D'Estaing do, and what was the result? 18. What did Lafayette do, and what was the effect? 19. What dangers now threatened England?

· · · ¹ *pu-las'-ki.*

spread much alarm in *Great Britain*, because of their depredations upon commerce in *British* waters.

20. The naval operations of the Americans during the
Revolution do not hold a conspicuous place in history, but
they were important. The *Americans* were not able to
build large ships of war, but vessels armed by private citizens, commissioned by the Congress, and known as **privateers,** captured a great many *British* vessels and so helped
the cause.

21. Arrangements were made for creating a navy in the

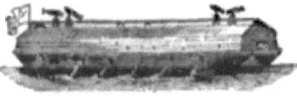

A GUN-BOAT AT BOSTON.

autumn of 1775. The first vessels
built were **gun-boats.** These
were used by *Washington* against
the *British* ships at *Boston*. They
were armed with heavy cannon at each end and lighter ones
on the top.

22. *Esek Hopkins* was the first commander-in-chief of
the naval forces, and performed good
service along our southern coasts and
among the *Bahama Islands*. There
were other commanders, such as *Man-
ly, Barry, McNeil,* and *Hinman,*
whose exploits made them famous.
But *John Paul Jones* became the
most famous of them all.

ADMIRAL HOPKINS.

23. Some vessels fitted out on the
coast of *France* were put under the
command of *Jones*. He cruised around *Great Britain* in

QUESTIONS.—20. What have you to say about the American navy? 21. What more
can you tell about the navy? 22. What can you tell about the first commander-in-
chief of the navy, and other leaders?

the summer of 1779, and filled the people of the coast towns with alarm because of his devasta-
tions.

24. In September, *Jones,* in a ship named *Bonhomme Richard* [1] (Good Man Richard), attacked and defeated the *British* ship of war *Serapis,* [2] off the eastern coast of *England*. The fight was in the moonlight, and it was a terrible one. At one time, when the ships were lashed together, they were

JOHN PAUL JONES.

both on fire. Jones was the victor. He took possession of the *Serapis,* and his own shattered vessel went to the bottom of the sea.

25. Although *England* was surrounded with many difficulties at the close of 1779, and many of her own people sympathized with the *Americans,* she put forth amazing strength and energy, and made ample provision of men and money to carry on the campaign against the *Americans* in 1780.

26. In this section we have considered—

(1) The *plans of the Americans;* (2) *military operations* in *Georgia* and *South Carolina;* (3) British *marauding expeditions;* (4) the conquests by *General Wayne* and *Major Lee;* (5) the war beyond the *Alleghanies;* (6) *Sullivan's campaign against the Indians;* (7) the *siege of Savannah,* and (8) the *naval operations.*

QUESTIONS.—23 and 24. What can you tell about John Paul Jones and his exploits? 25. What have you to say about England's troubles, strength, and actions? 26. What have we considered in this section?

¹ *bon-om′ ree′-shard.*   ² *se-ra′-pis.*

SECTION VII.

SIXTH YEAR OF THE WAR FOR INDEPENDENCE.

[1780.]

1. When *Clinton* was joined by the *British* troops from *Rhode Island,* he sailed for *Charleston* with a large force, to capture that city, leaving the remainder in *New York,* under the charge of the *Hessian* general, *Knyphausen.*[1] Early in the spring of 1780 *Washington* sent the *Baron De Kalb*[2] and other good officers to assist the *American* troops in the South.

2. The **chief seat of war** was now transferred to the South, and the people of the North had a little rest. *Clinton* and his troops were borne to *Charleston Harbor* in a

GOVERNOR RUTLEDGE.

fleet commanded by Admiral *Arbuthnot.*[3] Near the middle of February, they were landed on the islands and shores thirty miles below *Charleston.*

3. General *Lincoln* was then in *Charleston* with a few troops. The patriotic militia of *South Carolina* rallied at the call of Governor *Rutledge,* and when the invaders appeared before *Charleston* early in April, the force gathered there felt strong enough to resist them.

4. The patriots built strong military works across

QUESTIONS.—1. What did Sir Henry Clinton do? What did Washington do? 2. What can you tell about the seat of war and the movements of Clinton? 3. What can you tell about the Americans in Charleston?

[1] *nip-how'-zen.*   [2] *kawlb.*   [3] *ar-buth'-not.*

BATTLE FIELDS of the REVOLUTION. IN THE Southern States

SCALE OF MILES
10 20 30 40 50 60

Charleston Neck, and manned *Fort Moultrie,* in the harbor, with many soldiers. Near the town were six armed vessels under Commodore *Abraham Whipple,* and along the wharves batteries were constructed.

5. On the 9th of April, *Arbuthnot* sailed into *Charleston Harbor* with his fleet. At the same time *Clinton,* who had come up from below, approached the defences on *Charleston Neck.* He sent a summons to *Lincoln* to surrender his army and the city, and threatened to destroy the town and capture the troops in case he refused. *Lincoln* did refuse, and sent word to *Clinton* that he was **ready for war.**

6. The siege of *Charleston* continued for a month. Meanwhile Lord *Cornwallis* came from *New York,* with an army, to help *Clinton.* The *British* surrounded the town. On the night of the 9th of May, two hundred cannon opened fire upon the city. The fleet joined in the bombardment.

LORD CORNWALLIS.

7. For more than forty-eight hours the inhabitants of the city endured the **dreadful cannonade,** when, at about two o'clock in the morning of the 12th of May, **Lincoln offered to surrender.** The firing ceased. About six thousand citizens and soldiers were made prisoners of war, with four hundred cannon and a large quantity of provisions and stores.

210   *THE REVOLUTION.*

The British in South Carolina.   American Troops Sent to the South.

8. This was a heavy blow for the *Americans.* The *British* commander immediately sent large bodies of troops

SIEGE OF CHARLESTON, 1780.

into the country, in various directions, to **conquer and hold the State.** For awhile it seemed to the patriots that all was lost, and the quiet of despair prevailed throughout *South Carolina.*

9. Mistaking this quiet for permanent tranquillity, *Clinton* and *Arbuthnot,* with many troops, **sailed for New York** in June, leaving the remainder of the army in the South under the chief command of Lord *Cornwallis.*

GENERAL GATES.

10. The deceptive quiet was soon broken. *De Kalb* had moved too slowly to effect anything in favor of *Lincoln.* General *Gates* had also been sent to the South, and he took the **chief command** when he joined *De Kalb.* The news that the **conqueror of Burgoyne** was coming revived the spirits of

QUESTIONS.—8. What did the British commander then do ? What was the result ? 9. What did Clinton and Arbuthnot think and do ? 10. What can you tell about De Kalb and Gates, and Southern patriots ?

THE REVOLUTION. 211

Active Southern Partisans. Battle near Camden. Death of De Kalb.

the patriots, and partisan leaders like *Marion*,[1] *Sumter,*
Pickens and *Clarke* were soon in the field at the head of
daring men.

11. *Sumter* first appeared, with strength, on the *Ca-*
tawba River. At the same time
Marion was striking the *British*
and *Tories* in the swamps of the
lower country, on the borders of
the *Pedee;* and the other partisans were active.

GENERAL SUMTER.

12. When, in August (1780),
Gates marched down from the
hill country and approached *Cam-*
den, he was joined by many
patriots and felt strong. Lord *Rawdon* was then in command of *British* troops at *Camden.* *Cornwallis* hastened
to join him, and then moved forward to
meet *Gates.*

SANDERS' CREEK.

13. The two armies, marching silently
along a sandy road, met at midnight, unex-
pectedly to both, in a swamp on **Sanders'**
Creek, seven miles north of *Camden.*
They skirmished in the darkness, and at
daylight began a **fierce battle.** The
Americans were defeated and scattered.
De Kalb was killed, and *Gates* and a few
of his troops **fled into North Carolina.**

QUESTIONS.—11. Give an account of Sumter and Marion. 12. What can you tell
about Gates and Cornwallis? 13. Give an account of a march and a battle.

¹ *mah'ri-on.*

14. This was another severe blow for the patriots.

Within the space of three months **two of their armies** in the South had been destroyed, and the armed bands of the partisans were now scattered to the winds by *Tarleton* and other *British* leaders. All seemed hopeless, and yet the patriots were hopeful.

BARON DE KALB

15. With the foolish idea that **extremely harsh treatment** would secure submission, *Cornwallis* employed very oppressive measures. The exasperated patriots despised and defied him, and instantly prepared to strike an effectual **blow for freedom.**

16. Believing *South Carolina* to be thoroughly conquered, *Cornwallis* marched into *North Carolina,* and sent out armed parties to frighten the *Whigs* and encourage the Tories. The patriots in *Western Carolina* rallied, and at **King's Mountain** they fought, early in October, and defeated Colonel *Ferguson.* He lost a thousand men and fifteen hundred guns.

17. As the battle at *Bennington* was a severe blow to *Burgoyne,* so this was a hard blow for *Cornwallis.* Meanwhile *Marion*

GENERAL MARION.

was annoying the *British* and *Tories* near *Charleston;*

and *Sumter* and *Marion* again appeared at the head of brave patriots. So stealthy were the movements of one, and so full of fight was the other, that the *British* called *Marion* **The Swamp Fox**, and *Sumter* **The Carolina Game Cock.**

18. *Cornwallis* hastened back to *South Carolina,* and encamped between the *Broad* and *Catawba* Rivers, about the middle of October. Here we will leave him while we consider military movements in the North.

19. Extensive military operations were almost suspended in the North during the summer of 1780. As we have seen, *Knyphausen* was left in command at *New York.* That officer sent a force of five thousand men into *New Jersey,* under General *Mathews,* early in June, on a marauding expedition.

20. Mathews crossed over from *Staten Island* to *Elizabethtown,* and near that village burned a small settlement, and commenced **plundering the inhabitants.** *Washington* sent a detachment from his camp at *Morristown* to drive them back. This was effectually done.

21. A fortnight afterward, *Clinton,* who had returned from *Charleston,* joined *Mathews,* and marching toward *Morristown,* tried to drive *Washington* out of his encampment. They were met at *Springfield* by *Americans* under General *Greene,* on the 23d of June, when a **severe skirmish ensued.** The *British* set fire to the village and fled back to *Staten Island.*

22. Early in the same month a *French* fleet arrived at

QUESTIONS.—18. What did Cornwallis do? 19. What have you to say about military operations in the North? 20. What can you tell about an invasion of New Jersey? 21 What can you tell about a second invasion of New Jersey, and a battle?

214 THE REVOLUTION.

Arrival of French Forces. A Bargain for Treason. Price to be Paid.

Newport, Rhode Island, with six thousand soldiers under

the Count de *Rochambeau.*[1] A part of the *French* army wintered at *Lebanon,* near the residence of Governor *Trumbull.* The *British* were alarmed, and did not send out any more marauding expeditions. At that time *Clinton* was hoping to accomplish, through the agency of a **traitor**, what he could not secure by **force of arms.**

GOVERNOR TRUMBULL.

23. General *Benedict Arnold,* a brave and active officer, was the **traitor.** He was a quarrel-

some man and a spendthrift. He became soured toward many officers, and his expensive living involved him deeply in debt. Dishonest practices caused him to be publicly reprimanded by *Washington,* by order of the Congress.

24. Irritated and pressed for money, he resolved to **betray his country**

BENEDICT ARNOLD.

for a price. He bargained, through correspondence with Major *André,*[2] *Clinton's* adjutant-general, to receive **fifty thousand dollars and the commission of Brigadier-General in the British army,** as the price of his treason.

25. To accomplish his wicked purpose, *Arnold* obtained

QUESTIONS.—22. What can you tell about a French fleet with troops? What can you tell about the British? 23. Give an account of Benedict Arnold. 24. What moved Arnold, and what did he do? 25. What was the plan of his treason? With whom did he confer?

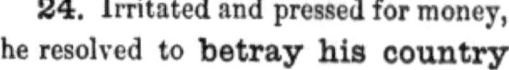

[1] *rosh'-awm-bo'.*   [2] *an'-dray.*

Conference Between Arnold and André.

command of the important military post of *West Point,* on the *Hudson River.* He bargained to betray that post and its dependencies into the hands of the *British.* In September, 1780, he and Major *André* had a conference at *Haverstraw,* on the *Hudson,* to complete the arrangements.

26. The ship in which *André* had ascended the *Hudson* was driven back by *American* cannon on the shore, and *André* was compelled to go back by land. He crossed the river, and was making his way on horseback toward *New York,* when he was arrested, near *Tarrytown,* by three militia-men, who searched him and found papers in his boots which convicted *Arnold* of Treason.

27. By a stupid blunder, *Arnold* was allowed to escape. He heard of the arrest of *André* while at breakfast in his house opposite *West Point.* Kissing his wife and babe farewell, he hurried to his barge, and offering his oarsmen a reward for speed, they took him swiftly down the river to the *British* sloop-of-war *Vulture,* and so he escaped.

28. Major *André* was **tried and executed** as a **spy.** If the *Americans* could have caught *Arnold,* they would have let the youthful *André* go.

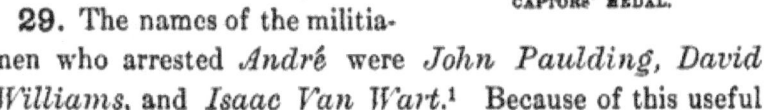

CAPTORS' MEDAL.

29. The names of the militia-men who arrested *André* were *John Paulding, David Williams,* and *Isaac Van Wart.*[1] Because of this useful

QUESTIONS.—26. What can you tell about Major André? 27. Tell about a blunder, and the escape of Arnold. 28. What more can you tell about André and Arnold? 29. What about André's captors?

[1] *wart.*

act the Congress voted them each a silver medal and two hundred dollars a year for life.

30. And now, as another year of the war drew to a close, the patriots were firm and hopeful. *Great Britain* had made really no progress toward conquering the *Americans*, after spending much blood and treasure. Yet the King and Parliament **went blindly on.** They declared war against *Holland,* which had favored *America,* and made extensive preparations to **crush the rebellion** in the colonies.

31. In this section we have considered—

(1) The *campaign of Clinton* against *Charleston;* (2) the *defeat of Gates* and the career of *Cornwallis* in *South Carolina;* (3) the *partisan leaders* in the South ; (4) the *invasion of New Jersey* by *British* troops ; (5) the *arrival of French allies,* and (6) the *treason of Arnold.*

SECTION VIII.

SEVENTH YEAR OF THE WAR FOR INDEPENDENCE.

[1781.]

1. The **patriotism of the Americans** had a trial and a triumph at the beginning of 1781. The troops had suffered every want. The paper money with which they had been paid had become worthless, and the Congress was not able to be prompt in redeeming its promises.

2. The soldiers had **asked for relief** in vain. Finally

QUESTIONS.—30. What can you tell about Great Britain and the King and Parliament ? 31. What have we considered in this section ?

QUESTIONS.—1. What can you tell about a trial of the patriotism of the Americans ?

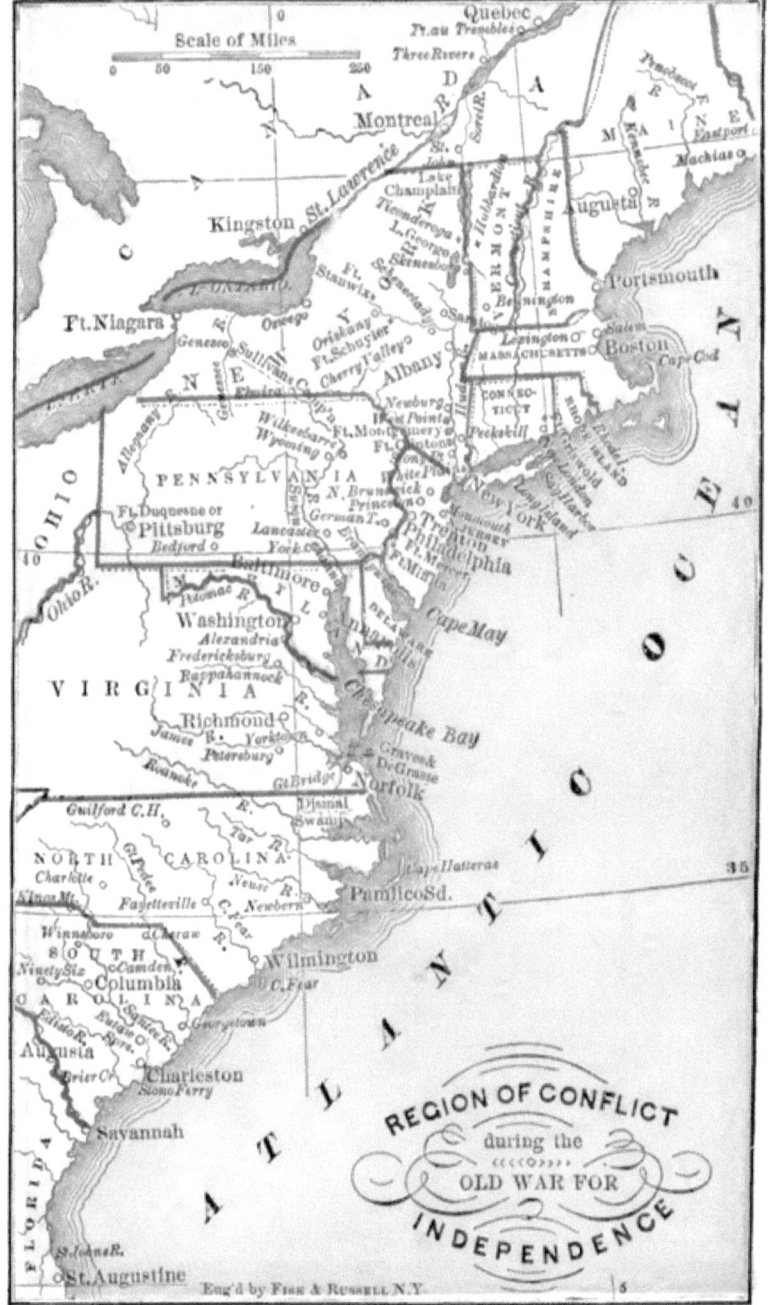

on the 1st of January, more than a thousand left the camp at *Morristown* and started for *Philadelphia* to **compel the Congress** to do something for them.

3. General *Wayne* was sent to bring them back. He *coaxed* and *threatened* them. When he pointed his pistol at the leader, they said : "We love and respect you, but if you fire you are a dead man. We are **not going to the enemy;** on the contrary, if they were now to come out, you should see us **fight under your orders** with as much cheerfulness as ever."

4. Their promise was soon redeemed in another way. Sir *Henry Clinton* heard of the mutiny, and sent agents to **entice the discontented soldiers to his army.** These agents went among the mutineers at *Princeton.* The indignant patriots seized them and handed them over to *Wayne* to be punished as spies.

5. The Congress satisfied the demands of the soldiers, and offered to reward them for this mark of their fidelity. They nobly replied : "Our necessities compelled us to **demand justice** from our government ; we ask no reward for **doing our duty** to our country against its enemies."

ROBERT MORRIS.

6. The Congress saw the necessity of promptly meeting the wants of the soldiers. They imposed taxes which were cheerfully paid. They borrowed money in *Europe ;* and a

national bank was established in *Philadelphia* under the management of *Robert Morris,* Secretary of the Treasury, which was a great help in that time of need. Mr. *Morris* used his own private fortune freely for the public good.

7. At the beginning of this year (1781) *Arnold* the traitor was **desolating lower Virginia** with a band of *British* and *Tory* soldiers. *Lafayette* was sent to *Virginia* to catch the traitor, but *Arnold,* after doing all the mischief he could, escaped to *New York* in April.

8. *Arnold* was cautious, for he knew his countrymen would show him no mercy if they should catch him. One day he asked a captive *Virginian,* "What would the *Americans* do with me if they should catch me?" The prisoner replied: "They would bury your leg that was wounded at *Quebec,* with military honors, and hang the rest of you."

9. Turning toward the *Carolinas,* where most of the  fighting was done in 1781, we see General *Greene,* the brave soldier from *Rhode Island,* at the **head of the Southern army.** A part of it he sent toward the sea, eastward of the *Pedee,* and the remainder, under General *Morgan,* he caused to be encamped at the junction of the *Pacolet* and *Broad* rivers.

GENERAL GREENE.

10. *Greene* had succeeded *Gates* in the autumn of 1780.

Cornwallis, who now lay between the two portions of the *American* army, found in *Greene* a much better soldier than *Gates.* He was just preparing to march into *North Carolina,* when he found himself menaced by this active leader.

11. Unwilling to leave *Morgan* in his rear, *Cornwallis* sent Colonel *Tarleton,* a fiery *British* soldier, to capture or scatter the *Americans.* The foes met in a desolate place in Western *South Carolina,* called **The Cowpens,** where they had a severe battle. The British were **beaten and scattered,** and many of them were made prisoners This was on the 17th of January, 1781.

COLONEL TARLETON.

12. At the close of the battle *Morgan* started for *Virginia* with his prisoners. *Cornwallis* tried to head him off. He was a little too late, for *Morgan* had crossed the Catawba river before *Cornwallis* reached its banks. The *British* commander felt sure of catching the "rebel" leader in the morning, so he halted.

GENERAL MORGAN.

13. As at *Trenton,* the active foe of *Cornwallis* escaped. A heavy rain during the night so swelled the river, that the *British* troops could not cross. *Morgan,* meantime, had pushed forward and joined Greene on the *Yadkin.*

QUESTIONS.—11. What can you tell about a battle between Morgan and Tarleton? 12. What did Morgan and Cornwallis do? 13. What more can you tell about the movements of Morgan and Cornwallis?

14. Now began a wonderful **flight and pursuit,** which extended from the *Yadkin* to the *Dan.* *Greene* was joined by the forces eastward of the *Pedee.* Three times the rivers were **filled by rains** after the *Americans* had crossed, leaving the *British* on the other side. The

Americans finally crossed the *Dan* into *Virginia* (February 3, 1781), and *Cornwallis* **gave up the chase.**

15. *Greene* remained in *Virginia* only long enough to allow his troops to rest, and with some recruits he recrossed the Dan and pursued *Cornwallis,* who had gone into the interior of *North Carolina.* He

COLONEL HENRY LEE.

sent forward Colonel *Henry Lee* with cavalry or horsemen to **foil Tarleton** and scatter the *Tories.*

16. On the 15th of March the two armies met near *Guilford Court-house,* and there they fought one of the most **severe battles of the war.** Both suffered dreadfully. The *Americans* lost four hundred men and the *British* six hundred.

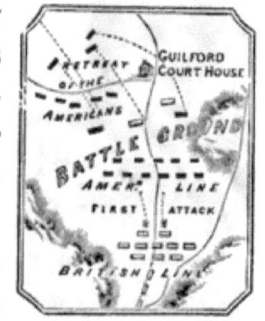

BATTLE OF GUILFORD.

17. Neither party gained a victory. *Cornwallis,* badly crippled, marched, with his shattered army, toward Wilmington, on the *Cape Fear,* and *Greene* marched into *South*

Carolina to attack the *British* under Lord *Rawdon* at *Camden.*

18. *Greene* encamped on **Hobkirk's Hill,** a mile from *Camden,* where *Rawdon* attacked him on the 25th of April,  1781. A desperate fight ensued, each party losing nearly three hundred men. In that battle Colo-

HOBKIRK'S HILL.

nel *William Washington* was conspicuous for his bravery. He *captured*

COLONEL WASHINGTON. *fifty British soldiers.* With these prisoners and all of his cannon, *Greene* retreated a few miles and encamped.

19. *Rawdon,* alarmed, **set fire to Camden** early in May, and retreated down to *Nelson's Ferry,* on the *Santee River.* At about the same time the *Americans* captured **four important British posts** in the interior of *South Carolina;* and *Greene,* with his whole army, marched against the strong post of *Ninety-Six,*  between the *Saluda* and *Savannah* rivers.

FORT NINETY-SIX.

20. *Greene* besieged *Fort Ninety-Six* for a month. Meanwhile *Lee, Pickens,* and others, had attacked the *British* and *Tories* at *Augusta,* in *Georgia,* and took pos-

QUESTIONS.—18. Give an account of a battle between Greene and Lord Rawdon. What have you to say about Colonel Washington? 19. What did Rawdon do? What had the Americans done, and where did Greene go? 20. What did Greene do? What did other leaders do?

session of that place on the 5th of June. They then hastened to help *Greene,* before *Ninety-Six,* which place the *Americans* were compelled to leave on the approach of *Rawdon,* and flee beyond the *Saluda.*[1]

GENERAL PICKENS.

21. *Rawdon* fell back toward *Orangeburg,* and *Greene* became his pursuer. The summer heats were now approaching, and *Greene* marched his army to the **High Hills of Santee,**[2] below *Camden,* where they were encamped during a portion of the sickly season. *Rawdon,* leaving his troops at *Orangeburg* in charge of Colonel *Stewart,* went to *Charleston* and sailed for *England.*

22. Many *North Carolina* troops joined *Greene,* in August, and at the close of that month his entire army were in motion toward *Orangeburg.* The *British* fled down the *Santee* and encamped at **Eutaw**[3] **Springs,** two miles from that river, where *Greene* attacked them on the 8th of September, 1781.

23. The battle raged for four hours. At night the *British* held the field, but the advantage was with the *Americans.* The *British* had lost about seven hundred men, and the *Americans* about five hundred and fifty. The victory was claimed by both parties in this **Battle of Eutaw Springs.**

24. On the night after the battle the *British* fled toward

QUESTIONS.—21. What can you tell about the movements of Greene and Rawdon? 22. What can you tell about the movements of hostile troops? 23. Tell about a battle and its results.

[1] *sah-lu'-dah.*   [2] *san-tee'.*   [3] *u'-taw.*

Charleston, pursued by the main *American* army and by the partisans, *Marion, Sumter, Lee,* and others. The *British* took refuge in *Charleston*, and at the close of 1781 they held only that city and *Savannah* in all the country, excepting the city of *New York*.

25. Of all the Southern partisans, *Marion* became the most famous. He was bold but cautious, and was generally successful. His followers were ready to endure any privations demanded by their leader. At one time his camp was upon an island at the junction of the *Pedee* [1] and *Lynch's Creek.*

26. To that camp a *British* officer was once sent with a flag of truce. He was conducted to *Marion* with his eyes covered. The partisan invited the young officer to dine with him. All that he could offer his guest were a few roasted potatoes served on pieces of bark.

27. The officer was informed that this was better than the usual fare to which *Marion* and his men were accustomed. When the young man returned to his camp he gave up his commission, declaring that such a people could not and ought not to be conquered.

28. While these events were occurring in *South Carolina, Cornwallis* was trying to subdue *Virginia*. He marched from *Wilmington,* and at the close of May he was at *Petersburg,* in *Virginia*, with a considerable army. *Lafayette* was then in that State, but his troops were too few to do much against the stronger *British* force.

QUESTIONS.—24. What did the British do? 25. What have you to say about Marion? 26. Tell the story about a British officer in Marion's camp. 27. What did Marion say, and what did the officer do? 28. What was Cornwallis then trying to do? What can you tell about him and Lafayette?

[1] *pe-dee'.*

29. *Virginia* seemed, for awhile, to be doomed to absolute submission to the enemy. *Cornwallis* marched to *Richmond* and beyond, destroying an immense amount of property. Then turning toward the sea, he marched slowly down the *James* River, followed by Generals *Lafayette, Wayne,* and *Steuben.*[1]

30. Crossing the *James* at old *Jamestown,* where the first *English* settlement was made, *Cornwallis* marched to *Portsmouth,* opposite *Norfolk,* in July. In August he went to *Yorktown,* on the *York River,* and there, building strong fortifications around his camp, he gathered together all the *British* troops in *Virginia.*

31. *Washington* so deceived Sir *Henry Clinton,* at *New York,* that the *British* commander had no suspicion that the *French* and *American* armies were going to *Virginia* until they were so far on the way that pursuit would be useless. Then *Clinton* sent the traitor *Arnold* to desolate the *New England* coasts, hoping thereby to cause the *Americans* to return for their defence.

32. *Arnold* performed the task willingly. He burned *New London,* almost in sight of his birth-place at *Norwich.* He allowed a horrid massacre of prisoners captured at *Fort Griswold.* But these cruelties did not turn *Washington* from his purpose; and late in *September* the allied armies, twelve thousand strong, appeared before *Yorktown.*

33. Meanwhile the *French* admiral, Count de *Grasse,*[2]

QUESTIONS.—29. What seemed to be the doom of Virginia? What did Cornwallis do? 30. What more can you tell about the movements of Cornwallis? 31. How did Washington deceive Clinton? What did Clinton do? 32. Give an account of Arnold's doings. What did the allied armies do?

[1] *sty'-ben.*   [2] *deh-grass'.*

had arrived with a *French* fleet, and, after battling with the *British* fleet under Admiral *Graves,* at the entrance to *Chesapeake Bay,* blockaded the *York* and *James* Rivers. He was now ready to assist the land forces in besieging *Yorktown.*

COUNT DE GRASSE.

34. After careful preparations the allied armies began a general attack upon the *British* fortifications and shipping. Several of the *British* vessels were burned by hot shot, and *Cornwallis* was driven out of his quarters in Governor *Nelson's* stone house, to the shelter of a cave in the high river-bank.

SIEGE OF YORKTOWN.

35. For awhile, *Cornwallis* hoped for aid from *Clinton.* This hope failed, and he attempted to escape by crossing the *York River* in the darkness of a stormy night. He failed in this, and then, in despair, offered to surrender.

36. Arrangements were soon made, and on the **19th of October, 1781,** *Cornwallis* and his troops, about seven thousand in number, with his vessels and seamen, were surrendered to *Washing-*

COUNT DE ROCHAMBEAU.

ton and *Rochambeau.* *Clinton,* who had just arrived with as many more troops, amazed at the event, returned to *New York* thoroughly disheartened.

37. The **surrender of Cornwallis** was a signal and crowning victory for the *Americans.* It was the final blow which secured their independence of the political rule of *Great Britain.* The King and his ministers, the parliament and the people, were confounded by the disaster.

38. Throughout the *United States* there was universal joy, such as had never been felt before. From churches and legislative halls; from the army and from the Congress, and at wayside gatherings of the people, went up a shout of thanksgiving and praise to the *Lord God Omnipotent* for the success of the *allied troops.*

39. The news reached *Philadelphia* at midnight. The watchmen cried out, with their loudest voices: "Twelve o'clock, and *Cornwallis* is taken!" Very soon lights were seen moving in all the houses. The inhabitants poured into the streets and filled the air with huzzas. The news had been nearly five *days* coming from *Yorktown* to *Philadelphia.* Now it could be sent in five *seconds.*

40. The next morning (Oct. 24, 1781), the secretary of the Congress then in session in *Philadelphia,* read a letter from *Washington,* to that body, giving an account of the

QUESTIONS.—37. What have you to say about this victory and its effects in England? 38. What were the effects of the victory in the United States? 39. What can you tell about the arrival and effect of the news in Philadelphia? 40. What did the Congress do?

surrender. Then the members all went in procession to the Lutheran Church, and there returned thanks to *God* for the great victory. Yet the war was not quite ended

41. We have considered in this section—

(1) The character of the *American patriots;* (2) *justice toward the army* and the establishment of a *National Bank;* (3) doings of the *traitor Arnold;* (4) the *Campaign* of *Greene* in the *Carolinas;* (5) the *battle at the Cowpens,* and the *race between Greene and Cornwallis;* (6) the *battles at Guilford Court House, Hobkirk's Hill,* and *Eutaw Springs;* (7) the *camp of Marion;* (8) *Cornwallis in Virginia;* (9) the *siege of Yorktown,* and (10) the *surrender of Cornwallis.*

SECTION VIII.

CLOSING EVENTS OF THE WAR FOR INDEPENDENCE.

[1782–1789.]

1. The news of the **surrender of Cornwallis** reached General *Greene* on the *High Hills* of the *Santee* on the 30th of October. It was an omen of peace to the patriots of *South Carolina,* and Governor *Rutledge* soon called a legislative assembly. Yet vigilance was necessary, for there was a considerable body of *British* troops yet in *Charleston,* and *Tories* were plentiful everywhere.

2. *Marion* kept watch near *Charleston; Greene* and his army took a position on the *Edisto; Wayne,* always wide awake, kept the *British* in *Georgia* close within the city of *Savannah; St. Clair,* marching down from *Yorktown,* made the *British* troops at *Wilmington* flee into *Charleston;* and *Washington,* who had returned to the North with his army, made Sir *Henry Clinton* and his troops close prisoners in the city of *New York.*

3. It was now the spring of 1782. The *British* government now gave up the *American* colonies as lost to the realm, and ordered the *British* commanders in *America* to stop fighting and prepare to leave the country. At midsummer the *British* left *Savannah,* but those in *Charleston* did not depart until near the close of the year.

4. General *Leslie,* in command at *Charleston,* tried to seize food for his army in the interior of *South Carolina.*

Late in August, 1782, a *British* foraging party attempted to ascend the *Combahee* [1] *River*, when they were met by some *Americans* under Colonel *John Laurens*, and in a skirmish on the 25th that young officer was killed. In September following, the *American* captain *Wilmot*, was killed in a skirmish at *Stono Ferry*, below *Charleston*. This was the **last blood shed** in the old War for Independence.

5. Meanwhile commissioners, appointed by the *United States* and *Great Britain*, had met at *Paris* to make arrangements for peace. A preliminary treaty to that effect was signed there on the 30th of November, 1782. A final and definitive treaty was signed on the 3d of September, 1783. Then the *British* monarch acknowledged the independence of the *United States*.

6. While these peace measures were going on, the *British* held *New York* with a military force, and *Washington*, with a small army at *West Point* and *Newburgh*, on the Hudson, watched them. In the spring of 1783, the suffering *American* troops were tempted to revolt, but the prudence of *Washington* and their own patriotism prevented the calamity.

GENERAL KNOX.

7. On the 25th of November, 1783, the *British* troops left *New York* and sailed for *England*. On the same day *American*

QUESTIONS.—4. What can you tell about skirmishes in South Carolina and the last blood shed in the war? 5. What can you tell about negotiations for peace? 6. What can you tell about the two armies and the temptations of the American troops? 7. Give an account of the movements of British and American troops at New York.

¹ *kom-ba-hee'*.

troops under General *Knox*, accompanied by *Washington*, marched into the city, and Governor *George Clinton* established civil government there.

8. On the 2d of November *Washington* issued a *Farewell Address to the Armies of the United States,* about to be disbanded. A few days after the *British* left *New York,* he called his principal officers together there, and in person bade them an affectionate farewell.

GOVERNOR CLINTON.

Then he went to *Annapolis,* in *Maryland,* where the Congress was in session, and resigned his commission as commander-in-chief into the hands of General *Mifflin,* then their President.

GENERAL MIFFLIN.

9. A little while before the disbanding of the Continental army, the officers formed an association, for mutual friendship and assistance, which they called the **Society of the Cincinnati.** They adopted an "order," or badge, made of gold and enamel, which, with membership, was to descend to their nearest masculine representative for all time. This society is yet in existence.

THE ORDER.

QUESTIONS.—8. What did Washington do? 9. What can you tell about the Society of the Cincinnati? 10. What have you to say about the first plan of a national government?

10. The States, in 1781, by their representatives in Congress, had adopted a plan for a national government, called **Articles of Confederation.** It was simply a *League of States,* with no real sovereign power, and was not fitted for the foundation of a nation. The people in some places refused to pay taxes at the call of the general government, and in Massachusetts they were in armed rebellion, led by *Daniel Shays.* This is known as Shays's Rebellion.

11. Leading men soon perceived the necessity for another plan of government, and in the course of a few years a convention was called at *Philadelphia* to consider the subject. Representatives from all the States excepting *Rhode Island* met there in the summer of 1787, and framed what is known as our **National Constitution.** *Washington* was President of the Convention, and **Dr.** *Franklin,* then more than eighty-one years of age, was one of the most active of its members.

12. For several days the Convention could not agree upon a plan, and it seemed as if their labors would be fruitless. One morning Dr. *Franklin* proposed that the proceedings should be opened each day with prayers to *Almighty God* for guidance. This was not done, because there was no money which could be appropriated for the payment of a minister of the Gospel for the sacred service.

13. The Constitution then formed was submitted to the people of the several States for consideration. It was agreed to by a majority of them, and on the 4th of March, 1789, the old Continental Congress expired, and the National Constitution became the Great **Law of the Republic.**

QUESTIONS.—11. What did leading men perceive, and what was done? 12. What did Franklin do in the Convention, and what was the result? 13. What was done with the National Constitution, and what did it become?

Washington was inaugurated the first President of the United States on the 30th of April following.

FRANKLIN OFFERING HIS MOTION FOR PRAYERS IN THE NATIONAL CONVENTION.

14. This was the final act of the Revolution; and was the closing work of the patriots. Then the **United States of America** commenced their glorious national career.

QUESTIONS.—14. What have you to say about the effects of the Constitution on the national character?

THE REVOLUTION. 233

Character of the National Government. Outline of Important Events.

They were no longer a mere League of States, but united under one **General Government.** Then, for the first time, did *England* fully acknowledge our independence, by sending a representative of the *British* government to reside at our national capital.

15. We have considered in this section—
(1) The *vigilance of the Americans* after the *surrender of Cornwallis;* (2) the *action of the British government;* (3) the last *skirmishes of the war;* (4) the *negotiations for peace;* (5) the *abandonment of the country* by the British; (6) the formation of the *Society of the Cincinnati;* and (7) the establishment of a *national government.*

OUTLINE OF IMPORTANT EVENTS FROM 1763 TO 1789.*

1765. Stamp Act Congress meets in New York in *October.* Patrick Henry's great speech in the Virginia Assembly.

1766. Stamp Act repealed in *March.*

1768. Tax-gatherers sent to Boston and opposed by the people.

1770. Massacre of citizens in Boston by British troops in *March.*

1771. The " Regulator" movements in North Carolina.

1772. The British schooner *Gaspé* burned in Narraganset Bay, by Americans, in *June.*

1773. Cargoes of tea destroyed by a mob in Boston Harbor in *December.*

1774. The port of Boston closed against commerce by the British ministry in *June.* A general or Continental Congress assemble in Philadelphia in *September.* Minute-men organized in different colonies.

1775. Attention of Parliament called to American affairs in *January.* Skirmishes at Lexington and Concord in *April.* A second Continental Congress assembles at Philadelphia in *May.*

QUESTIONS.—15. What have we considered in this section?

* See foot-note on page 32.

Capture of Ticonderoga and Crown Point by the Americans in *May*. A considerable British army in Boston in *June*. Battle of Bunker's (Breed's) Hill, and Washington appointed commander-in-chief of the Americans, in *June*. Washington takes command of the army at Cambridge in *July*. The Congress issues Bills of Credit, or paper money. Revolutionary movements throughout the colonies. Governor Dunmore driven from Virginia. St. Johns, on the Sorel, and Montreal captured by the Americans in *November*. Quebec besieged and Americans repulsed in *December*. Americans declared to be "rebels." German troops hired by the British government to fight the Americans.

1776. The British army driven out of Boston in *March*. German troops arrive at Quebec in *May*. A British land and naval force attack the fort on Sullivan's Island in the harbor of Charleston and are repulsed in *June*. British troops under General Howe near New York in *June*. Declaration of Independence adopted by the Congress in *July*. Battle on Long Island near New York, in *August*. British take possession of New York, and battle on Harlem Plains, in *September*. Battle at White Plains in *October*. Capture of Fort Washington in *November*. Flight of Washington across New Jersey, pursued by Cornwallis, in *November* and *December*. The Congress flee to Baltimore from Philadelphia, and the Americans capture Hessians or Germans at Trenton in *December*. Commissioners sent to France to ask for aid for the Americans.

1777. Battle at Princeton, and march of Americans to Morristown, in *January*. Danbury burned by Governor Tryon, and battle near Ridgefield, in *April*. Raid by Colonel Meigs on the British vessels at Sag Harbor in *May*. Capture of the British General Prescott on Rhode Island by Colonel Barton, in *July*. Burgoyne collects a force at St. Johns in Canada, in *June* and *July*. British plans for the campaign of 1777 revealed. Crown Point, Ticonderoga, and Skenesborough captured by Burgoyne, and the battle at Hubbardton, in *July*. Lafayette joins the army under Washington in *July*. Battle near Bennington and at Oriskany in *August*. Battle on the Brandywine; Congress flee to Lancaster and York; and battle on Bemis' Heights, in *September*. Battle on Bemis' Heights and capture of Burgoyne and his army at Saratoga, in *October*. Battle at Germantown, and capture of Forts Clinton and

Montgc.aery by the Americans in *October*. Capture of Forts Mifflin and Mercer by the British in *November*. Washington's army marches to Valley Forge in *December*.

1778. A treaty of alliance between the United States and France completed in *February*. Commissioners to treat for peace came from England in *April*. The British army and navy retreat from Philadelphia in *June*. The army under Clinton chased by Washington across New Jersey, and fight a battle at Monmouth Court-House, in *June*. D'Estaing arrives with a French fleet in *July*, and sails for Rhode Island to help General Sullivan drive the British from there. Tories and Indians desolate the Wyoming Valley in *July*. French and English fleets off Rhode Island, scattered by a storm, and the Americans defeated in a battle on Quaker Hill, Rhode Island, in *August*. Cherry Valley desolated by Brant and Tories in *November*. Savannah captured by the British in *December*.

1779. The British under Campbell take possession of Augusta in *January*, and George Roger Clarke captures British posts in the Illinois country the same month. Tories defeated at Kettle Creek in *February*. Americans under Colonel Ashe defeated at Brier Creek in *March*. The British under General Prevost threaten Charleston, but decamp, in *May*. Southern Virginia ravaged, and Stony Point captured by the British the same month. Americans defeated at Stono Ferry in *June*. Tryon burns East Haven, Fairfield, and Norwalk, and Stony Point recaptured by General Wayne, in *July*. British post at Paulus' Hook captured by Major Henry Lee in *August*. General Sullivan chastises the Indians in Western New York, and Paul Jones gains naval victories, in *September*. The American and French troops besiege and abandon Savannah, where Pulaski was killed, in *October*.

1780. Charleston, S. C., besieged by the British under Clinton in *April*, and surrendered to him in *May*. Clinton returns to New York; a French fleet with an army under Rochambeau arrives at Newport, Rhode Island; New Jersey invaded by the British, and a battle at Springfield in that State, in *June*. Battle at Sanders' Creek between Gates and Cornwallis, the former defeated, in *August*. Arnold's treason discovered in *September*. Battle of King's Mountain, and Major André hung as a spy, in *October*.

1781. Mutiny in the American army at Morristown, and noble display

236   *THE REVOLUTION.*

Outline of Important Events.   Principal Battles of the Revolution.

of patriotism, in *January.* The traitor Arnold desolates Virginia during the winter and spring. Battle of the Cowpens in *January.* Race of Greene and Cornwallis across the Carolinas in *February.* Battle at Guilford Court-House, in North Carolina, in *March.* Battle at Hobkirk's Hill in *April.* Capture of four British posts in South Carolina in *May.* Siege of Fort Ninety-Six in *June.* Cornwallis at the head of British troops in Virginia in *June* and *July.* Greene on the High Hills of Santee in *July* and *August.* Cornwallis forms a fortified camp at Yorktown in *August.* Battle at Eutaw Springs, and New London burned by Arnold the traitor, in *September.* Surrender of Cornwallis and his army to Washington and Rochambeau in *October.*

1782. In *March* the British government order the troops in America to stop fighting and prepare to leave the country. The British leave Savannah in *July.* Colonel Laurens killed on the Combahee in *August.* The last blood of the Revolution shed near Stono Ferry in *September.* Preliminary treaty of peace signed at Paris in *November.*

1783. Temptation to mutiny in the army at Newburgh in the spring, opposed by patriotism. Washington issues his Farewell Address to the Armies of the United States, and the British troops leave New York, in *November.* Washington takes leave of his officers the same month. Resigns his commission into the hands of the President of Congress in *December.*

1787. A convention at Philadelphia frames a national constitution in *September.* Northwestern territory organized.

1789. The Continental Congress expires and a national government begins its career in *March.* Washington inaugurated first President of the United States in *April.*

The following is a list of the principal battles of the Revolution, with the dates of their occurrence:

NAME.	DATE.	NAME.	DATE.
1775.		Long Island	Aug. 27
Lexington	April 19	White Plains	Oct. 28
Bunker Hill	June 17	Fort Washington	Nov. 16
Siege of St. Johns	Nov.	Trenton	Dec. 26
Quebec	Dec. 31	**1777.**	
1776.		Princeton	Jan. 3
Fort Moultrie	June 28	Ridgefield	April 27

Principal Battles of the Revolution.

NAME.	DATE.	NAME.	DATE.
Hubbardton	July 7	Savannah	Oct. 9
Oriskany	Aug. 6		
Bennington	Aug. 16	**1780.**	
Brandywine	Sept. 11	Monk's Corner	April 14
Bemis's Heights	Sept. 19	Santee Ferry	May 6
Paoli	Sept. 20	Charleston	May 12
Germantown	Oct. 4	Waxhaw	May 29
Forts Clinton and Montgomery.	Oct. 6	Springfield	June 23
Saratoga	Oct. 7	Rocky Mount.	July 30
Fort Mercer	Oct. 22	Hanging Rock	Aug. 6
Fort Mifflin	Nov. 16	Sauders' Creek	Aug. 16
		Fishing Creek	Aug. 18
1778.		King's Mountain	Oct. 7
Monmouth	June 28	Fish Dam Ford	Nov. 12
Wyoming	July 3	Blackstock	Nov. 20
Quaker Hill, on Rhode Island	Aug. 29		
Savannah	Dec. 29	**1781.**	
		Cowpens	Jan. 17
1779.		Guilford Court-House	March 15
Sunbury	Jan. 9	Hobkirk's Hill	April 25
Kettle Creek	Feb. 14	Ninety-Six	June 18
Brier Creek	March 3	Fort Griswold	Sept. 6
Stono Ferry	June 20	Entaw Springs	Sept. 8
Stony Point	July 15	Yorktown	Oct. 19
Penobscot	Aug. 13		
Paulus' Hook	July 19	**1782.**	
Indian Country in New York	Aug. 29	Combahee	Aug. 25
Flamboro' Head	Sept. 23	Near Stono Ferry	September.

WASHINGTON HONORED AT TRENTON, WHEN ON HIS WAY TO BE INAUGURATED.

CHAPTER V.

THE NATION, OR UNION OF STATES.

SECTION I.

WASHINGTON'S ADMINISTRATION.

[1789-1797.]

WASHINGTON AND HIS RESIDENCE.

1. *Washington* reluctantly left the quiet of his home at *Mount Vernon,* on the *Potomac*[1] *River,* travelled to the city of *New York,* and was there **inaugurated the first President of the United States** by publicly taking the required oath, administered by the chancellor of the State of *New York, R. R. Livingston,* on the 30th of April, 1789.

2. The **National Congress** was then in session in the same city. It was composed of two bodies of men from the several States. One body, the most numerous, were called Representatives,

QUESTIONS.—1. What have you to say about Washington being made President of the United States? 2. Of what is the National Congress composed?

[1] *po-to'-mak.*

who were chosen by the people. The smaller body, chosen by the State Legislatures of the various States, were called Senators, each State having two senators in the National Congress.

3. The **Representatives** were chosen to serve two years, and the **Senators** six years. The two bodies meet in separate rooms. As the National Congress was then organized, so it remains now—composed of the Senate and House of Representatives.

4. An act of either house, or body, can become a law only when it shall be agreed to by the other house, and be signed by the President of the *United States;* or if the President shall refuse to sign it, it may become a law by receiving two-thirds of the votes of both houses in favor of it. Such refusal of the President is called his **Veto.**

5. The Congress meets once a year, each Congress having two sessions. The President, whose business is to execute the laws made by the Congress, is authorized to have advisers or assistants in the management of the affairs of the government. They are called cabinet ministers, and, at first, were only four in number.

6. The minister for the transaction of business with other nations was called *Secretary of State.* The one who had charge of the money affairs of the nation was named *Secretary of the Treasury.* Military matters were entrusted to a *Secretary of War;* and the legal adviser of the President was called *Attorney-General.*

7. Afterward, when a navy was authorized, a *Secretary*

QUESTIONS.—3. What can you tell about Senators and Representatives? 4. What can you tell about the making of laws? 5. What have you to say about the sessions of Congress and the President's advisers? 6. Give the titles of the cabinet ministers and tell what are their duties.

of the Navy was added to the Cabinet. Then the one who had the general management of postal affairs was called *Postmaster-General,* and added to the Cabinet. Finally another cabinet officer was created, called *Secretary of the Interior,* who manages the Indian and other internal affairs of the government.

8. A Supreme Court of the United States was formed, consisting of several able lawyers. Whatever may be its decrees, in the line of its duty, is law, for it is the highest tribunal in the land. It is composed of a *Chief Justice* and five *Associate Justices,* appointed by the President and Senate. There were also circuit and district courts established in different parts of the country.

9. The President, Congress, and the Supreme Court formed the three co-ordinate branches of the government, which the National Constitution authorizes. In the Constitution, which was put into proper shape by the pen of *Gouverneur Morris,* the duties of the members of each branch of the government are clearly defined, as we shall see hereafter.

GOUVERNEUR MORRIS.

10. *Alexander Hamilton* was made the first Secretary of the Treasury. As soon as the new government was set in motion, he devised a plan for the management of its receipts and expenditures, which has always been considered a wise one, and which, with some slight changes, is yet used.

11. Very soon a **Mint** for coining money was established; also a **National Bank.** The seat of the national government was permanently fixed in a territory ten miles square, lying on each side of the *Potomac River.* Part of it was in *Virginia* and part in *Maryland.* It was named by *Washington, The District of Columbia.*

ALEXANDER HAMILTON.

12. In 1791 *Vermont* was admitted into the Union as the fourteenth State, and in 1792, *Kentucky* as the fifteenth State. Already settlements had been made north of the *Ohio River,* beyond the limits of the original thirteen States. The region now covered by the States of *Ohio, Indiana,*[1] *Illinois,*[2] *Michigan,*[3] and *Wisconsin*[4] was put under a governor in 1787, and called The *North-Western Territory.*

13. Meanwhile the *British* held forts in that region, and urged the *Indians* to make war on the *Americans.* They did so. General *Harmer* was defeated by them in October, 1790. General *St. Clair* was defeated by them in November, 1791; but in August, 1794, troops under General *Wayne* made them beg for peace, and keep quiet for more than a dozen years.

14. Political parties were formed in the Republic during the administration of *Washington*. Those who were in favor of giving great power to the general government were called **Federalists**. Those who wished to give more power to the people and State governments were called **Republicans**.

15. At about the time our national government was established, the people of *France* rebelled against their King. They finally cut off his head, and set up what they called a republican government. They made bad work of it, and soon found themselves involved in war with England and several other nations of Europe.

16. The *American Republicans* wished to help the *French Republicans*. *Washington,* desiring to keep his people from the danger of meddling with the affairs of other nations, issued a proclamation, declaring that the *United States* would not take part in the foreign quarrels, and warning the people not to engage in them.

17. That proclamation offended the *Republicans*, and they encouraged the *French* minister, to our government, to defy the President, and to fit out ships of war here to fight the *English*. The President asked the *French* government to call him home and send a less mischievous man. They did so.

18. Just as this trouble was passing away, a little rebellion broke out in Western *Pennsylvania*. Congress had taxed liquors which were made in this country. The whiskey distillers in Western *Pennsylvania* declared that they would not pay the tax. They armed themselves, and ill-

QUESTIONS.—15. What have you to say about a revolution in France? 16. What did American republicans do? What did Washington do? 17. What was the effect of his proclamation? What can you tell about a French minister? 18. What can you tell about a little rebellion?

treated the tax-collectors.   In 1794, *Washington* sent troops there to enforce the laws.   That is known as **The Whiskey Insurrection.**

19. Bad feeling was beginning to grow between the *Americans* and *British*, because the latter did not act according to the agreement made by the treaty of 1783.   The

President sent *John Jay* to *England* to adjust all matters in dispute. *Jay* negotiated a new treaty, which some *Americans* condemned and some approved.   This treaty was a subject for hot disputes for some time.

20. American commerce was now working its way into the *Mediterranean Sea,* where it met

JOHN JAY.

the *African* sea-robbers of *Algiers*,[1] who seized the ships and made slaves of the sailors.   Congress authorized ships to be built to protect *American* commerce, and this was the beginning of our **Navy.**   For several years our government was compelled to pay tribute to the *Algerine*[2] ruler, to keep his pirates from *American* merchantmen.

21. *Washington* was twice elected President.   The people wished to elect him for a third term of four years, but he would not consent.   In the autumn of 1796, they were compelled to make choice of a new man.   The political parties had a sharp contest.   *John Adams,* the Vice-President, and a *Federalist*, was elected President.

QUESTIONS.—19. What have you to say about the conduct of the British and a new treaty? 20. What can you tell about American commerce in the Mediterranean Sea? 21. What can you tell about a choice for President?

[1] *al-jeers'.*   [2] *al-je reen'.*

THE UNION OF STATES. **245**

Washington's Farewell Address.   President Adams and his Troubles.

22. Before retiring from office, *Washington* issued his **Farewell Address** to the people of the *United States.* It was a noble exhortation to the people to preserve their national union. On the 4th of March, 1797, he returned to *Mount Vernon*, with no expectation of being called into public life again.

23. In this section we have considered—

(1) *Washington* as the *first President;* (2) the structure of the *national government;* (3) organization of the *North-West Territory;* (4) war with the *Indians;* (5) the *French Revolution* and its effects here ; (6) the *Whiskey Insurrection;* (7) *Jay's Treaty;* (8) the *Algerine pirates;* and (9) the retirement of *Washington.*

SECTION II.

ADAMS'S ADMINISTRATION.

[1797–1801.]

1. *John Adams,* of Massachusetts, was inaugurated the **second President** of the *United States* on the 4th of March, 1797. He had to contend with serious troubles from the beginning. There was opposition from parties at home and enemies abroad.

2. The rulers of *France* were offended because the *American* government would not help them in their struggle against Kings. *Jay's* treaty seemed to show friendliness on

---

QUESTIONS.—22. What have you to say about Washington's Farewell Address, and his retirement from office ? 23. What have we considered in this section ?

QUESTIONS.—1. What have you to say about John Adams ? 2. What can you tell about the rulers of France and the Americans ?

the part of *America* to *England,* with whom *France* was at war.

3. The President called Congress together in May, 1797, to consult upon the matter. They sent three agents to *France* to adjust all matters in dispute. These were insulted by the **Directory,** as the five men who ruled *France,* were called.

4. War with France seemed probable, and our government prepared for it. Provision was made for an army with *Washington* at its head. Soon afterward *Napoleon Bonaparte,* an ambitious soldier, took the government of *France* into his own hands. He was wise and courteous, and the difficulty was soon settled after a few contests between *American* and *French* war-vessels on the ocean.

ADAMS, AND HIS RESIDENCE.

5. *Washington* did not live to see this happy result. He died at *Mount Vernon* on the 14th of December, 1799, and was mourned by *Americans* and *Europeans,* who loved the **liberty** for which he had struggled. Statues have been erected to his memory, and people of all lands, who know of his deeds, revere his name.

6. In the *District of Columbia*, a capital, or chief town of the nation was laid out, and named the *City of Washington*. It was made the **seat of the national government** in the year 1800, and has remained so ever since.

7. In the autumn of the year 1800, the Federalists and Republicans had a severe contest for power. The Republicans finally won the victory by electing *Thomas Jefferson*, of *Virginia*, President of the *United States*, and *Aaron Burr*, of *New York*, Vice-President.

8. We have considered in this section—

(1) The *inauguration of John Adams* as President of the United States ; (2) the relations of the *United States with France* ; (3) preparations for *war with France*, and a settlement of the difficulties ; (4) the death of *Washington* ; (5) the *establishment of a seat of government* at *Washington City*, and (6) the *election of a new President*.

SECTION III.

JEFFERSON'S ADMINISTRATION.

[1801–1809.]

1. *Thomas Jefferson* was inaugurated the **third President** of the *United States* on the 4th of March, 1801. The ceremony took place at the new *capitol*, in *Washington*

QUESTIONS.—6. Tell about the national capitol and seat of government. 7. What can you tell about an election ? 8. What have we considered in this section?

QUESTIONS—1. What have you to say about Mr. Jefferson and the place where he was inaugurated ?

248   THE UNION OF STATES.

Purchase of Louisiana and its Division.   The African Sea-Robbers.

City, a building not nearly so large as it is now. Mr. *Jefferson* was the man who wrote the Declaration of Independence.

2. Much was done for the prosperity of the *United States* during the administration of Mr. *Jefferson.* In the autumn of 1802 *Ohio* was admitted into the Union of States. The next year the vast region west of the *Mississippi* River from the *Gulf* to *Minnesota* and westward to the *Pacific*, known as *Louisiana*, was purchased from *France* by the *United States* for $15,000,000.

JEFFERSON, AND HIS RESIDENCE.

3. This great territory was divided. The southern part was called the *Territory of New Orleans,* and the northern part the *District of Louisiana.* Since then several States and many Territories have been formed from this domain.

4. The *African* sea-robbers were again troublesome, and our government resolved not longer to pay tribute for their forbearance from plunder. The ruler of *Tripoli* on the north *African* coast finally declared war against the *United States.*

QUESTIONS.—2. What can you tell about the country, and the purchase of Louisiana? 3. How was that territory divided? 4. What can you say about the African sea-robbers and rulers?

American Vessel Captured at Tripoli.

5. In the year 1801, *American* war vessels were sent to the *Mediterranean* to protect *American* commerce there. They did not effect much. Finally, in 1803, Commodore *Preble*[1] was sent with a number of vessels to **chastise the pirates.**

UNITED STATES FRIGATE.

6. One of *Preble's* vessels, the frigate *Philadelphia,* struck upon a

COMMODORE BAINBRIDGE.

rock in the harbor of *Tripoli,*[2] and was captured by the enemy. Her commander, Captain *Bainbridge,* and his officers were made prisoners of war, and the sailors were made slaves, and suffered dreadfully.

7. Early in 1804 Lieutenant *Decatur*[3] sailed into the harbor of *Tripoli* with a small vessel on a dark night, drove the *Tripolitans* from the *Philadelphia,* set her on fire, and escaped. This bold act alarmed the governor of *Tripoli.*

LIEUTENANT DECATUR.

8. That governor had no right to his office. It belonged to his brother *Hamet,* whom he had

QUESTIONS.—5. What did Americans do? 6. Tell about the capture of an American frigate and her officers and crew. 7. What did Decatur do? 8. What have you to say about the governor of Tripoli?

[1] *preb'-l.* [2] *trip'-o-le.* [3] *de-ka'-tur.*

driven into *Egypt.* *Hamet* joined the *Americans* against his usurping brother.

MOHAMMEDAN
SOLDIER.

9. In the spring of 1805 some *American* seamen and *Mohammedan* soldiers led by General *William Eaton* and accompanied by *Hamet,* traversed the Egyptian deserts from *Alexandria,* captured the *Tripolitan* city of *Derne,*[1] and were pressing on *Tripoli* when the governor made peace with the agent of the *United States,* who was there.

10. The *American* navy restrained, but did not subdue the pirates. That task was left for *Decatur* to perform in after years.

11. In the summer of 1804, *Alexander Hamilton* and *Aaron Burr,* rival political leaders, fought a duel. *Hamilton* was killed, and *Burr* became a fugitive. Beyond the *Alleghany* Mountains he devised a scheme for self-elevation which has never been fully revealed.

AARON BURR.

12. It was believed that *Burr* contemplated a **division of the Union,** and setting up a separate nation westward of the *Alleghany* Mountains, with himself at its head. He was arrested on a charge of treason in 1807, tried, and acquitted. He, however, lost the respect of his countrymen forever.

QUESTIONS.—9. What can you tell about an expedition under Eaton? 10. What did the American forces effect? 11. Give an account of Hamilton and Burr. 12. What have you to say about Burr and his scheme?

[1] *der'-ne.*

13. The same year, *Robert Fulton,* an *American* artist and inventor, having made machinery for driving vessels by steam, performed a successful voyage on the *Hudson River,* from *New York* to *Albany,* with a steamboat. This was the beginning of successful **navigation by steam** in the world.

ROBERT FULTON.

14. Now there was serious trouble in *Europe.* War was raging in many parts. *Bonaparte*

FULTON'S STEAMBOAT.

had made himself Emperor of *France* and three of his brothers Kings of other countries. The Continent of *Europe* and *Great Britain* were in arms against him.

15. The *United States* kept aloof from the strife, and, for a long time, *American* merchant vessels were allowed to trade in all parts of the world. They were called **neutrals,** because they did not take sides with any party.

16. A change came in the year 1806. *England* and *France,* in order to injure each other, closed many *European* ports, and both parties **seized American vessels.** *American* commerce was soon ruined. Our government had but few large ships to protect it, and the swarm of gunboats which Congress ordered were hardly sufficient to form a coast-guard.

QUESTIONS.—13. Tell about the first successful steamboat. 14. What have you to say about affairs in Europe, and Bonaparte? 15. What did the United States do, and what was the effect? 16. Tell about the treatment of American vessels, and the action of our government.

17. *Americans* naturally felt bitter toward the *English,*

with whom they had treaties of friend-
ship. This feeling was increased by the
British claiming the right to enter
American vessels and take away any
English seamen found on board of
them. This was called the **right of**
search.

A FELLUCA GUN-BOAT.

18. The exercise of the claimed
right of search finally led to war between the *United States*
and *Great Britain.* *British* cruisers became so insolent
that the *Americans* could not endure their insults.

19. In June, 1807, the *British* ship *Leopard,* attacked
the *American* ship *Chesapeake,* off the coast of *Virginia,*
because the commander of the latter would not allow the
British to search his vessel. The Chesapeake was badly
injured, and British seamen were taken from her by force.

20. This outrage made the *Americans* very angry. The
President issued a decree, in which he ordered every *British*
armed vessel to **leave American waters** immediately,
and not to return until the *British* government should give
full satisfaction for the outrage.

21. Meanwhile, *England* and *France* did all they could
to injure each other. *American* commerce continued to
suffer at their hands. The *British* would not give up the
right of search. Therefore, late in 1807, Congress passed
an Embargo Act, which forbade vessels of all kinds leaving
or entering *American* ports.

QUESTIONS.—17. What caused ill-feelings between the Americans and the English?
18. What right did the British claim, and how did they exercise it? 19. What can
you tell about a British outrage? 20. What did the President do? 21. How did
England and France act? What have you to say about the action of the English and
Americans?

22. This was a hard blow against **American commerce.** It killed it, without seeming to do good, for *England* and *France* cared very little what the *Americans* did or said. Early in the spring of 1809 the **Embargo Act** was repealed, and Congress forbade commercial intercourse with France and England.

23. Mr. *Jefferson* had now been President of the *United States* eight years. He was succeeded in office by *James Madison* of Virginia.

24. In this section we have considered—
(1) The *inauguration of Mr. Jefferson ;* (2) the addition of a *State and Territories ;* (3) the doings of the *African sea-robbers*, and a war with them ; (4) the *duel of Hamilton and Burr ;* (5) *Burr's conspiracy ;* (6) the first successful *steamboat ;* (7) affairs in *Europe*, and their *influence on Americans ;* (8) events tending to *war between Great Britain and the United States,* and (9) the *Embargo Act.*

SECTION IV.

MADISON'S ADMINISTRATION.

[1809–1817.]

1. It was a time of great commotion in the political world when, on the 4th of March, 1809, *James Madison,* the **fourth President of the United States**, took his oath of office. He had been a member of the Continental

---

QUESTIONS.—22. How was American commerce destroyed, and what was done?
23. What have you to say about Mr. Jefferson and a new President? 24. What have we considered in this section?

QUESTIONS.—1. What have you to say about President Madison?

Congress and an earnest advocate of the National Constitution.

2. On account of continued troubles with *France* and *Great Britain*, he called Congress together soon after he entered the office of President, to consult upon public matters.

3. Mr. *Madison* was assured by the *British* minister at *Washington City* that a special envoy or agent would soon come from the King, to settle all existing difficulties between the two governments. Thereupon the President proclaimed a renewal of commercial relations with the *British*.

4. The *British* ministry, in spite of the good intentions of the King, proceeded in their unrighteous course, and the President felt compelled to proclaim **commercial non-intercourse** with *Great Britain*.

5. *British* war-ships seized *American* vessels and sent

MADISON, AND HIS RESIDENCE.

them to England as prizes. About the middle of April, 1811, the *British* sloop-of-war *Little Belt* attacked the *American* ship *President,* off the coast of *Virginia.*

QUESTIONS.—2. What did Madison do? 3 How was the President deceived? 4. What did the British ministry and the President do? 5. What can you tell about British war-ships and a fight?

They had a severe fight. This event created much ill-feeling.

6. *British* officers and traders in the northwest again tried to get the *Indians* to make war on the *Americans.* A *Shawnoese*[1] chief named *Tecumtha*[2] formed a **confederacy of tribes**, for the purpose of driving the *Americans* from the country northwest of the *Ohio River*

7. General *Harrison* (afterward President of the *United States*) was then governor of the *Indiana* Territory. He saw the impending danger, and caused the settlers there to arm themselves. In the summer of 1811, he marched a considerable force into the *Indian* country to watch the movements of the savages.

8. Early in November, when *Harrison* and his men were encamped near the *Tippecanoe*[3] *River*, the *Indians* fell upon them on a dark night. A **hard fight** ensued, which lasted until near morning, when the *Indians* were driven away. That was on the 7th of November. *Tecumtha's* plan was ruined.

9. The people now felt that longer forbearance with the insults and injuries of *Great Britain* would be to make themselves slaves to that government. They resolved to fight again for their **independence**. *British* newspapers had insolently asserted that "the Americans can't be kicked into a war."

10. Abhorring an appeal to arms, yet accepting it with cheerfulness when it became necessary, the President, on

QUESTIONS.—6. What did British officers and traders do? What did an Indian chief do? 7. What can you tell about General Harrison and the Indians? 8. What can you tell about an encampment and battle? 9. What have you to say about the Americans and the British? 10. What did the President now do? What may that war be properly called?

[1] *shaw-no-ees'.*   [2] *teh-kum'-tha.*   [3] *tip pe-ca-noo'.*

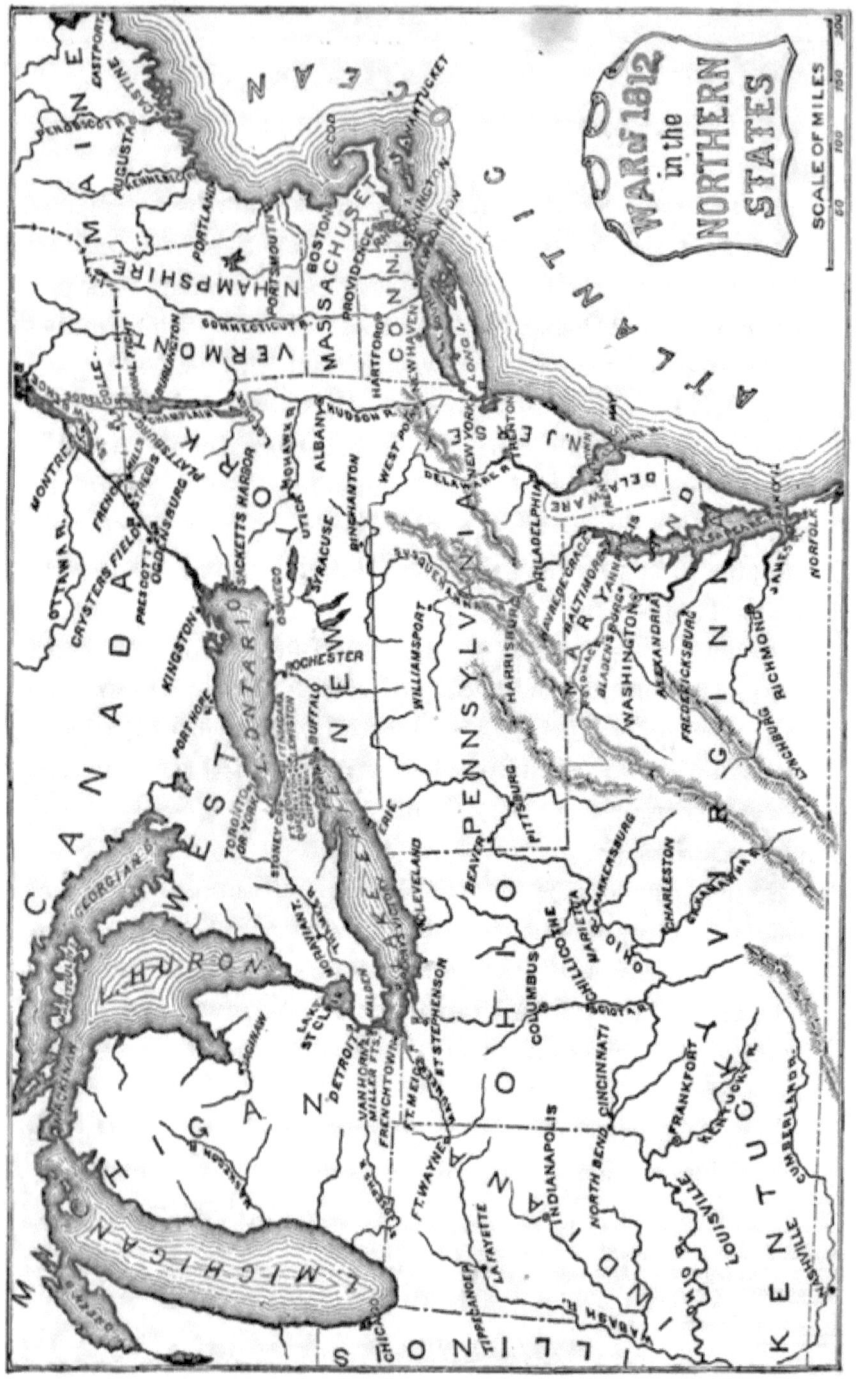

the 19th of June, 1812, **declared war against Great Britain,** by the authority of the National Congress. That conflict, known in history as The War of 1812, may properly be called

THE SECOND WAR FOR INDEPENDENCE.

11. Congress made ample provisions for prosecuting the war on land. The *American* Navy was then feeble compared to that of *Great Britain,* it having only twelve large war vessels, while the Royal Navy contained over nine hundred of all kinds. Yet the *Americans* went into the war with a confidence that they would win.

12. General *Dearborn*[1] of *Massachusetts,* an officer of

the old war for independence, was chosen general-in-chief of the armies, with other old army officers as his assistants. A plan for the invasion and **capture of Canada** was arranged, and General *William Hull,* then governor of the Territory of *Michigan,* was instructed to carry it out.

GENERAL DEARBORN.

13. *Hull* was ordered to cross the *Detroit*[2] *River* into *Canada,* capture *Fort Malden,*[3] and take possession of the province. He went over in July, but soon felt compelled to return. Hearing of the **capture of Fort Mackinaw,**[4] a strong barrier against the *Indians* of the northwest, the defeat of a detachment which he had sent out, under Major

QUESTIONS.—11. What did Congress do? What can you tell about the American and British navies? 12. What have you to say about the appointment of officers and plan of a campaign? 13. What was general Hull ordered to do? What did he hear of, and what did he do?

[1] *dehr'-burn.*   [2] *deh-troit'.*   [3] *mawl'-den.*   [4] *mak'-i-naw.*

Van Horne, to escort a provision train to *Detroit;* and confronted by a strong *British* force, he thought it prudent to take shelter in the fort at *Detroit.*

14. The *British* General *Brock* followed *Hull* across the river and demanded the surrender of the fort at *Detroit.* He threatened to take it by force, and let his *Indians* loose upon the garrison. *Hull* believed that he would carry out his threat, and, for the sake of his people, he **surrendered** the fort, army and territory on the 16th of August.

15. Because of this loss the *Americans* were greatly mortified and irritated. *Hull* was charged with cowardice and treason ; and by a court-martial was sentenced to be shot. He was pardoned by the President. In after years his conduct was commended by the *American* people as humane and right.

16. A plan was arranged in the summer of 1812 for **invading Canada** across the *Niagara*[1] *River.* On the morning of the 13th of October, about three hundred *American* troops, under Colonel *Solomon Van Rensselaer,*[2] crossed from *Lewiston* to attack the *British* on *Queenstown Heights.*

17. The battle was severe. Colonel *Van Rensselaer* was badly wounded and carried across the river. The British were driven from the *Heights,* and there General *Brock* was killed. Other *British* troops attacked and beat the *Americans* the same day. Both armies suffered much. Many *Americans* were made prisoners.

QUESTIONS.—14. What did General Brock do and threaten? and what did Hull do? 15. What can you tell about the feeling of the Americans and the treatment of Hull? 16. What plan of invasion was arranged, and what was done? 17. What can you tell about battles on Queenstown Heights?

[1] *ni-ag'-a-rah,*   [2] *rens'-e-lehr.*

18. Very little more was done on land during the remainder of that year. On the ocean the little *American* navy was winning great honors by its victories. In August the *American* frigate *Essex*, Captain *Porter*, captured the *British* sloop *Alert*, and the *American* frigate *Constitution*, Captain *Hull*, destroyed the *British* frigate *Guerriere*.[1] Two months afterward the sloop-of-war *Wasp*, Captain *Jones*, captured the *British* brig *Frolic*, but in the afternoon of the same day (October 18), the *Wasp* was taken by another British vessel.

A SLOOP-OF-WAR.

19. A week later (October 25) the frigate *United States*, Captain *Decatur*, captured the *British* frigate *Macedonian;* and on the 20th of December, the *Constitution*, Captain *Bainbridge*, captured the *British* frigate *Java*[2] off the coast of *Brazil*.

20. These victories made the *Americans* feel strong and joyful. Their privateers were rapidly increasing on the ocean ; and during the year 1812, they captured about three hundred merchant-ships, three thousand prisoners, and valuable cargoes, from the *British*. Thus encouraged, the *Americans* prepared for the next campaign with great vigor.

21. During the excitement of the war, Mr. *Madison* was again chosen President of the *United States*. A portion of

QUESTIONS.—18. What have you to tell about the war on land and sea? 19. What more can you tell about the war on the sea? 20. What was the effect of victories? What did American privateers do? 21. What have you to say about Madison and the Federalists?

[1] *geh-ree-ehr'.*   [2] *jah'-vah.*

the *Federalists* opposed the war, but the better class of them patriotically supported the measures necessary to carry it on.

22. In this section we have considered—

(1) The *inauguration of Mr. Madison;* (2) *dealings with the British government;* (3) the *conduct of British vessels;* (4) *troubles with the Indians* and their defeat ; (5) the *declaration of war* against Great Britain ; and (6) the *conduct of the war on land and sea.*

SECTION V.

THE SECOND WAR FOR INDEPENDENCE.

[1813.]

1. The campaign of 1813 opened early. The military forces were in three divisions. The **Army of the West** was under General *W. H. Harrison;* the **Army of the Centre** was under General *Henry Dearborn,* and the **Army of the North** was under General *Wade Hampton.*

2. *Harrison* had his headquarters in *Ohio; Dearborn's* were on the *Niagara River,* and *Hampton's* were in the neighborhood of *Lake Champlain.* Sir *George Prevost,*[1] who succeeded General *Brock* in command of *Canada* and the *British* army, had his headquarters at *York* or *Toronto.*

3. The campaign was opened in the West at the begin-

QUESTIONS.—22. What have we considered in this section?

QUESTIONS.—1. What have you to say about the army in 1813? 2. Where were the headquarters of the generals?

[1] *pra-vost'.*

ning of the year. There were hundreds of young men in that region, in the field, eager to drive the *British* from *Michigan*.

4. In January, General *Winchester*, with a fine body of *Kentuckians*, was encamped at *Frenchtown* (now *Monroe*), on the River *Raisin*, from which they had driven a *British* force. The *British* General *Proctor*, who was at *Malden*, marched against them. He crossed the *Detroit River*, with a force of white men and *Indians*, to attack *Winchester*.

5. A hard battle was fought on the morning of the 22d of January, and the *Americans*, defeated, surrendered on the condition that they should be well-treated. *Proctor* marched away without leaving a guard to keep his promise. The *Indians* soon turned back, fired the houses, murdered many of the prisoners, and kept others alive for torture in the woods.

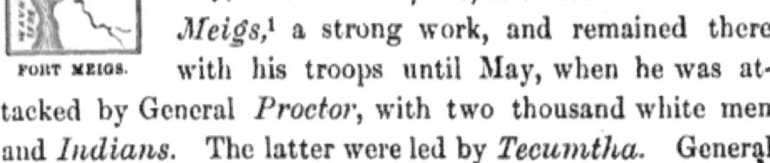

6. General *Harrison* was at the *Maumee Rapids* when he heard of this massacre. He and his troops were very indignant. After that the war-cry of the Kentuckians was: **"Remember the River Raisin!"**

7. At the *Rapids, Harrison* built *Fort Meigs*,[1] a strong work, and remained there

FORT MEIGS.

with his troops until May, when he was attacked by General *Proctor*, with two thousand white men and *Indians*. The latter were led by *Tecumtha*. General

QUESTIONS.—3. Where was the campaign opened, and with what spirit? 4. What can you tell about troops on the River Raisin? 5. What about a battle and of Indian cruelties? 6. What can you tell about Harrison and a war cry. 7. What did Harrison do? What occurred at Fort Meigs?

[1] *mēgz*

Green Clay came with troops to assist *Harrison,* and *Proctor* was soon driven to *Canada.* He fled on the 8th of May.

8. General *Clay* was left in command of *Fort Meigs.* Late in July the post was again besieged by *Proctor* and *Tecumtha,* with four thousand men. They were driven off, and then marched swiftly toward *Fort Stephenson,* at *Lower Sandusky.*[1]

9. **Fort Stephenson** was commanded by *Major Croghan,*[2] a brave young soldier, only twenty-one years of age, and having with him only one hundred and fifty men. When *Proctor* summoned him to surrender immediately, *Croghan* replied : "**Never, while I have a man left.**"

FORT STEPHENSON.

10. A terrible conflict ensued on the 2d of August. Finally the *British* and *Indians,* thoroughly beaten, fled from *Fort Stephenson* in great confusion. One shot from a cannon in a block-house of the fort swept a ditch filled with *British* troops, and killed or wounded one hundred and fifty of them. *Croghan* lost only one man killed and seven wounded.

MAJOR CROGHAN.

11. Lakes *Erie* and *Ontario* now became theatres of important events. In the autumn of 1812 the *Americans* completed a small **fleet on Lake Ontario.** In the sum-

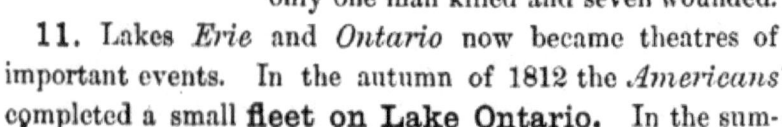
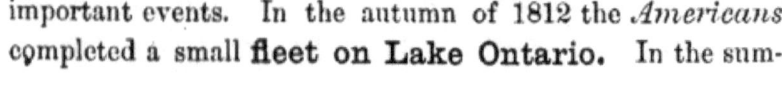

QUESTIONS.—8. What more can you tell about events at Fort Meigs? 9. What have you to say about Fort Stephenson? 10. Tell about a battle there. 11. What can you tell about Lakes Erie and Ontario?

[1] *san-dusk'-ee.*   [2] *kro'-an.*

THE UNION OF STATES. 263

Victory of Americans on Lake Erie.   Perry's Famous Despatch.

mer of 1813 another had been constructed on *Lake Erie,* and placed under the command of Commodore O. H. *Perry.*

COMMODORE PERRY.

12. The *British* also had a fleet on Lake *Erie,* under Commodore *Barclay.* The two fleets met near the western end of the lake on the 10th of September, 1813. They fought a **hard battle** from morning till evening; and before the twilight every *British* vessel had surrendered to *Perry.*

13. General *Harrison* was then near the western shores of *Lake Erie* with a small army. To him *Perry* wrote : " **We have met the enemy and they are ours!** " A few days afterward *Harrison* was joined by the brave veteran, Governor *Shelby,* with four thousand *Kentuckians.*

GENERAL SHELBY.

14. These land troops were borne across the lake in some of *Perry's* vessels to attack *Malden.* The *Americans* found the place deserted. *Proctor,* with his *British* troops, and *Indians,* under *Tecumtha,* were flying toward the interior of western *Canada.* A part of the *American* army **took possession of Detroit,** and the remainder pursued the fugitives.

15. The *Americans,* about three thousand in number, led by *Harrison,* overtook *Proctor* and his army on the little river *Thames,* and there, on the 5th of October, they **fought a desperate battle.** *Tecumtha* was killed, and *Proctor,* defeated, fled toward the head of *Lake Ontario.*

16. All that *Hull* had lost was now recovered, and the war ceased in that region. *Harrison* left *Detroit* in charge of Colonel *Cass* and a few soldiers, dismissed many of the volunteers from *Kentucky,* and with the remainder of his force marched to *Niagara,* and there joined the *Army of the Centre.*

17. General *Dearborn* was at **Sackett's Harbor** toward the close of April. *Ogdensburgh* had been attacked by the *British* in February, who destroyed much property there. *Dearborn* had not troops sufficient to send any in that direction, so he determined to attack *York* (now *Toronto*[1]), on the northern shore of Lake *Ontario.*

18. Commodore *Chauncey*[2] was there in command of the little fleet on Lake *Ontario.* These vessels conveyed land troops under General *Pike* across the lake. They attacked the *British* post at *York* and captured it.

19. The *British,* commanded by General *Sheaffe,*[3] **fled from York** (April 27, 1813), after blowing up the fort there. Some stones set flying by the explosion mortally wounded General *Pike.* He died on *Chauncey's*

GENERAL PIKE.

flag-ship, with the captured *British* flag under his head.

QUESTIONS.—16. What was recovered? What did Harrison do? 17. What have you to say about doings at Ogdensburgh, and Dearborn's determination? 18. What did Commodore Chauncey and his vessels do? What have you to say about York or Toronto? 19. What did the British do? Tell about the death of Pike.

[1] *to-ron'-to.*   [2] *chan'-se.*   [3] *sheef.*

20. A month later (May 27, 1813) the same troops, borne by the same ships, attacked the *British Fort George,* at the mouth of the *Niagara* River. The garrison **abandoned the fort** and fled westward to *Burlington Heights,* at the western end of Lake *Ontario,* closely pursued by the conquering *Americans.*

21. While *Chauncey* and his ships were at the western end of Lake *Ontario,* Sir *George Prevost* proceeded to attack *Sackett's Harbor,* on its eastern border, with a land and naval force. On the 27th of May he landed more than a thousand men. General *Jacob Brown* had hastily gathered the *American* militia, and these appeared so formidable that *Prevost* **fled with his ships and men.**

22. The *Americans* who had followed the flying British from *Fort George,* were now encamped at **Stoney Creek,** not far from the present city of *Hamilton,* where they were attacked in the dark, on the 6th of June. The assailants were repulsed, but Generals *Chandler* and *Winder,*[1] the *American* commanders, were made prisoners.

23. Late in the autumn of 1813 an attempt was made to capture *Montreal.* General *Wilkinson* had taken command, *Dearborn* being sick. Early in November he assembled about seven thousand soldiers at *French Creek,* on the *St. Lawrence.* After a brief skirmish there (November 13), he proceeded with his army down the *St. Lawrence* in a flotilla of boats.

24. A portion of the army under General *Brown* landed

[1] *wine'-der.*

on the *Canada* side of the *St Lawrence*, near *Williams-burg*, and at a place known as **Chrysler's** [1] **Field**, he fought a severe battle with the *British* on the 11th of November.

25. Neither party won a victory in the fight. *Wilkinson* passed on, expecting to find General *Hampton* at *St. Regis*,[2] with a co-operating force. *Hampton* failed to be there, and the expedition against *Montreal* was abandoned. The *Americans* encamped for the winter at *French Mills*, nine miles from the *St. Lawrence.*

26. At about this time some exciting events occurred on the banks of the *Niagara River.* The *Americans* burned the *Canadian* village of *Newark*, near *Fort George*, on the 10th of December. The *British* retaliated by burning several villages on the *American* side of the river and capturing Fort *Niagara.*

At that time *Buffalo* was destroyed. Thus ended the campaign in the North.

FORT NIAGARA, 1813.

27. Meanwhile a fierce war had been kindled in *Alabama.*[3] *Tecumtha* had been among the **Creek Indians** in the spring of 1813, to arouse them to hostilities against the *Americans.* They listened to him ; and late in August they captured *Fort Mimms*,[4] on the *Alabama River*, and murdered almost three hundred men, women, and children who were in the fort.

28. General *Andrew Jackson*, with twenty-five hundred

QUESTIONS.—25. What did Wilkinson do? What did his army do? 26. What can you tell about the destruction of villages on the Niagara River? 27. Give an account of war in Alabama.

¹ *krise'-ler's.*   ² *ree'-jis.*   ³ *ah-lah-bah'-mah.*   ⁴ *mims.*

Tennesseans, immediately marched into the *Creek* country. He won battle after battle against the *Indians.* Finally, toward the close of March, 1814, in a battle at the **Great Horse-Shoe Bend** of the *Tallapoosa*[1] *River,* he slew six hundred *Indian* warriors, and so **crushed forever** the power of the *Creek* nation.

29. War on the ocean was carried on vigorously in 1813. On the 24th of February, the sloop *Hornet,* commanded by Captain *Lawrence,* captured the *British* ship *Peacock,* off the eastern coast of *South America.* On his return home Captain *Lawrence* was placed in command of the frigate *Chesapeake.*

30. On the first of June the *Chesapeake* sailed out of

CAPTAIN LAWRENCE.

the harbor of *Boston* to attack the British ship *Shannon.* A hard battle was fought. Captain *Lawrence* was mortally wounded, and as he was conveyed below to die, he said : **" Boys, don't give up the ship ! "** But they were compelled to surrender.

31. On the 14th of *August* the *British* sloop *Pelican* captured the *American* brig *Argus.* On the 5th of September the *American* brig *Enterprise* captured the *British* brig *Boxer;* and five days afterward occurred the victory of *Perry* on *Lake Erie.*

32. During the spring and summer of 1813 the *British*

QUESTIONS.—28. How was the Creek Nation subdued ? 29. Give an account of war on the ocean in 1813. 30 and 31. Give further accounts of war on the ocean.

[1] *tahl-lah-poo'-sah.*

Admiral *Cockburn* plundered and destroyed towns and property on the coast of *Chesapeake Bay* and vicinity.   In

LAWRENCE CARRIED BELOW.

March he destroyed *American* shipping on the *Delaware*.   In May he plundered and burned *Havre de Grace*,[1]

QUESTIONS.—32. What can you tell about the depredations of Admiral Cockburn on the shores of the Chesapeake?

[1] *hav'-er-deh-grass'*.

THE UNION OF STATES. 269

The British in Hampton Roads. Cruise and Capture of the Essex.

Frenchtown, Georgetown, and *Frederickton,* on the *Chesapeake Bay.*

33. In June *Cockburn* was in *Hampton Roads* with the intention of taking *Norfolk.* The *Americans* had fortified *Craney*[1] *Island,* in the *Elizabeth River,* and successfully disputed the passage of the *British* up that stream on the

COMMODORE PORTER.

22d of June. The **British, repulsed**, plundered *Hampton* and then went southward, desolating the *Carolina* coasts to the *Savannah River.*

34. The frigate *Essex,* Captain *David Porter,* made a long cruise in the *Atlantic* and *Pacific* Oceans in 1813, and was finally captured in the harbor of *Valparaiso,*[2] on the 28th of March, 1814, by the *British*

frigate *Phœbe* and sloop-of-war *Cherub. Porter* wrote to the Secretary of the Navy : **" We have been unfortunate, but not disgraced."**

35. In this section we have considered—

(1) The disposition of the *American army;* (2) *military operations* in northern Ohio ; (3) the *victory on Lake Erie;* (4) *pursuit of the British* into Canada ; (5) operations on the borders of Lake *Ontario* and the *St. Lawrence River;* (6) events on the *Niagara River* and in the *Creek country;* (7) *war on the Ocean,* and (8) the marauding expeditions of *Admiral Cockburn.*

QUESTIONS.—33. Tell about Cockburn's career at and near Hampton, and on the Carolina coasts. 34. What can you tell about Captain Porter and the Essex ? 35. What have we considered in this section ?

[1] *kra-ne.*   [2] *vahl-pah-ri'-so.*

SECTION VI.

SECOND WAR FOR INDEPENDENCE CONTINUED.

[1814, 1815.]

1. *Great Britain,* at the beginning of the year 1814, was at war with the Emperor *Napoleon,* and could not spare many ships or soldiers for war in *America.* But in the spring *Napoleon* was driven out of *France,* and it was believed that war with him was at an end.

2. With this belief, the *British* sent many veteran troops

GENERAL BROWN.

to *Canada* to fight the *Americans.* The *American* troops near the *St. Lawrence River* moved early. General *Wilkinson* led some of them to *Plattsburg,* on *Lake Champlain,* and was defeated by the *British* in an engagement at La Colle. General *Brown* marched with others to *Sackett's Harbor.*

3. At the beginning of May a *British* fleet and three thousand troops **attacked Oswego,** on the southern shore of *Lake Ontario.* After a conflict that lasted two days, they were driven off on the 7th of May, with considerable loss.

4. About the same time General *Brown* led his troops to the *Niagara* frontier. On the morning of the 3d of

QUESTIONS.—1. What have you to say about Great Britain and Napoleon? 2. What did the British do? What did American commanders do? 3. What can you tell about events at Oswego? 4. What did General Brown do? What can you tell about an invasion of Canada and a battle there?

Battles at Chippewa and Bridgewater.

July, *American* troops under Generals *Scott* and *Ripley* crossed the river, and captured *Fort Erie,* opposite *Buffalo.* The next day the *Americans* and *British* had a very severe **battle at Chippewa.** Both armies suffered much.

5. The *British* were badly beaten, and fled to *Burlington Heights,* where they were joined by troops under General *Drummond,* and turned back. At the close of a hot day (July 25, 1814), they attacked the *Americans* under General *Brown* at **Bridgewater,** near *Niagara Falls.*

6. This battle was a severe one, each party losing about eight hundred men. The **Americans were victors**; and on the following day they fell back to *Fort Erie.*

7. On the 15th of August *Drummond,* with five thousand men, attacked *Fort Erie.* He was **repulsed,** with a loss of almost a thousand men. He fled to *Fort George.* The *Americans,* in September, drove the *British* from *Fort Erie,* destroyed that work, crossed the *Niagara River,* and went into winter quarters at *Buffalo* and in its neighborhood. They never invaded *Canada* again.

NIAGARA FRONTIER.

8. The *Americans* at *Plattsburg,* late in the summer of 1814, were commanded by General *Macomb.*[1] There was a small *American* navy on *Lake Champlain* at the same time, commanded by Commodore *Macdonough.*[2] The *British,* also, had a small fleet at the lower end of the lake.

QUESTIONS.—5. What have you to say about British troops and their movements? 6. What can you tell about the battle at Bridgewater? 7. Give an acount of an attack on the Americans in Fort Erie. What did the British and Americans do? 8. What have you to say about the Americans and British near Plattsburg?

[1] *mah-koom'.*   [2] *mak-don'-oh.*

9. In August, General _Prevost,_ with fourteen thousand men, marched from _Canada,_ to drive the _Americans_ from _Plattsburg._ At the same time the _British_ fleet sailed up _Lake Champlain._ A hard-fought battle ensued on the 11th of September, 1814, when the **Americans beat the British army and navy.** _Prevost_ fled in haste to _Canada._

10. The victories at _Plattsburg_ created great joy throughout the country. At the same time the _Americans_ had to lament severe losses further south.

COMMODORE MACDONOUGH.

11. About the middle of August, the _British_ General _Ross_ landed on the shores of _Maryland_ with six thousand troops. They were borne by a large fleet. _Ross_ marched toward _Washington City,_ our national capital.

12. General _Winder_ summoned the militia of that region to the field, to repel the invasion. They met _Ross_ at _Bladensburg,_ four or five miles from _Washington City,_ where a battle was fought, and the **Americans were beaten.**

13. On the 24th of August, the _British_ entered _Washington City,_ **burned the Capitol and the President's house,** and came near making President _Madison_ a prisoner. Then they went back to their ships.

14. Early in September General _Ross,_ with his conquer-

QUESTIONS.—9. Give an account of the invasion of New York State by the British in September, 1814. 10. What have you to say about the victory at Plattsburg? 11. Give an account of a British invasion of Maryland. 12. What did General Winder do? What can you tell about a battle? 13. What did the British do at Washington City? 14. What can you tell about an attempt to capture Baltimore? What did Americans do?

ing army, landed a few miles from *Baltimore,* to co-operate with Admiral *Cochrane*[1] in an attempt to capture *Baltimore* city. Troops under General *Stricker* went out to meet *Ross;* and *Fort McHenry,* in the harbor of *Baltimore,* commanded by Colonel *Armistead,*[2] was bravely defended.

15. While marching on *Baltimore, Ross* was killed in a skirmish. A conflict, known as the **Battle of North Point,** ensued on the 12th of September. At the same time the *British* fleet **bombarded Fort McHenry.** The *British* army and navy were both repulsed, and soon left the neighborhood to repose.

16. During the summer of 1814, a *British* blockading squadron annoyed the people on the *New England* coasts. From the 9th to the 12th of August, 1814, *British* ships bombarded *Stonington,* but were finally driven away. After the repulse at *Stonington* and *Baltimore,* the war almost ceased in the north.

17. The *Spaniards* now possessed *Florida,*[3] and favored the *British.* The latter were allowed to fit out ships at *Pensacola*[4] with which to fight the *Americans;* and the *Spaniards* encouraged the remnant of the *Creek* Nation to join the *British.*

18. The fleet from *Pensacola* attacked the American *Fort Bowyer,*[5] at the entrance to *Mobile Bay,* on the 11th of September, 1814. The *British* and their *Indian* allies were finally **driven away,** with considerable loss.

QUESTIONS.—15. What have you to say about General Ross, and a battle and a bombardment? 16. Tell about a British blockading squadron off New England, and events at Stonington. 17. What can you tell about events at Pensacola? 18. Tell about an attack on Fort Bowyer.

[1] *kok'-ran.* [2] *ar'-mis-ted.* [3] *flor'-i-dah.* [4] *pen-sah-ko'-lah.* [5] *bo'-yer.*

19. General *Jackson,* then at *Mobile* with troops, held the *Spanish* governor responsible for aiding the *British.*

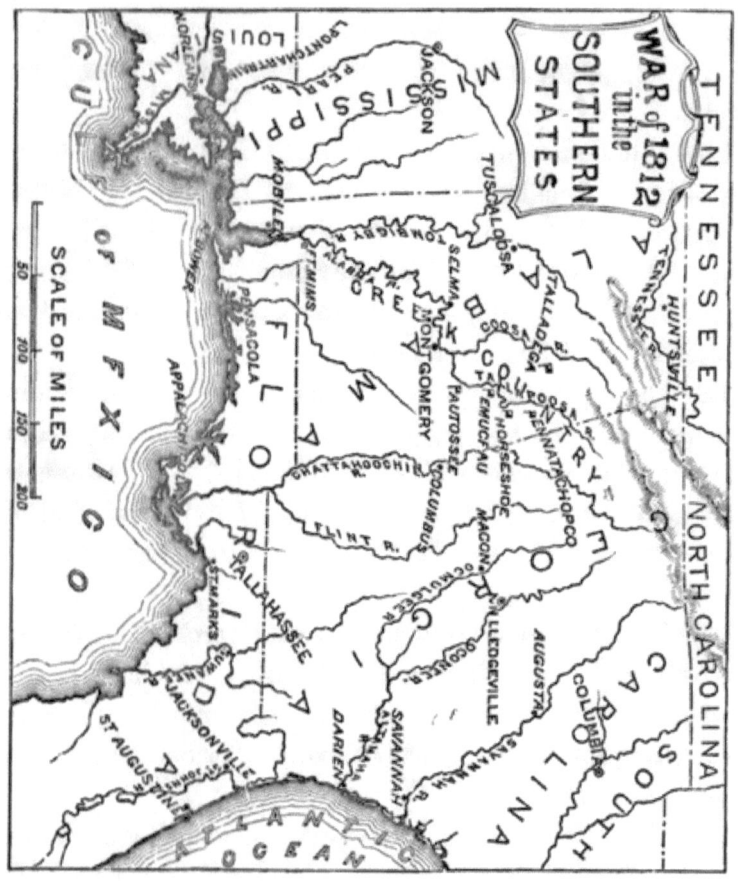

He marched upon *Pensacola* with two thousand *Tennesseeans,* drove the *British* to their shipping on the 7th of November, and **captured the town.**

20. When *Jackson* returned to *Mobile,* he met an urgent call for help from the citizens of *New Orleans.* A large *British* land force were in vessels on the *Gulf of Mexico,* for the purpose of invading *Louisiana.*[1] *Jackson* hastened to *New Orleans,* and soon afterward General *Pakenham,*[2] with twelve thousand *British* soldiers, was landed below that city, after capturing an *American* flotilla of gun-boats in Lake *Borgne.*[3] That was in December, 1814.

21. After some skirmishing, and casting up entrenchments by *Jackson,* the two armies met in battle array a few miles below *New Orleans,* on the 8th of January, 1815. A **very severe battle** was fought there on that day, in which the *British* lost their general and about seventeen hundred men killed and wounded. The *Americans,* protected by breastworks, lost only eight killed and thirteen wounded.

22. The **Battle of New Orleans** was the last one of the war, on land. The war continued a little longer on the ocean. During the year 1814, it had been prosecuted vigorously on the sea.

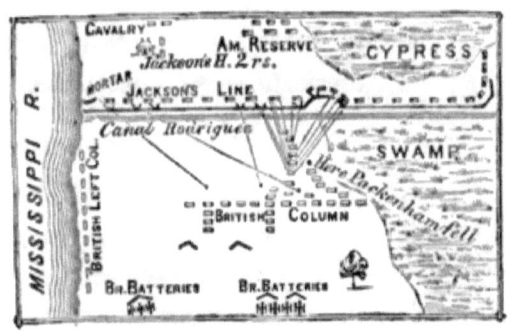

BATTLE OF NEW ORLEANS.

23. On the 29th of April, 1814, the *Peacock* captured the *Epervier*[1] off the coast of *Florida.* During the year, the *American* sloop *Wasp,* Captain *Blakely,* captured no less than **thirteen British vessels.** After capturing

---

QUESTIONS—21. Give an account of the Battle of New Orleans. 22. Which was the last land battle of the war? 23. Give an account of naval actions.

[1] *loo'-e-ze-ah'-na.*   [2] *pak'-'n-am.*   [3] *born.*   [4] *ep-ehr'-ve-are.*

her thirteenth prize—the *Avon*—on the first of September, she was never heard of.

24. On the 15th of January, 1815, the *President,* under command of Commodore *Decatur,* was captured by a *British* squadron off the coast of *Long Island.* On the 20th of February following, the *Constitution,* Commodore *Stewart,* captured the *British* frigate *Cyane,*[1] and sloop *Levant.*[2] On the 23d of March, the *Hornet* captured the *Penguin.*[3] The **naval operations were closed** then, excepting by privateers.

25. Before the Battle of *New Orleans,* a treaty of peace had been concluded between the *United States* and *Great Britain.* It was signed at *Ghent,*[4] in *Belgium,* on the 24th of December, 1814. When the treaty reached *America,* the President proclaimed peace, and the nation rejoiced.

26. The contest with *Great Britain* had just ended, when the Americans were compelled to engage in a short

WAR WITH ALGIERS.[5]

27. *Algerine* sea-robbers continued their depredations on *American* commerce in the *Mediterranean Sea.* The ruler of *Tripoli,* as we have seen, had been humbled. The ruler of *Algiers,* believing that the *American* navy had been destroyed by that of *Great Britain,* was now more exacting and insolent than ever.

28. President *Madison* declared war against *Algiers;* and sent Commodore *Decatur,* with a naval force, in May

QUESTIONS.—24. Give a further account of naval actions. 25. What have you to say about a treaty of peace? 26 and 27. What have you to say about Algiers, Tunis and Tripoli? 28. What did President Madison do? What did Decatur do?

¹ *si-an'.* ² *le-vant'.* ³ *pen'-gwin.* ⁴ *gant.* ⁵ *ahl-jeers'.*

1815, to humble the *Algerines*.[1] Our naval forces captured some of their pirates, and then appeared before their city.

29. The haughty governor was astonished. *Decatur* demanded the release of all *American* prisoners and payment for property which the *Algerine* pirates had seized or destroyed. "Do this," said the brave Commodore, "or I will **destroy your ships and your city.**"

30. The affrighted governor complied with *Decatur's* demand. Then the Commodore visited the cities of *Tunis* and *Tripoli,* and made their governors do the same thing. So, in a very short space of time, *Decatur* did what the Christian powers of *Europe* had not been able to do. The **Barbary**[2] **Powers,** as the piratical communities were called, were completely humbled.

31. And now the eventful administration of President *Madison* was drawing to a close. *Louisiana* had been admitted into the Union of States in 1812. *Indiana*[3] entered in 1816, and the same year *James Monroe* of Virginia was elected President of the *United States.*

32. In this section we have considered—

(1) The *movements of British forces* against the Americans ; (2) movements of *American troops on the Canada frontier;* (3) *victories at Plattsburg;* (4) *capture of Washington City* and repulse of the British at *Baltimore;* (5) *blockade of New England;* (6) *career of General Jackson* in the South ; (7) *peace;* and (8) *war with Algiers.*

QUESTIONS.—**29.** What did Decatur demand of the Algerines? **30.** What did the Algerine governor do? What did the governors of Tunis and Tripoli do? What did Decatur accomplish? **31.** What have you to say about the close of Madison's administration, and the admission of States? Who was elected President? **32.** What have we considered in this section?

[1] *ahl-je-reens'.* [2] *bahr'-ba-ry.* [3] *in-de-an'na.*

The following is a list of the principal land and naval battles fought during the second war for independence :

LAND BATTLES.

NAME.	DATE.
1812.	
Van Horne's	Aug. 5
Detroit	Aug. 15
Queenstown	Oct. 13
1813.	
Frenchtown	Jan. 22
York, or Toronto	April 27
Fort Meigs	May 5
Stoney Creek	June 6
Craney Island	June 22
Sackett's Harbor	May 29
Fort Stephenson	Aug. 2
Thames	Oct. 5
Creek War	November.
Chrysler's Field	Nov. 11
1814.	
Oswego	May 6
Chippewa	July 5
Niagara, or Bridgewater	July 25
Stonington	Aug. 10
Fort Erie	Aug. 15
Bladensburg	Aug. 24
Plattsburg	Sept. 11
North Point	Sept. 12
Fort McHenry	Sept. 13
Fort Bowyer	Sept. 15
Fort Erie (sortie)	Sept. 17
Below New Orleans	Dec. 23
1815.	
New Orleans	Jan. 8

NAVAL BATTLES.

NAME.	DATE.
1812.	
Essex,* Alert,	Aug. 13
Constitution, Guerriere,	Aug. 19
Wasp, Frolic,	Oct. 18
United States, Macedonian,	Oct. 25
Constitution, Java,	Dec. 29
1813.	
Hornet, Peacock,	Feb. 24
Chesapeake, Shannon,	June 1
Argus, Pelican,	Aug. 14
Enterprise, Boxer,	Sept. 5
Lake Erie	Sept. 10
1814.	
Essex, Phœbe,	March 28
Peacock, Epervier,	April 29
Wasp, Reindeer,	June 28
Wasp, Avon,	Sept. 1
Lake Champlain	Sept. 11
Lake Borgne	Dec. 14
1815.	
President, British Squadron,	Jan. 15
Constitution, Cyane and Levant,	Feb. 20
Hornet, Penguin,	March 23

* The American vessels are first named, each time.

SECTION VII.

MONROE'S ADMINISTRATION.

[1817–1825.]

1. James Monroe, the fifth President of the *United States,* took the oath of office on the 4th of March, 1817. With his able cabinet he worked zealously to extricate the country from the confusion caused by the war.

MONROE, AND HIS RESIDENCE.

2. During the war the *Americans* had manufactured many things which they had before bought in *France* and *England.* They had **established manufactories** here at considerable expense, and thousands of persons were employed in them.

3. When the war was closed, foreign goods came in abundance. Manufacturing in *America* was made an unprofitable business, and a multitude of people were idle. Many of these went to the fertile regions west of the *Alleghany* Mountains, and became **founders of States.**

QUESTIONS.—1. What have you to say about President Monroe and his cabinet? 2. What can you tell about American manufactories? 3. What was the state of business after the war, and what caused emigration to the West?

4. During the administration of President *Monroe*, the Territories of *Mississippi, Illinois, Alabama*,[1] and *Missouri*[2] were admitted into the Union as States. Settlements increased very rapidly all over the West. **Great prosperity** in the future was hoped for, when difficulties appeared in the South.

5. Mischievous *British* subjects in *Florida* were exciting the *Indians* to make war on the *Americans.* Toward the close of 1817 a large number of *Creek* and *Seminole Indians* and fugitive slaves began to **plunder and murder** the *American* settlers on the borders of *Georgia* and *Alabama.*

6. Troops were sent to protect the settlers. The *Indians* became more and more hostile, when General *Jackson,* with a thousand *Tennessee* volunteers, went to assist the regular troops. The General hung two of the men who had excited the Indians to plunder and murder. Then he marched to *Pensacola* and **captured it,** and sent offending *Spaniards* and others to *Cuba.*[3]

7. For these acts *Jackson* was at first censured, and then he was commended. By a treaty with *Spain, Florida* came into the **possession** of the *United States* soon afterwards, and *Jackson* was appointed its first governor. That was in February, 1821.

8. At that time the question of admitting *Missouri* into the Union as a State was settled. It had caused violent discussions in Congress and out of it. The main point in dispute was the question, Shall it be a **free** or **slave-labor** State ? For two years the discussion continued.

9. It was finally agreed to allow slaves to be held in *Missouri.* It was also agreed that a line should be drawn from the southern boundary of *Missouri* to the *Pacific Ocean,* north of which **slavery should never exist.** This agreement is known as the *Missouri Compromise.* It was effected in 1820.

10. In the autumn of 1820 the President (Mr. *Monroe*) and Vice-President (*Daniel D. Tompkins*) were re-elected. There was very little opposition to them, for the old *Federal party* had almost disappeared as an organization.

11. *Monroe's* administration was popular. A law was passed giving a pension to soldiers of the Revolution yet living. An agreement with *Great Britain* in relation to coast fisheries, favorable to *Americans,* was made ; and our government recognized the **independence** of *South American* republics.

12. On that occasion the President proclaimed, as a principle, that the *American* continents " are henceforth not to be considered as **subject for future colonization** by any European Power." This is known as " The **Monroe Doctrine.**"

13. The **sea-robbers** were not all in the *Mediterranean.* They greatly annoyed *American* merchantmen among the *West India* Islands. In 1819 Commodore *Perry* was sent to disperse them ; he died there soon after. In

1823 Commodore *Porter* **completed their destruction.** The previous year a small *American* squadron had destroyed more than twenty piratical vessels on the coast of Cuba.

14. The last year of *Monroe's* administration was marked by the visit of *Lafayette*[1] to this country as the **Nation's guest.** He went back from our shores in the frigate *Brandywine,* so named in his honor, he having fought his first battle for us on the banks of the *Brandywine Creek.*

15. A new President of the Republic was chosen in the autumn of 1824. *John Quincy Adams,* son of the second President, was chosen; with *John C. Calhoun,*[2] of *South Carolina,* as Vice-President.

16. In this section we have considered—

(1) The *condition of the country* after the war; (2) the *settlement and organization of Territories;* (3) *British emissaries* among the Southern Indians, and the result of their work; (4) *Jackson and Florida;* (5) *Missouri Compromise;* (6) *pensions, fisheries,* and the *Monroe Doctrine;* (7) *pirates,* and (8) the *visit of Lafayette.*

QUESTIONS.—14. Tell about the visit of Lafayette. 15. What have you to say about an election for President? 16. What have we considered in this section?

[1] *lah-fa-et'.*　　　[2] *kal-hoon'.*

THE UNION OF STATES. 283

Inauguration of President Adams. The Indians and State Supremacy.

SECTION VIII.

J. Q. ADAMS'S ADMINISTRATION.

[1825-1829.]

1. John Quincy Adams, the sixth President of the United States, entered upon the duties of his office on the 4th of March, 1825. Our country was at **peace with all the world,** and everything seemed prosperous. His administration is remarkable for its lack of very stirring incidents.

J. Q. ADAMS, AND HIS RESIDENCE.

2. The subject of the removal of the *Creek* and *Cherokee Indians* from *Georgia* ruffled the general serenity for a while. The assumption of State supremacy, put forth at that time, produced some uneasy feeling.

3. In 1825 a great work of internal improvement was completed. It was the canal which connects the waters of **Lake Erie and the Hudson River.** Governor *De Witt Clinton* acquired great honor by his zealous promotion of the work.

QUESTIONS.—1. What have you to say about President J. Q. Adams, and the state of the country? 2. Tell about trouble in Georgia. 3. What have you to tell about the Erie Canal?

4. On the 4th of July, 1826, *Thomas Jefferson* and *John Adams* died. They were both on the Committee that drew up the Declaration of Independence and signed it, just **fifty years before** ; both had been foreign ambassadors and both had been President of the Republic. The coincidence was remarkable.

DEWITT CLINTON.

5. In order to assist *American* manufacturers a protective system was adopted in 1828. It imposed a duty on foreign manufactures so high as to enable the *Americans* to make and sell their productions as low as those which came over the sea. This was called **The American System.**

6. This policy was popular with the manufacturers, but the cotton-growers of the Southern States, who found a ready market for raw cotton in *England,* opposed this **Protective Tariff.** Among

JOHN C. CALHOUN.

the most eminent of the political leaders in this opposition was *John C. Calhoun,* of *South Carolina.*

7. The serene administration of President *Adams* now drew toward its close. The nation was prosperous. The

THE UNION OF STATES. 285

Andrew Jackson Elected President.   The Character of Jackson.

government was **very little in debt,** and was at peace with all the world. It was the calm before a storm.

8. In the autumn of 1828, a bitter political contest was carried on. *Adams* was a candidate for a second term. He was defeated by *Andrew Jackson, of Tennessee,* who was elected President, with *John C. Calhoun* as Vice-President.

9. In this section we have considered—

(1) The *state of the country* when Adams became President ; (2) the case of the *Indians in Georgia;* (3) the *Erie Canal;* (4) deaths of *Adams and Jefferson;* (5) the *American System* and its opposers ; (6) the election of *Andrew Jackson* to the Presidency.

SECTION IX.

JACKSON'S ADMINISTRATION.

[1829–1837.]

1. Andrew Jackson, the seventh President of the *United States,* was the last but one of the chief magistrates of the Republic, who had lived during the Revolution. He became President on the 4th of March, 1829.

2. *Andrew Jackson* was an honest man, with a strong will, and was always ready to do what he believed to be right, without regard to the opinions of others. His administration was a quiet one at first, and then it encountered serious troubles.

QUESTIONS.—8. What can you tell about a political contest? 9. What have we considered in this section ?

QUESTIONS.—1. Who was the seventh President of the United States? What have you to say about the character of Jackson?

3. A speck of rebellion appeared in *Georgia* in 1832. The governor of that State claimed the right to possess the lands of the *Cherokee Indians*. The President favored the claim. The Supreme Court of the *United States*—the expounder of the law—decided against the claim.

4. The authorities of *Georgia* **defied the Supreme Court,** and great trouble was expected. There was an amicable settlement, and a few years afterward the *Cherokees* were removed from their lands in that State.

5. The *Bank of the United States,* chartered during the presidency of *Washington,* and re-chartered during the presidency of *Madison,* asked for a new charter, to go into effect in 1836. The President opposed the measure, because he believed it to be an institution that might be made injurious to the government.

JACKSON AND HIS RESIDENCE.

6. The government money was deposited in the *United States Bank.* In 1832, Congress passed a bill for a renewal of the Bank Charter. *Jackson* **vetoed** the bill. He recommended the **withdrawal of the public funds** ($10,000,000) from the bank. Congress refused to sanction that measure, and the President took the responsibility of doing so, in the autumn of 1833.

7. This act produced great business embarrassments for awhile, but it was beneficial to the country finally.

8. In the summer of 1832, *Black Hawk,* a bold chief of the *Sac*[1] tribe of *Indians,* made war upon the white people on the borders of the *Mississippi River,* in *Illinois.* He and his followers were soon subdued by *United States* troops, and the chief was made a prisoner.

BLACK HAWK.

9. More serious trouble now appeared in *South Carolina.* We have observed that there was strong opposition in the cotton-producing States to a **Protective Tariff.** The political leaders in *South Carolina* declared that the duty, or impost tax, should not be paid on foreign goods entering the port of *Charleston.*

10. This defiance of law was promptly met by President *Jackson.* He told the people of *South Carolina* that if they did not pay the tax voluntarily, he would send troops to compel them to do so.

11. For a time the defiant movements of these nullifiers of law threatened civil war. Finally, in 1833, through the influence of *Henry Clay* of *Kentucky,* a plan for a **settlement of the difficulty** was adopted, and the cloud passed away in the spring of 1833.

12. In the autumn of 1832, *Jackson* was again chosen

QUESTIONS.—7. What was the effect of removing the public money from the Bank? 8. What can you tell about a war with Indians in the West? 9. What can you tell about trouble in South Carolina? 10. What did the President do? 11. What further have you to say about difficulties in South Carolina?

[1] *sawk.*

288   THE UNION OF STATES.

Prosperity Succeeded by Adversity.   War with the Southern Indians.

President of the *United States*, and continued to conduct public affairs with vigor. His **removal of the government deposits** from the *United States Bank* produced intense excitement throughout the country ; and great prosperity was followed by great adversity in business.

13. This excitement was disappearing, when another event caused much trouble. The President attempted, by force, to **remove the Southern Indians** to a country beyond the *Mississippi*. He sent troops into *Florida* and *Georgia* for that purpose in the autumn of 1835, and the *Seminole Indians* flew to arms.

HENRY CLAY.

14. Led by *Osceola*,[1] a brave and sagacious chief, the *Seminoles* made fierce war upon the white people, which continued several years. Many *United States* troops were sent against them from time to time, under Generals *Thompson, Clinch, Gaines, Scott, Jessup,* and Colonel *Taylor,* but could not subdue them in their dark swamps.

OSCEOLA.

15. In the spring of 1836, the *Creeks* joined the *Seminoles,* and made the war still more

[1] os-se-o'-la.

distressing. Thousands of white inhabitants, in Western *Georgia* and Eastern *Alabama,* fled from their homes in terror. Mail coaches, steamboats and villages were attacked.

SEAT OF SEMINOLE WAR.

16. At length General *Winfield Scott* took command of the troops in that region. The *Creeks* were soon subdued and sent beyond the Mississippi. That was in 1836. But the *Seminoles* still held out, and **kept up the war** through the ensuing winter. The little map shows the position of the forts and places of battles in *Florida,* that are mentioned in larger histories.

17. In the spring of 1837, President *Jackson's* administration closed. The government of the *United States* never before held a more exalted position in the opinion of the world. The President had always acted upon the principle—**Ask nothing but what is right, and submit to nothing that is wrong.** During that administration *Arkansas* and *Michigan* were admitted into the Union as States.

18. In the autumn of 1836, *Martin Van Buren* of *New York* was elected President of the *United States,* and *Richard M. Johnson* of *Kentucky* was chosen Vice-President.

19. In this section we have considered—

(1) *President Jackson* and his character ; (2) *troubles*

QUESTIONS.—16. What can you tell about General Scott and the Seminoles? 17. What have you to say about Jackson's administration and the admission of States? 18. What about an election? 19. What have we considered in this section?

in Georgia; (3) *Bank of the United States;* (4) *Black Hawk War;* (5) *defiance of law* in South Carolina ; (6) *war with the Southern Indians;* and (7) the country at the close of *Jackson's administration.*

SECTION X.

VAN BUREN'S ADMINISTRATION.

[1837–1841.]

1. Martin Van Buren became the eighth President of the *United States* on the 4th of March, 1837. He was then about fifty-five years of age.

2. The business of the country was in great confusion at that time. The **money of the government** had been deposited in State Banks. These banks had lent it freely to the people. Speculations and extravagance in living followed.

3. All over the country the people seemed almost wild in their anxiety to **build villages and fine houses** with their borrowed money. Finally, when there was no more to be borrowed, and the government wanted its money from the banks, the banks called upon the borrowers to pay. They were unable to do so, and **great trouble in business followed.**

4. So great was the trouble that the new President **called a meeting of Congress** in September, 1837, to consider the financial condition of the country. Aid was not extended to the people in business, but *Congress* **took the money from the State Banks** and placed it in the hands of agents appointed by the government.

QUESTIONS.—1. What have you to say about President Van Buren ? 2. What can you tell about the government money, the State Banks, and the way of living ? 3. What did the people do, and what happened ? 4. What did the President do ? What did Congress do ?

5. This prevented the banks from lending money so freely and checked speculation and extravagance. So far the measure was good in its effects. The government agents kept the money at the principal seaports and marts of business. The plan was called **The Independent Treasury System.**

VAN BUREN, AND HIS RESIDENCE.

6. Meanwhile the war with the *Seminoles* was continued. Nor did it cease during the administration of President *Van Buren.* By a treacherous act *Osceola* was seized and imprisoned in a fort in *Charleston* harbor, where he died of a fever.

7. On Christmas day, 1837, Colonel *Zachary Taylor,* who was afterward President of the United States, gained a **victory over the Seminoles** on the borders of *Macaco*[1] *Lake,* but for more than two years longer he continued to fight them. The war was finally ended in 1842, having continued seven years.

8. The peaceful relations between the *United States* and

QUESTIONS.—5. What were the effects of the action of Congress? What did government agents do? 6. What have you to tell about the war with the Seminoles? 7. What have you to say about Colonel Taylor and the Seminole War? 8. What have you to tell about the relations between the United States and Great Britain?

[1] *mah-ka'-ko.*

Great Britain were a little disturbed by revolutionary movements in *Canada,* begun in 1837. Many sympathizing *Americans* crossed into *Canada* to help the insurgents, in spite of the efforts of our government to prevent them.

9. These movements continued three or four years, until the insurrection was suppressed by the *British* government. At the same time a dispute arose respecting the eastern boundary line between the *United States* and the *British* provinces.

10. Much unpleasant feeling was produced by the aid given to the *Canadians* by *Americans;* and the **dispute respecting the boundary**, at one time, threatened to end in war. General *Scott* was sent by our government to *New Brunswick* to make peace, and the matter was **settled** in a friendly manner in 1842.

11. In the autumn of 1840 General *William Henry Harrison,* of *Ohio,* was elected President of the *United States,* with *John Tyler,* of *Virginia,* as Vice-President. At that time the two political parties were called, respectively, **Whigs** and **Democrats.** The Whigs were friends of *Harrison;* the Democrats were friends of *Jackson* and *Van Buren.*

12. We have considered in this section—

(1) The *confusion of business* in the country, and the *causes* of it ; (2) the *Independent Treasury System ;* (3) the continuance of the *war with the Seminoles;* (4) *unpleasant relations* between the United States and Great Britain, and (5) the *names of parties* and the newly chosen President.

QUESTIONS.—9. What did Americans do? What trouble appeared on the eastern boundary of the United States? 10. What have you to say about unpleasant feelings? 11. What can you tell about an election of a new President, and names of parties? 12. What have we considered in this section?

SECTION XI.

HARRISON'S AND TYLER'S ADMINISTRATIONS.

[1841–1845.]

1. William Henry Harrison, the ninth President of

the *United States,* was inaugurated on the 4th of March, 1841. He was then past sixty-eight years of age. He was the last of the Presidents who had witnessed scenes in the old war for independence.

2. Precisely one month after he took the chair of State, **President Harrison died.** In accordance with the provisions of the National Constitution, the Vice-President, *John Tyler*, then became President.

3. Mr. *Tyler* became the tenth President by taking the oath of office on the 6th of April, 1841. He was then fifty-one years of age.

4. President *Harrison* had,

HARRISON, AND HIS RESIDENCE.

on the last day of March, called an extraordinary meeting of Congress, mainly for the purpose

QUESTIONS.—1. What have you to say about General Harrison? 2. Tell about the death of the President, and who was his successor, and how. 3. What have you to say about Mr. Tyler? 4. What can you tell about an extraordinary meeting of Congress, and the result?

of considering the question of chartering a new **United**

States Bank, with a hope of relieving the country from embarrassment. They met and passed a law for this purpose, but President *Tyler* refused to sign it.

5. This action offended the political friends of the President, and his cabinet or advisers **all left him,** excepting *Daniel Webster,* who was Secretary of State. As he was engaged in negotiating a treaty with *Great Britain,* he thought it best for the country that he should remain in his place.

6. Changes were made in the tariff laws, during Mr. *Tyler's* administration, which secured reconciliation for a time. Disputes arose in *Rhode Island*

TYLER, AND HIS RESIDENCE.

concerning a change of the old charter given by *Charles* the Second, for a new constitution.

7. Two parties were formed, one for and the other against a **new charter.** At one time each party appeared in arms, and a civil war seemed imminent. The President sent troops there to restore order. A new constitution was **adopted** in 1842.

QUESTIONS.—5. What have you to say about President Tyler's cabinet? 6. What have you to say about tariff laws and disputes in Rhode Island? 7. Give an account of the affair in Rhode Island.

8. In 1844 the country was much agitated by a proposition for the annexation of the Republic of *Texas* to the *United States.* That State had been separated from *Mexico* by **revolution.** It had been effected chiefly by settlers from the *United States.*

DANIEL WEBSTER.

9. The people of *Texas* desired to become a part of our Republic. Arrangements were finally made for the annexation. It was advocated by the slaveholders of the South, and opposed by those who were opposed to the system of slave-labor.

10. The question of **annexation** was a prominent one at the election in the autumn of 1844. *James K. Polk,* of *Tennessee,* who was in favor of annexation, was chosen President, with *George M. Dallas,* of *Pennsylvania,* as Vice-President.

PROFESSOR MORSE.

11. At about the same time Professor *Samuel F. B. Morse* had perfected his invention of the **Electro-magnetic telegraph,** and had put up message-wires between *Baltimore and Washington.* The **first public message** sent over those wires was the announcement of the nomination of Mr. *Polk* for President.

12. In this section we have considered—

(1) The *inauguration and death of President Harrison;* (2) the *accession of Mr. Tyler* to the Presidency; (3) the action of Congress and the President concerning a *new bank charter;* (4) *changes in the cabinet;* (5) *difficulties in Rhode Island;* (6) *annexation of Texas;* and (7) the *election of Polk* and invention of the *magnetic telegraph.*

SECTION XII.

POLK'S ADMINISTRATION.

[1845–1849.]

1. James Knox Polk was fifty years of age when he became the eleventh President of the *United States*, on the 4th of March, 1845. He was a Democrat in politics, and was supported by a powerful party.

2. Three days before the expiration of his term of office, President *Tyler* had signed the bill providing for the **admission of Texas** into the Union. This subject required the immediate attention of the new President.

3. The government of *Mexico* had never acknowledged the independence of *Texas*, and claimed that country as a part of *Mexican* territory. The annexation of *Texas* was offensive to that government, and led to great difficulties.

QUESTIONS.—12. What have we considered in this section?

QUESTIONS.—1. What have you to say about President Polk? 2. What did President Tyler do? What did the subject require? 3. What were the relations between Mexico and Texas?

4. This offence, and an old quarrel about debts due from *Mexico* to people of the United States, became **a pretext**

for war. The President sent General *Zachary Taylor*, with a small force, into *Texas,* in July, 1845, which was called an **Army of Observation.**

5. *Taylor's* troops encamped not far from the *Rio Grande,*[1] the boundary between *Texas* and *Mexico,* and at the same time *American* ships of war went into the *Gulf of Mexico.*

6. A large force of *Mexican* troops were assembled at *Matamoras,* near the mouth of the *Rio Grande,*[1] at the close of 1845. Early in January, 1846, *Taylor* and his troops began building a fort opposite *Matamoras,*[2] when the *Mexican* commander, General *Ampudia,*[3] ordered him

POLK, AND HIS RESIDENCE.

to leave within twenty-four hours.

7. General *Taylor* refused to go. General *Arista*[4] was made chief commander of the *Mexicans.* He sent some *Mexican* troops across the river, and in a skirmish with

QUESTIONS.—4. What caused war between the United States and Mexico? What did the President do? 5. What have you to tell about American military and naval forces? 6. What can you tell about Mexican and American forces in and near Matamoras? 7. What did General Taylor refuse to do? What did the Mexicans do? What can you tell about the first blood shed in the war with Mexico?

[1] *re'-o-grahn-da.* [2] *mat-a-mo'-rus.* [3] *am-poo'-dhe-ah.* [4] *ah-rees'-ta.*

them late in April, some *Americans* under Captain *Thornton* were killed.   This was the **first blood shed** in

THE WAR WITH MEXICO.

8. Some *American* soldiers and provisions left at *Point Isabel* were now in danger.   General *Taylor* left the fort opposite *Matamoras,* which he called Fort *Brown,* and, with a greater part of his troops, marched toward *Point Isabel.*[1]

9. The *Mexicans* attacked Fort *Brown,* and *Taylor* turned back to protect it.   On his way back, with about two thousand men, he met the *Mexican* army under *Arista,* six thousand in number, at a prairie called **Palo Alto.**[2]

10. It was the 8th of May, 1846.   A hard fight was immediately begun, and lasted five hours.   The *Americans* won the victory, and the *Mexicans* retreated.   On the following day *Taylor* gained another victory over the same troops at **Resaca de la Palma,**[3] when the *Mexicans* lost a thousand men, and General La Vega was made prisoner.   The *Americans* lost only one hundred.

11. Before the news of these victories reached the *United States,* Congress had formally **declared war against Mexico,** and an extensive campaign had been planned for the invasion of that country, which extends from the Gulf to the *Pacific Ocean.*

12. A **fleet** was to sweep around *Cape Horn* and attack its *Pacific* coast ; an **Army of the West** was to gather

---

QUESTIONS.—8. What can you tell about the movements of General Taylor? 9. What did the Mexicans and General Taylor do? 10. What occurred at Palo Alto and Resaca de la Palma? 11. What did the Congress of the United States do? 12. Give an outline of the plan for a campaign.

[1] *iz-a-bel'.*   [2] *pah'-lo-ahl'-to.*   [3] *reh-sah'-ka dah lah pah'-mah.*

at *Fort Leavenworth,* invade *New Mexico,* and coöperate with the *Pacific* fleet; and an **Army of the Centre** was to invade Old *Mexico* from the north

13. It had been determined in council to take possession of *Mexico,* and the President was authorized to raise an army of **fifty thousand men.** Volunteers flocked to the camp in *Texas* at the call, and there General *Wool* prepared them, by thorough discipline, for invading the country.

14. After his two successful battles, *Taylor* crossed the *Rio Grande,* drove the *Mexican* troops from *Matamoras,* and marched against the strong *Mexican* town of *Monterey.*[1] It was **surrendered** to him on the 24th of September, 1846. General *Taylor* rested near this place, waiting for further orders from his government.

15. Meanwhile General *Wool* had been preparing the volunteers. By the middle of July, twelve thousand of them were mustered into service. Nine thousand of these *Wool* sent to reinforce *Taylor,* and with the remaining three thousand he prepared to **invade Mexico** from *San Antonio.*

16. *Wool* penetrated *Mexico* in October, with the design of taking possession of *Chihuahua,*[2] in the heart of the country, but hearing of the capture of *Monterey,* he turned in the direction of *Coahuila.*[3] His kindness to the people of the country won their affections.

17. About the same time General *Worth,* sent out by

QUESTIONS.—13. What was determined on and what was done concerning Mexico? 14. What can you tell about an invasion of Mexico and a victory there? What did Taylor then do? 15. What have you to say about General Wool and the volunteers? 16. What can you tell about Wool's invasion of Mexico? 17. What did General Worth do? What did Commodore Connor and General Taylor do?

[1] *mont-a-ra'.*   [2] *che-wah'-wah.*   [3] *ko'-ah-weel'-ah.*

General *Taylor,* took possession of *Saltillo,*[1] the capital of *Coahuila,* and near this place his army and *Wool's* were joined in December. Meanwhile Commodore *Conner,* with

REGION OF TAYLOR'S OPERATIONS.

his fleet, had captured **Tampico,**[2] on the coast. *Taylor* had moved, and encamped at *Victoria.*

18. General *Winfield Scott* was the commander-in-chief of the armies of the *United States.* He went to *Mexico* early in 1847, and prepared to attack the strong town of **Vera Cruz**[3] and the fort there. For that purpose he called troops from *Victoria* to strengthen his own.

19. *Taylor's* army was now reduced to five thousand men, and he was compelled to act on the defensive against twenty thousand *Mexicans* gathered at *San Luis Potosi,*[4] under General *Santa Anna.*

20. *Santa Anna* advanced upon the *Americans* early in February, 1847. The two armies met and fought desperately at a place called **Buena Vista**[5]— meaning a pleasant view—on the 23d of that month. The battle lasted all day.

SANTA ANNA.

The *Mexicans* were beaten with a loss of two thousand men. The *Americans* lost about seven hundred.

QUESTIONS.—18. What have you to say about General Scott and his movements? 19. What was now the condition of Taylor's army, and what was he compelled to do? 20. What can you tell about Santa Anna, and a severe battle?

[1] *sahl-teel'-yo.*   [2] *tam-pee'-ko.*   [3] *va-rah krooz'.*   [4] *sahn loo'-is po-to-see'.*
     [5] *bwa'-nah vees'-tah.*

Various Operations in Mexico.

21. All Northern *Mexico* was now in possession of the *Americans.* *Taylor's* army was inactive several months, and in September he gave the command of it to General *Wool* and returned home. Then the people, who admired him for his deeds, first began to talk about making him **President of the Republic.**

22. While these events were occurring in Eastern *Mexico,* the *Americans,* under different leaders, were taking possession of other parts of the country. General *Philip Kearney*[1] was then in chief command of the *Army of the West,* at Fort *Leavenworth.*

23. In August, 1846, *Kearney,* with a considerable force, drove the *Mexicans* from *Santa Fe,*[2] and took possession of *New Mexico.* He organized a government ; and leaving the main body of his troops there, with Colonel *Doniphan,*[3] he crossed the continent into *California.*

24. With a thousand *Missourians Doniphan* **invaded Northern Mexico.** After fighting a battle at *Braceto,*[4] in December, 1846, and another at *Sacramento,*[5] in February, 1847, he took possession of *Chihuahua,* one of the finest provinces of Mexico.

25. In the meantime Colonel **J. C.** *Fremont,*[6] the explorer of the Rocky Mountains, took possession of a portion of *California,* and on the 5th of July, 1846, declared that country **independent.** With the aid of an *American* fleet, under Commodore *Stockton, Fremont* subdued *California.*

QUESTIONS.—21. What did the Americans now possess? What have you to tell about Taylor and his army? 22. What have you to say about other American commanders? 23. What did General Kearney do? 24. What did Colonel Doniphan do? 25. What can you tell about the doings of Colonel Fremont?

[1] *kar'-nee.* [2] *sahn-tah fa'.* [3] *don'-i-fun.* [4] *brah-the'-to.* [5] *sah'-kra-men'-to.*
[6] *freh-mont'.*

302   THE UNION OF STATES.

Conquest of California Secured.   Americans Capture Vera Cruz.

26. General *Kearney* arrived in time to take part in the

final battle at *San Gabriel,* on the 8th of January, 1847, which secured the **conquest of California.** On the 8th of February, *Kearney,* assuming the office of governor, proclaimed the **annexation of California** to the *United States.*

COLONEL FREMONT.

SCOTT'S INVASION OF MEXICO.

27. Early in March, 1847, General *Scott* landed near *Vera Cruz* with about thirteen thousand men. They were borne to the shores of *Mexico* by a fleet under Commodore *Conner,* which assisted in the attack on *Vera Cruz.*

28. *Vera Cruz* was attacked on the 18th of March, after a siege of nine days, and on the 27th, the city, the strong castle of *San Juan d'Ulloa,*[1] and five thousand prisoners, with five

INTRENCHMENTS AT VERA CRUZ.

hundred cannon, were **surrendered** to the *Americans.*

29. On the 8th of April, *Scott's* army began their march toward the city of *Mexico.* At **Cerro Gordo,**[2] a difficult

QUESTIONS.—26. What have you to say about General Kearney, and the fate of California? 27. What can you tell about Scott's invasion of Mexico? 28. Tell about the capture of Vera Cruz and its castle. 29. What did Scott's army do? What can you tell about a battle?

[1] *sahn-hwan dah-oo'-loo'-ah.*   [2] *thar'-o-gor'-do.*

mountain pass, they were met by *Santa Anna* and an army of twelve thousand men. There they had a severe battle on the 18th. The *Mexicans* were defeated with a loss of more than four thousand men. *Santa Anna* escaped on the back of a mule.

GENERAL SCOTT.

30. Week after week *Scott's* army pressed steadily forward, taking possession of place after place, and resting at *Puebla*,[1] a town of eighty thousand inhabitants, from May until August. Within two months the *Americans* had made ten thousand *Mexicans* prisoners, and captured seven hundred cannon and a vast amount of small arms and munitions of war.

31. At *Puebla, Scott* was reinforced, and with ten thousand men he moved on over the lofty *Cordilleras*,[2] a chain of high mountains in *Mexico.* From the summits of these the *Americans* looked

ROUTE OF U. S. ARMY FROM VERA CRUZ TO MEXICO.

down into the vast and fertile valley, and saw, in the distance, the city of *Mexico,* the grand object of the expedition.

32. After fighting severe battles at **Contreras**[3] and

[1] *pweb'-lah.*   [2] *kor-dil'-yer-as.*   [3] *kon-tra'-ras.*

Churubusco,[1] in August, and always beating the *Mexicans,* the conquering *Americans* stood before the ancient capital, where *Cortez,* the Spanish conqueror, had stood almost three hundred years before.

33. *Santa Anna* was then in the capital with his army. *Scott* offered him terms of peace. While commissioners were considering the terms, the treacherous *Mexican* strengthened the defences of the city. Informed of this, *Scott* made a vigorous attack on the outer defences of the city on the morning of the 8th of September, 1847.

34. The fortress of *Molino del Rey*[2] and the fortified

OPERATIONS NEAR MEXICO.

hill of Chepultepec were carried by storm. *Santa Anna* and his officers fled from their capital, and on the morning of the 14th of September General *Scott* and his army **entered the city of Mexico** as victors.

35. The war soon closed. The last battle of the war occurred at Huamantla on the 9th of October. A **treaty of peace** was agreed to on the 2d of February, 1848. Although the *Americans* had fairly won, by battle, the whole of the old *Mexican* Empire, it was all given back excepting *New Mexico* and *California.* These

¹ *choo-roo-boos'-ko.*　² *mo-lee'-no del ra.*

provinces became and have remained portions of the *United States*. Our government allowed Mexico $15,000,000 for them, and assumed debts to the amount of $3,000,000, due from *Mexico* to *American* citizens.

36. In the same month in which this treaty was made, **gold** was first found on the *American* fork of the *Sacramento* [1] *River,* in *California*. It was discovered soon after in other places. When the news reached the *United States,* thousands of people hastened to *California* in search of gold.

37. Gold was found in abundance. Permanent settlements, by people of our Republic, were made there, and thus was planted, on a firm foundation, one of the most flourishing States of our Union.

38. The war with *Mexico* was the chief event of the administration of President *Polk*. A difficulty with *England* concerning the northern boundary of *Oregon* had been settled. *Florida* and *Texas* had been admitted as States in 1845, and *Iowa* [2] in 1846. *Wisconsin* [3] was admitted in 1848.

39. The deeds of General *Taylor* in *Mexico* made him very popular, and in the autumn of 1848 he was elected President of the *United States,* with *Millard Fillmore,* of *New York,* as Vice-President.

40. In this section we have considered—

(1) The *inauguration of President Polk;* (2) causes of the *war with Mexico;* (3) *beginning of the war*

QUESTIONS.—36. What can you tell about the discovery of gold in California? 37. What were the effects of the discovery of gold? 38. What was the chief event of Polk's administration? What can you tell about a difficulty with England, and admission of new States? 39. What about an election for President? 40. What have we considered in this section?

[1] *sah'-kra-men'-to.* [2] *i'-o-wah.* [3] *wis-kon'-sin.*

and its *progress ;* (4) *conquest of California ;* (5) capture of the *city of Mexico ;* (6) *treaty of peace ;* (7) *discovery of gold* in California ; (8) *admission of new States,* and (9) the election of a *new President.*

The following is a list of all the principal battles fought during the war with Mexico, in which the Americans were always victorious :

NAME.	DATE.	PAGE.	NAME.	DATE.	PAGE.
1846.			Sacramento	Feb. 28.	
Palo Alto	May 8.		Vera Cruz	March 27.	
Resaca de la Palmo	May 9.		Cerro Gordo	April 18.	
Monterey	Sept. 24.		Contreras	Aug. 20.	
Braceto	Dec. 25.		Churubusco	Aug. 20.	
1847.			Molino del Rey.	Sept. 8.	
Buena Vista	Feb. 23.		Chepultepec	Sept. 13.	
			Huamantla	Oct. 9.	

SECTION XIII.

TAYLOR'S ADMINISTRATION.

[1849–1850.]

1. **Zachary Taylor** entered upon his duties as President of the United States on the 5th of March, 1849. He was then sixty-five years of age. The 4th of March occurring on Sunday, the inauguration took place on Monday the 5th.

2. The thousands of people who went to **California** in search of gold, soon formed a sufficient population to entitle the territory to the dignity of a State, and in September,

QUESTIONS.—1. What have you to say about President Taylor? 2. What can you tell about the people of California, and the framing of a State constitution?

1849, they met in convention and framed a **State consti-tution.**

3. In February following the people of *California* asked

Congress to admit their territory into the Union as a State. This request made a great stir in Con-gress and throughout the coun-try; the people of *California* having in their constitution for-bidden the existence of **negro slavery** in their State.

4. Representatives of the slave-labor States in Congress **opposed the admission** of *California,* because of that article in its constitution, and they threatened to **break up the Union** if it should be admitted as a free-labor State. The debates on the subject were sometimes violent. Finally *Henry Clay* proposed a com-promise, which was agreed to.

TAYLOR, AND HIS RESIDENCE.

5. Five Acts, grouped in one bill, were passed, namely: for the admission of *California* as a free-labor State; for the organization of *New Mexico* and *Utah* into Territories, without mention of slavery; for the establishment of the boundaries of *Texas;* for the abo-

QUESTIONS—3. What else did the people of California do? What followed? 4. What occurred in Congress, and why? What was threatened? What was done? 5. Give an account of Henry Clay's proposition for a compromise.

308   THE UNION OF STATES.

Fugitive Slave Law.   Death of President Taylor.   New Territories.

lition of the slave-trade in the *District of Columbia;* and for the surrender to their masters of runaway slaves, escaping into free-labor States or Territories.

6. The last bill, known as the **Fugitive Slave Law,** deeply offended many of the people of the free-labor States. They wished for its repeal, but it remained on the national Statute Book until it was expunged by the **Civil War.**

7. While this **Omnibus Bill,** as it was called, was before Congress, President *Taylor* died. This was early in July, 1850. The Vice-President then became President, and on the tenth of that month began

FILLMORE'S ADMINISTRATION.

8. Mr. *Fillmore* was the thirteenth President of the *United States.* During *Taylor's* administration of sixteen months, one State (*California*), and three Territories (*New*

Mexico, Utah, and *Minnesota*), were added as members of the Republic. *Utah* was called, by the people who settled there, *Deseret,*[1] or the *Land of the Honey Bee.*

9. *Utah* was settled by *Mormons,* a sect founded by Joseph Smith, of *New York,* having a peculiar religious belief, and who have since greatly in-

JOSEPH SMITH.

creased in numbers. On account of their peculiar **social system** that Territory has not been admitted as a State.

[1] *dez-e-ret'.*

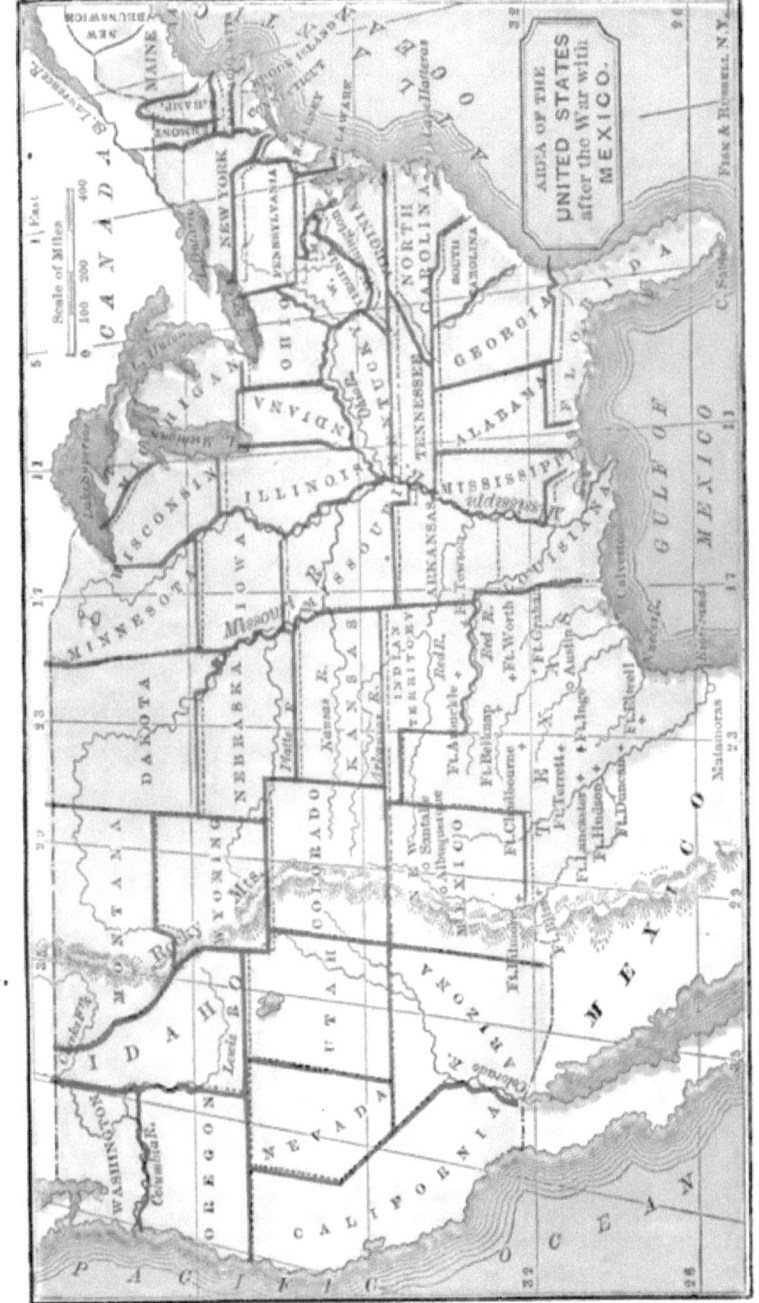

AREA OF THE
UNITED STATES
after the War with
MEXICO.

10. In the spring of 1850 trouble with *Spain* was threatened because of some offensive acts committed by citizens

of the *United States.* These consisted in expeditions to assist the *Cubans* in their efforts to free themselves from the dominion of *Spain.* These offences continued, more or less, for about ten years.

11. In 1852 a dispute arose between the *United States* and *Great Britain* in regard to the fisheries in the neighborhood of *Newfoundland.* Both parties sent armed ships to those waters, but the quarrel was settled by *negotiation,* which is far better than *fighting.*

12. In the same year a naval expedition was sent to *Japan,*[1] off the eastern coast of *China,* to carry a letter from the President. In this letter the President asked for the friendship of the *Japanese,* and that our countrymen might be permitted to trade with them.

FILLMORE, AND HIS RESIDENCE.

13. The privilege was granted, and the most friendly relations now exist between the governments of the *United*

QUESTIONS.—10. What have you to say about expeditions to assist the Cubans? 11. What can you tell about a dispute concerning fisheries? 12. What have you to say about an expedition to Japan? 13. What was the result?

[1] *Jah-pan'.*

States and *Japan.*　Many *Japanese* youths are educated in the schools of the *United States.*

14. During the administration of Mr. *Fillmore,* the Compromise measures had quieted the public mind, and the election for a new President, in the autumn of 1852, was a quiet

one. *Franklin Pierce,*[1] of *New Hampshire,* was chosen President, and *William R. King,* of *Alabama,* was elected Vice-President.

15. It was during the administration of Mr. *Fillmore* that the remarkable voyages toward the North Pole were made, in search of the English navigator, Sir *John Franklin,* in which Dr. *E. K. Kane* was

DR. KANE.

a principal actor.　His published journals of these voyages are very interesting histories.

16. In this section we have considered—

(1) The inauguration of *President Taylor;* (2) *admission of California* into the Union as a free-labor State; (3) *death of President Taylor,* and accession of *Mr. Fillmore;* (4) *additions to the Union;* (5) *Mormons;* (6) expeditions to help the *Cubans;* (7) the *fisheries,* and (8) the *relations with Japan.*

QUESTIONS—14. What have you to say about the compromise measures, and an election for President? 15. What have you to say about certain voyages? 16. What have we considered in this section?

[1] *peerce.*

SECTION XIV.

PIERCE'S ADMINISTRATION.

[1853–1857.]

PIERCE, AND HIS RESIDENCE.

1. Franklin Pierce took the oath of office on the 4th of March, 1853, when he was forty-nine years of age. He was the fourteenth President. The country was then prosperous, and nothing serious disturbed the public harmony.

2. In May, 1852, ships were sent to explore the eastern coast of *Asia;* and land explorations were in progress to select a good route for a **railway from the Mississippi to the Pacific Ocean.**

3. These explorations led to the establishment of a **line of steamships** which regularly cross the *Pacific Ocean* between *America* and *Asia,* and a **railway across our continent.** Now travellers can go from *New York* to *Japan* in a short space of time.

4. In 1854, Congress passed a bill for the organization of

QUESTIONS.—1. What have you to say about President Pierce, and the state of the country? 2. What can you tell about explorations by sea and land? 3. What are the results of those explorations?

312   THE UNION OF STATES.

Slavery in Congress.   Civil War in Kansas.   Foreign Nations Offended.

the Territories of *Kansas* [1] and *Nebraska*.[2] Its provisions
annulled the **Missouri Compromise**, and made slavery

possible in all the Territories.
This measure produced violent agitation all over the
country.

    5. The opponents of slav-
ery were aroused to action
by this measure. Emigrants
from the **free-labor States**

OCEAN STEAMSHIP.

flocked into *Kansas*. Many also went from the **slave-
labor States**. When the Territory was organized, the
two parties contended for the political mastery, and a **Civil
War** broke out in *Kansas*.

    6. The war was quieted for a time by an exciting election
for the Presidency, which took place in the autumn of 1856.
The Democrats were victorious, electing *James Buchanan*,[3]
of *Pennsylvania*, President, and *John C. Breckinridge*,
of *Kentucky*, Vice-President.

    7. Trouble with foreign nations was expected during the
administration of President *Pierce*. *Spain* was offended
because of expeditions from our shores to deprive her of
Cuba. *Great Britain* was offended because our government sent her minister at *Washington* home for breaking
our laws by enlisting men here for the *British* army ; and
the **Central American States** were offended because

QUESTIONS.—4. What can you tell about a bill for the organization of two new
Territories, and the effects ? 5. What did the opponents and friends of slavery do ?
What occurred in Kansas ? 6. What made quiet ? What can you tell about an election in 1856 ? 7. What have you to say about expected troubles with foreign
nations ? What nations were offended, and why ?

       [1] *kan'-zas.*   [2] *neh-bras'-ka.*   [3] *bu-kan'-nan.*

THE UNION OF STATES. 313

Ostend Manifesto. Troubles Settled. Outline of Important Events.

lawless men from the *United States* attempted to get possession of their country.

8. On account of these unfriendly movements against friendly nations, called **fillibustering,** a conference of *American* ministers in *Europe* was held at *Ostend,*[1] in *Belgium.* They issued a paper known as the **Ostend Manifesto,** which was discreditable to the *American* character. It was a plea in favor of the unrighteous doctrine, that **Might makes Right.** These troubles were, however, amicably settled.

9. In this section we have considered—

(1) The inauguration of *President Pierce ;* (2) our *direct communications* with Asia by land and water ; (3) the organization of the Territories of *Kansas and Nebraska,* and ensuing troubles ; (4) election of *President and Vice-President ;* (5) causes of expected troubles with *foreign nations,* and (6) the *Ostend Manifesto.*

OUTLINE OF IMPORTANT EVENTS FROM 1789 TO 1857.[2]

1790. General Harmar defeated by the Indians in *October.* District of Columbia organized as the seat of the national government.

1791. United States Bank chartered. Vermont admitted into the Union in *March.* St. Clair defeated by the Indians in *November.*

1792. Kentucky admitted into the Union in *June.*

1793. Federal and Republican parties formed. Washington proclaims the neutrality of the United States in *May.*

1794. Indians in the northwest subdued by Wayne in *August.* Whiskey Insurrection in Western Pennsylvania. Congress authorizes the creation of a navy.

QUESTIONS.—8. What can you tell about a conference at Ostend and the result ? 9. What have we considered in this section ?

[1] *os'-tend.* [2] See foot-note on page 32.

1795. John Jay's treaty with Great Britain ratified in *June*.

1796. Tennessee admitted into the Union in *June*.   Washington issues his Farewell Address in *September*.

1797. John Adams inaugurated President in *March*.   Extraordinary session of Congress beginning in *May*.

1798. Preparations for war with France.

1799. Washington dies in *December*.

1800. The city of Washington becomes the National Capital.   Treaty of peace concluded with France in *September*.

1801. Thomas Jefferson inaugurated President in *March*.   Tripoli declares war against the United States in *June*.

1802. Ohio admitted into the Union in *November*.

1803. Louisiana purchased of France in *April*.   Commodore Preble sent to the Mediterranean sea.

1804. Decatur destroys the *Philadelphia* in the harbor of Tripoli in *February*.   Alexander Hamilton killed by Aaron Burr in a duel in *July*.

1805. Derne, in Africa, captured by American and Mohammedan soldiers in *April*.   Treaty of peace made with Tripoli in *June*.

1806. European forts blockaded.

1807. Burr tried for treason and acquitted.   First navigation by steam. The *Leopard* attacks the *Chesapeake* in *June*.   British war vessels ordered to leave American waters in *July*.   Embargo Act passed in *December*.

1809. Embargo Act repealed, and commercial intercourse with France and England forbidden by Congress, in *March*.   James Madison inaugurated President in *March*.

1811. Action between the *President* and *Little Belt* in *May*.   Indians defeated near the Tippecanoe in *November*.

1812. Louisiana admitted into the Union in *April*.   War declared against Great Britain in *June*.   General Hull invades Canada, and Fort Mackinaw is taken by the British, in *July*. Van Horne is defeated and Detroit is surrendered in *August*. The American frigate *Essex* captures the *Alert*, and the American frigate *Constitution* captures the *Guerriere* in *August*. Battle at Queenstown occurs in *October*.   The American sloop-of-war *Wasp* captures the *Frolic*, and the American frigate *United States* captures the British frigate *Macedonian*, in *October*.   Madison re-elected President in *November*.   The American frigate *Constitution* captures the *Java* in *December*.

1813. Americans defeated at Frenchtown and massacred in *January*. American sloop *Hornet* captures the *Peacock* in *February*.

Toronto captured by the Americans and General Pike killed in *April.* Fort Meigs besieged by the British, Fort George taken by the Americans, and the British repulsed at Sackett's Harbor, in *May.* The *Shannon* captures the *Chesapeake*, a battle is fought at Stony Creek, and the British are repulsed at Craney Island, in *June.* Fort Meigs again besieged and the British repulsed in *July.* The British and Indians driven from before Fort Stephenson in *August.* The British sloop *Pelican* captures the *Argus*, and the Americans are massacred at Fort Mims, in *August.* The American brig *Enterprise* captures the *Boxer*, and Perry gains a victory on Lake Erie, in *September.* The Battle of the Thames occurs in *October.* The Battle of Chrysler's Field is fought in *November.* Villages on the Niagara River are burned in *December.*

1814. The Creek Indians subdued in *March.* The American frigate *Essex* captured in the harbor of Valparaiso, and Americans defeated at La Colle, in *March.* The American sloop *Peacock* captures the *Epervier* in *April.* Fort Erie is captured and the battles of Chippewa and Bridgewater are fought in *July.* The British are repulsed at Fort Erie and at Stonington, the Americans are defeated at Bladensburg, and Washington City is burned in *August.* The American sloop *Wasp* captures the *Avon* in *September.* The British are defeated on land and water at Plattsburg, and repulsed at and near Baltimore and from Fort Bowyer, near Mobile, in *September.* The British are driven from Fort Erie in *September*, and from Pensacola in *November.* American gunboats captured by the British in Lake Borgne, and a treaty of peace is signed at Ghent, in *December.*

1815. The British are defeated at New Orleans and the American frigate *President* is captured by the British in *January.* The American frigate *Constitution* captures two British vessels, and peace proclaimed by the President, in *February.* The American sloop *Hornet* captures the *Penguin*, and Congress declares war against Algiers, in *March.* Decatur is sent against the Algerines in *May*, and humbles them and others of the "Barbary States" in *July* and *August.*

1816. Indiana is admitted into the Union in *December.*

1817. James Monroe inaugurated President in *March.* Indians in the Gulf region commit depredations. Mississippi admitted into the Union in *December.*

1818. Jackson goes against the Seminole Indians, and pensions granted to soldiers of the Revolution, in *March.* Jackson hangs two British subjects in Florida in *April.* Arrangements about the coast fisheries made in *October.* Illinois is admitted into the Union in *December.*

1819. Alabama admitted into the Union in *December.* Commodore Perry sent against the West India pirates.

1820. Maine admitted into the Union, and " Missouri Compromise " act passed, in *March.* Monroe re-elected in *November.*

1821. Florida annexed to the United States in *July.* Missouri admitted into the Union in *August.*

1823. Pirates among the West India islands dispersed by Commodore Porter.

1824. Lafayette comes to the United States in *August.*

1825. John Quincy Adams is inaugurated President in *March.* Erie Canal finished.

1826. John Adams and Thomas Jefferson died in *July.*

1828. " American System " adopted.

1829. Andrew Jackson is inaugurated President in *March.*

1832. Troubles in Georgia concerning the Indians. The Black Hawk war occurs. United States Bank charter vetoed in *July.* Nullification doctrines avowed in South Carolina.

1833. Henry Clay's compromise measure is made a law in *March.* Government money removed from the United States Bank in *October.*

1835. War commenced by the Seminole Indians in *December.*

1836. Creeks subdued and sent beyond the Mississippi. Arkansas is admitted into the Union in *June.*

1837. Michigan is admitted into the Union in *January.* Martin Van Buren is inaugurated President in *March.* Extraordinary session of Congress is held in *September.* Seminoles defeated by Taylor in *December.* Insurrection in Canada breaks out.

1841. William Henry Harrison is inaugurated President in *March* and dies in *April.* John Tyler becomes President in *April.* Extraordinary meeting of Congress in *May.* The Cabinet resigns in *September.*

1842. War with the Seminoles and the troubles about a new constitution in Rhode Island are ended.

1844. The Electro-magnetic Telegraph is perfected in *June.*

1845. Bill for the annexation of Texas is signed by Tyler, Florida is admitted into the Union, and James K. Polk is inaugurated

President, in *March*. General Taylor sent to Texas with troops in *July*. Texas admitted into the Union in *December*.

1846. Taylor begins building Fort Brown in *January*. First blood shed in the war with Mexico in *April*. Fort Brown attacked in *May*. Battles of Palo Alto and Resaca de la Palma fought, and Mexico invaded, in *May*. Congress declares war against Mexico in *May*. California declared independent by Fremont in *July*. New Mexico conquered in *August*. Taylor captures Monterey in *September*. General Wool invades Mexico in *October*. Wool's and Worth's armies unite near Saltillo, and the Battle of Braceto occurs, in *December*. Iowa is admitted into the Union in *December*.

1847. Battles at Buena Vista and Sacramento are fought in *February*. Vera Cruz surrendered to the Americans under General Scott in *March*. Battle at Cerro Gordo is fought in *April*. Battles at Contreras and Churubusco occur in *August*. Americans win victories at Molino del Rey and Chepultepec in *September*. The American armies enter the city of Mexico in *September*. Battle at Huamantla fought in *October*.

1848. Treaty of peace signed in Mexico in *February*. Wisconsin admitted into the Union in *May*.

1849. Zachary Taylor inaugurated President in *March*.

1850. President Taylor dies and Millard Fillmore becomes President in *July*. California is admitted into the Union in *September*. The Fugitive Slave Law passed in *September*.

1852. Disputes about coast fisheries settled. Commercial intercourse with Japan opened.

1853. Franklin Pierce inaugurated President in *March*.

1854. Kansas-Nebraska bill is passed in *May*.

1855. Civil war in Kansas. Invasion of Central American States by citizens of the United States.

1856. James Buchanan elected President in *November*. The Ostend Manifesto issued.

CHAPTER VI.

THE CIVIL WAR AND THE SOCIAL REVOLUTION.

SECTION I.

BUCHANAN'S ADMINISTRATION.

[1857–1861.]

BUCHANAN, AND HIS RESIDENCE.

1. **James Buchanan** was inaugurated the fifteenth President of the United States on the 4th of March, 1857. He was then sixty-six years of age. From the beginning to the end of his administration the **slavery question** violently agitated the people in all parts of the country.

2. The struggle for political ascendancy in *Kansas,* between the people of the free-labor and the slave-labor States, continued, the President giving the weight of his influence in favor of the latter. The conflict was ended in 1858 by an overwhelming vote of the

QUESTIONS.—1. What have you to say about President Buchanan and his administration? 2. What have you to say about a struggle in Kansas?

inhabitants of *Kansas* in favor of making it a **free-labor State.**

3. In 1857 a rebellious movement was made by the **Mormons** in *Utah,* but it was soon put down by the presence of a military force which was sent into the Territory. Quiet was restored in April, 1858.

4. The quarrel about *Kansas* had caused much bitter feeling. A great party, opposed to slavery, arose in 1856, called the **Republican Party.** Under its banner were rallied the opponents of slavery. The contest of words waxed hotter and hotter as the time for the election of a new President drew near.

5. In 1858 public attention was arrested for awhile by the successful connection of the *American* and *European* continents by telegraphic wires. After a message from the Queen of *England* and a reply from the President of the *United States* had passed over the **"Atlantic Cable,"** the connection was broken and remained so for some years.

6. In 1859 the agitation about slavery was aroused to great vehemence by the foolish attempt of an enthusiast named *John Brown* to free. the slaves of *Virginia*. He entered that State with a small band of armed followers, and seized the government arsenal at *Harper's Ferry*. He was captured and hung. This was like an electric spark that exploded the magazine of **Civil War.**

7. In 1860 an embassy from *Japan ;* also the *Prince of Wales,* visited the *United States.* They directed public attention from political affairs for awhile ; but when, in the

QUESTIONS.—3. What can you tell about the Mormons in 1857? 4. What have you to say about a new party, and a political contest? 5. What can you tell about the magnetic telegraph between America and Europe? 6. What have you to say about John Brown? 7. Tell about an embassy from Japan, and visit of the Prince of Wales. What have you to say about political affairs, and Mr. Lincoln?

320   THE CIVIL WAR.

Enemies of the Union.   "Star of the West."   Secession Movements.

autumn of that year, *Abraham Lincoln,* the candidate of the Republican party, was elected President, there was intense excitement all over the land.

8. The friends of the **slave system** thought that institution and their entire social system was in danger, and they resolved to **secede from the National Union** and found a new nation composed of the inhabitants of the slave-labor States.

9. The political leaders in *South Carolina* took the first step toward retiring from the Union. On the 20th of December, 1860, they met in convention and declared that *South Carolina* was no longer a member of the Union.

10. It being evident that the *South Carolinians* intended to seize the forts in *Charleston* Harbor, Major *Anderson,* in command of a few troops, left *Fort Moultrie* [1] and took possession of *Fort Sumter.*

11. In January, 1861, the steamer *Star of the West,* with

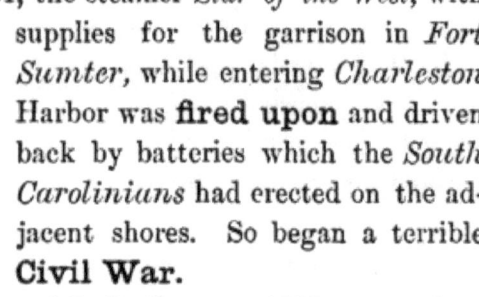

supplies for the garrison in *Fort Sumter,* while entering *Charleston* Harbor was **fired upon** and driven back by batteries which the *South Carolinians* had erected on the adjacent shores. So began a terrible **Civil War.**

12. In January, 1861, conventions in the States of *Mississippi, Florida, Alabama,* [2] *Georgia,* and

JEFFERSON DAVIS.

Louisiana declared that their respective States were no

QUESTIONS.—8. What did the friends of the slave system think and do? 9. What did the political leaders in South Carolina do? 10. What was evidently about to happen in Charleston harbor, and what did Major Anderson do? 11. With what circumstances was the Civil War begun? 12. What have you to say about conventions in certain States, and in what States?

[1] *mool'-tre.*   [2] *ah'-lah-bah'-mah.*

longer members of the Union. Their acts were called **Ordinances of Secession.** A convention in *Texas* did the same thing early in February.

13. On the 4th of February, 1861, a Congress, composed

of delegates from these several States, excepting *Texas*, met at *Montgomery, Alabama,* organized a provisional government under the title of the **Confederate States of America,** and elected *Jefferson Davis,* of *Mississippi,* President, and *Alexander H. Stephens,* of *Georgia,* Vice-President.

14. Forts, arsenals, navy-yards, custom-houses, and other property belonging to the *United States,* within these States, were seized and appropriated to the use of the insurgents. They created an army, authorized a navy, and took measures for seizing

LINCOLN, AND HIS RESIDENCE. *Washington City* and taking

possession of the general government. In this effort *Virginia* soon assisted, and became the seventh State of the Confederacy.

15. On the 4th of March, 1861, *Abraham Lincoln* was

QUESTIONS.—13. Give an account of the formation of the government of the " Confederated States of America." 14. What was done with public property in certain States? What did the Confederate government do? What did Virginia do?

inaugurated President. His address on that occasion was conciliatory. The Southern leaders, however, would listen to no words of kindness, but ordered General *Beauregard*,[1] at the head of troops in *Charleston,* to **attack and seize Fort Sumter.** Then began the great

CIVIL WAR.—[1861.]

16. On the 12th of April the insurgents attacked *Fort Sumter.* After sustaining a fierce bombardment for thirty-four hours, with a small garrison; and when his food was exhausted, Major *Anderson,* its commander, withdrew with his troops and sailed for *New York,* carrying with him the flag of *Sumter.* The fort was *evacuated,* not *surrendered.*

17. The evacuation took place on the 14th of April. On

FORT SUMTER.

the following day the President issued a proclamation calling for **seventy-five thousand volunteers** to suppress the insurrection. More than that number almost immediately started from the **free-labor States** in obedience to the call.

QUESTIONS.—15. What have you to say about Abraham Lincoln and his inaugural address? What did the Southern leaders do? 16. What did the insurgents at Charleston do? What have you to say about the evacuation of Fort Sumter? 17. What did the President then do? What have you to say about the people in the free-labor States?

¹ *bo'-re-gard'.*

18. This was followed by a proclamation from Mr. *Davis,* offering commissions to privateers to depredate on the commerce of the *United States.* Mr. *Lincoln* also issued another proclamation, declaring all the ports of the Confederate States in a state of **blockade.**

19. About the same time the *Virginians* attempted to seize the arsenal at *Harper's Ferry* and the navy-yard at *Gosport,* when each was set on fire by its respective commander. The *Virginians* obtained about two thousand cannon at the navy-yard.

20. In May national troops crossed the *Potomac River* into *Virginia,* and occupied *Arlington Heights* and the city of *Alexandria.* The Confederate soldiers were then pressing northward, and very soon about one hundred thousand of them occupied a line through *Virginia,* from *Norfolk* to *Harper's Ferry.*

21. On the 10th of June, 1861, a battle was fought at *Big Bethel,* where the Nationals were defeated. On the following day the Confederates were beaten at *Romney,* in *West Virginia.* About the same time a convention in *West Virginia* declared its independence of old Virginia, and organized a provisional government

22. In July, 1861, the Confederates made *Richmond, Virginia,* their capital. Confederate troops under General *Beauregard* now pressed toward *Washington City.* They were met in *Fairfax County, Virginia,* by National troops under General *McDowell.*

QUESTIONS.—18. What did Jefferson Davis and Mr. Lincoln do? 19. What have you to say about public property at Harper's Ferry and Gosport Navy-yard? 20. What did National troops do in May? What have you to say about the Confederates? 21. What have you to tell about battles in West Virginia and political movements there? 22. What have you to tell about the Confederate capital and the meeting of Confederate and National troops?

23. In a severe conflict, known as the **Battle of Bull Run**, on the 21st of July, the Nationals were defeated.

They fled in haste and confusion toward *Washington*. General *McClellan*, who had hastened from *West Virginia*, now took the chief command of the army.

GENERAL M'CLELLAN.

24. Congress met on the 4th of July, and voted a **hundred million dollars** in money and **five hundred thousand** men to carry on the war against the secessionists. The insurrection had now assumed the character of a **Civil War.**

25. The area of conflict rapidly widened. There was a severe contest in *Missouri* [1] between the Secessionists and the Unionists for the control of that State. At *Carthage* [2] in July ; and at *Dug Springs,* near the *Arkansas* [3] borders, and at *Wilson's Creek,* in August, there were severe conflicts. At the latter place the Union General *Lyon* was killed.

26. In September the Nationals under *Colonel Mulligan* were compelled to surrender to a large Confederate force at *Lexington, Missouri.* After that the war continued in *Missouri,* with varying success, for a long time.

27. At the close of August General *Butler* and Commo-

QUESTIONS.—23. What have you to say about the battle of Bull Run, movements of troops and General McClellan? 24. What did the National Congress do? What have you to say about the insurrection? 25. What can you tell about the area of the conflict? What about battles in Missouri in July and August? 26. What have you to say about a battle in September and the continuance of war in Missouri?

[1] *mis-soo'-re.*   [2] *kar'-thage.*   [3] *ark'-an-saw.*

dore *Stringham*,[1] with a land and naval force, captured forts, constructed by the Confederates, at *Hatteras*[2] *Inlet*.

28. General *Rosecrans*[3] defeated the Confederate General *Floyd* at *Carnifex*[4] *Ferry*, in *West Virginia*, in September. Late in October the Nationals were beaten in a battle at **Ball's Bluff**, on the Upper *Potomac*.

29. Early in November troops under General *Grant* were beaten at **Belmont**,[5] in *Missouri;* and on the same day (November 7, 1861), the forts at **Port Royal** entrance, hundreds of miles east of *Missouri,* on the *Atlantic* coast, were captured by the National Navy under Admiral *Dupont*.[6]

30. The latter victory secured to the Nationals all the fine islands on that Southern coast for the remainder of the war.

31. In November, Captain *Wilkes*,[7] who was in command of a National frigate, captured *James M. Mason* and *John Slidell*,[8] Confederate ambassadors, on their way to *Europe,* on board an English vessel. They were released by our government because the seizure, according to the **American doctrine**, was in violation of the rights of neutrals.

32. From the beginning of the conflict the attitude of *France* and *Great Britain* was unfriendly toward our national government. They helped the Confederates all they

QUESTIONS.—27. What can you tell about operations at Hatteras Inlet? 28. What have you to say about Generals Rosecrans and Floyd in West Virginia? What about events at Ball's Bluff? 29. What have you to say about General Grant in Missouri, and naval operations at Port Royal entrance? 30. What did a national victory at Port Royal secure? 31. What have you to tell about the capture of Mason and Slidell, and its effect? 32. What have you to say about France and Great Britain? What did the seizure of Mason and Slidell produce, and what was the result?

[1] *string'-um.*   [2] *hat'-te-ras.*   [3] *rose'-krance.*   [4] *kar'-ne-fex.*   [5] *bel-mont'.*   [6] *doo-pont'.* [7] *wilks.*   [8] *sli-del'.*

could.　This seizure led *England* to threaten war ; but the justice of our government soon shamed that government into silence.

33. At the close of 1861 the war was raging at places several hundred miles apart.　Congress had authorized the issue of an immense amount of **paper money** to carry on the war, and the banks had generally suspended the payment of specie.

34. In this section we have considered—

(1) The inauguration of *President Buchanan ;* (2) the *civil war in Kansas* and the result of the struggle ; (3) the *Atlantic cable ;* (4) *John Brown's raid ;* (5) *visitors from abroad ;* (6) the *insurrectionary movements* and beginning of *civil war ;* and (7) the *progress* of that war.

SECTION II.

THE CIVIL WAR CONTINUED.

[1862.]

1. On the 19th of January, 1862, General *George H. Thomas* gained a victory over the Confederates at *Mill Spring, Kentucky,* which gave the National forces much advantage in that region.

2. On the 8th of February General *Burnside* and Commodore *Goldsborough* [1] took *Roanoke* [2] *Island* from the

QUESTIONS.—33. What have you to say about the war at the close of 1861 ? 34. What have we considered in this section ?

QUESTIONS.—1. What have you to say about a battle in Kentucky ? 2. Give an account of the capture of Roanoke Island and New Berne, and the effects.

[1] *golds'-bur-rah.*　　[2] *ro-a-noke'.*

Confederates, and soon afterward *New Berne*, in *North Carolina*. These victories gave the National army control of a large region of country, extending even above the *Dismal Swamp*, and imperilled *Norfolk*.

3. In February General *Grant* and Commodore *Foote* were operating on the *Tennessee* and *Cumberland* rivers. On the 16th of that month *Grant*, assisted by *Foote*, captured **Fort Donelson**, with over thirteen thousand men under General *Buckner*. This victory opened the way to *Middle Tennessee*, and caused the Confederates to leave *Kentucky*.

4. Toward the western part of *Arkansas*, among the *Ozark* [1] *Mountains*, is a place called **Pea Ridge**. There National troops under Generals *Curtis* and *Sigel* [2] beat the Confederates under General *Van Dorn* on the 8th of March.

5. On the same day a vessel-of-war, named the *Merrimack*, which had been seized by the Confederates at the *Gosport* Navy-yard and covered with iron plates; went down from *Norfolk*, and at the mouth of the *James River* destroyed two National frigates, the *Congress* and the *Cumberland*.

THE "RAM" MERRIMACK.

6. This "ram," as it was called, was expected to destroy

QUESTIONS.—3. Give an account of the operations of General Grant and Commodore Foote on the Tennessee and Cumberland rivers, and the effects. 4. What have you to say about a battle in Arkansas? 5. Give an account of the doings of the Merrimack. 6. What have you to say about the *Merrimack* and a strange vessel?

[1] o-zark'. [2] see'-gel.

other vessels near *Hampton* the next morning. During the

THE MONITOR.

night a strange-looking vessel, lying deep in the water and with a revolving turret, appeared and drove off the *Merrimack* in the morning. She was called the **Monitor,** and was commanded by Lieutenant *John L. Worden.*

7. On the 22d of February, *Washington's* birthday, the President, as commander-in-chief of the army and navy, ordered all of the National forces on land and sea to **move against the Confederates** at all points. The Army of the *Potomac* was then commanded by General *McClellan;* and the Confederates, who were not far from the *Bull Run* battlefield, moved off toward *Richmond,* expecting he would follow. In March the Nationals under General *Pope* captured *New Madrid,*[1] in *Missouri.*

8. General *Grant* went up the *Tennessee River* to *Pittsburgh Landing,* near the borders of *Alabama,* and there and at *Shiloh Church* he fought and defeated the Confederates under *Beauregard* and *A. S. Johnston,* on the 7th of April, 1862. This is known as the **Battle of Shiloh.**

9. At the same time Commodore *Foote,* with a fleet of gun-boats, attacked and captured Island No. 10, in the *Mississippi River.* On the 11th, *Fort Pulaski,*[2] at the

QUESTIONS.—7. What can you tell about a general forward movement of the armies?   What about the Confederates in Virginia and Pope's victory in Missouri? 8. Give an account of the battle of Shiloh. 9. What have you to say about a victory on the Mississippi and the surrender of a fort at the mouth of the Savannah? What did General Mitchel do?

¹ *mah-drid'.*   ² *pu-lawz'-ki.*

mouth of the *Savannah River*, was surrendered by the Confederates to General *Gillmore*. On the same day General *Mitchel* took possession of *Huntsville*, in Northern *Alabama*.

COMMODORE FOOTE.

10. The Confederates retreated from *Shiloh* to *Corinth*, in Northern Mississippi. General *Halleck* led the National army very slowly in pursuit, and on its arrival at *Corinth* in May, he found the place deserted.

11. The summer was passed in quietude. On the 19th of September the Nationals under *Rosecrans* gained a victory over *Price*, in a battle near **Iuka Springs,** a few miles eastward of *Corinth*. He repulsed a large body of Confederates who attacked *Corinth,* on the 4th of October following. *Memphis, Natchez* and other places had been captured by the Nationals during the summer.

12. In the spring of 1862 the Nationals were successful on the Lower *Mississippi*. The gun-boats, under Commodore *Farragut,*[1] assisted by Commodore *Porter* and others, attacked and ran by two forts below *New Orleans,* and ascended the river. Twenty thousand Confederates under General *Lovell* retired from **New Orleans,** and on the 25th of April General *Butler,* with National troops, took possession of the city.

13. During the summer of 1862 there was a large Con-

QUESTIONS.—10. What have you to say about a retreat and pursuit of the Confederates? 11. What have you to say about the doings of Rosecrans in Northern Mississippi? 12. Give an account of passing forts and capturing New Orleans. 13. What have you to say about a Confederate army in Kentucky?

[1] *far'-ra-gut,*

federate army in *Kentucky* under General *Bragg*. He threatened *Cincinnati* and *Louisville*, but was foiled, and finally defeated in battle by General *Buell* at **Perryville**, in *Kentucky*.

14. There was a general movement against *Richmond* in the spring of 1862. General *McClellan* took the Army of the *Potomac* to *Fortress Monroe*; General *Fremont* commanded a body of troops in *West Virginia* and *East Tennessee*; General *Banks* was at the head of a force in the *Shenandoah Valley*; and General *McDowell* was with another force on the *Rappahannock River*.

15. Early in April *McClellan* moved slowly up the peninsula between the *York* and *James* rivers, and at *Williamsburg*, on the 5th of May, had a severe battle with the Confederates, which he won. On the 10th of the same

GENERAL LEE.

month General *Wool* **captured Norfolk,** and the Confederates destroyed the ram *Merrimack,* which they had named the *Virginia.*

16. *McClellan* crossed the *Chickahominy River;* and on the 31st of May fought an indecisive battle at **Fair Oaks.** The Confederates were commanded by General *Joseph E. Johnston,* who was wounded. He was succeeded in command by General *Robert E. Lee.*

QUESTIONS.—14. What can you tell about forces engaged in a general movement toward Richmond? 15. What can you tell about McClellan on the Virginia Peninsula, a battle at Williamsburg, and the capture of Norfolk? 16. What did McClellan do, and what can you tell about a severe battle and Confederate leaders?

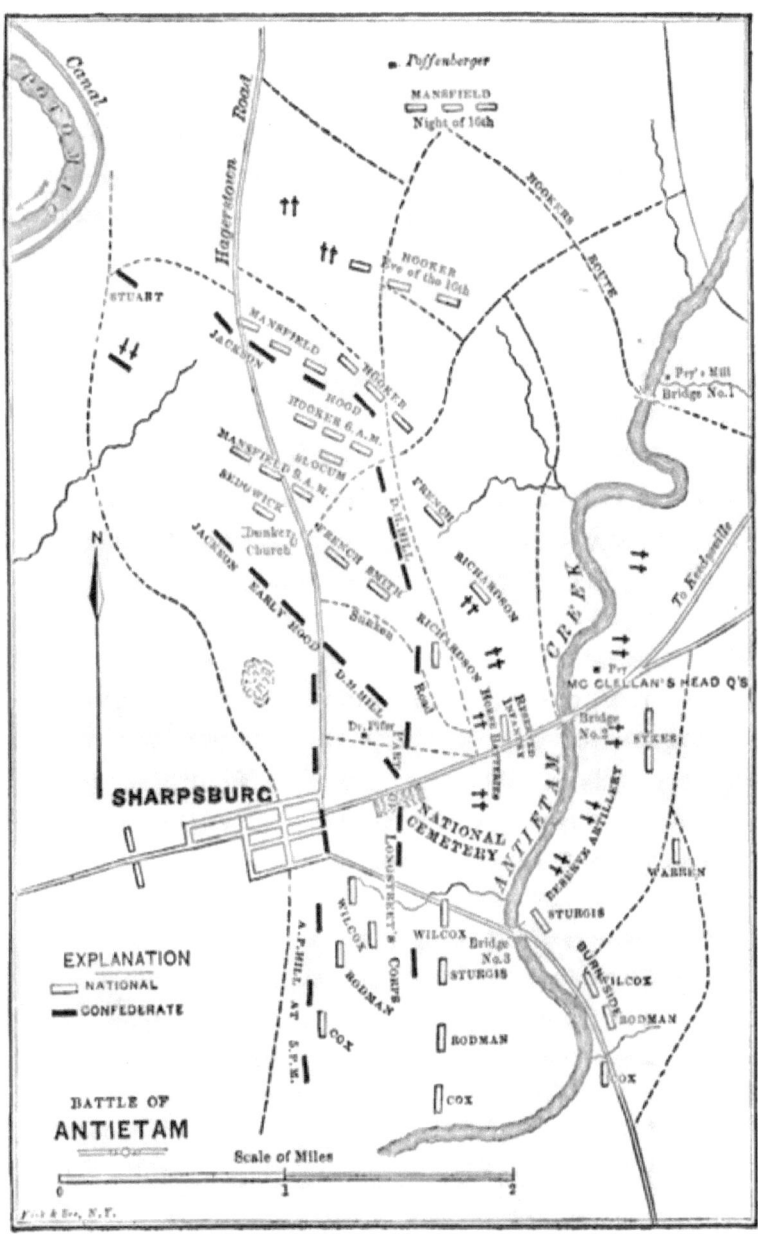

BATTLE OF
ANTIETAM

332   *THE CIVIL WAR.*

Battles near Richmond.   Movements of Lee and his Opponents.

17. The Confederates now pressed on toward *Washington City.* *Banks* fled down the *Shenandoah Valley* pursued by Confederates under "*Stonewall*" *Jackson.* *McClellan* now thought it prudent to change his base of supplies to the *James River.*

18. From the 25th of June to the close of that month several very **destructive battles** were fought not far from *Richmond* without decisive results, though two hundred thousand men were engaged.

19. Meanwhile the forces of *Fremont, Banks,* and *McDowell* were placed under General *Pope* as a consolidated army, and stood between the Confederates and *Washington City.* *McClellan* was ordered to assist *Pope,* but he did not arrive in time to help him in his extremity.

20. *Lee* pressed on toward *Washington.* At **Cedar Mountain** *Jackson* was defeated by *Banks* on the 9th of August. After that the contention between the two armies was very severe. At the close of the summer of 1862, the National forces under *Pope,* near *Bull Run,* were defeated, and driven to the fortifications around *Washington City.*

21. *Lee* now pressed forward, not toward *Washington City,* but across the *Potomac* into *Maryland.* *McClellan,* who had been appointed to the command of all the troops near *Washington,* followed and gained a victory over the Confederates at **South Mountain,** in *Maryland,* on the 14th of September.

QUESTIONS.—17. What did the Confederates do? What did Banks and McClellan do? 18. What have you to say about a series of battles near Richmond? 19. What can you tell about the joining of National forces, and General Pope? 20. What did General Lee do? What have you to say about Banks and Jackson, and a battle near Bull Run? 21. What did Lee and McClellan now do?

¹ *shen'-an-do'-ah.*

22. On the following day, **Harper's Ferry**, with eleven thousand men, was surrendered to the Confederates. On the seventeenth, in a hard fought battle on **Antietam Creek**, *Lee* was defeated with heavy loss. He retreated across the *Potomac* into Virginia.

23. In November, 1862, General *Burnside* succeeded *McClellan* in command of the **Army of the Potomac**. He pursued *Lee* to the *Rappahannock;* and at *Fredericksburg*, after a very severe battle, he was driven back across the river by the Confederates. Here the National army remained until late the next April.

24. At the close of December, 1862, General *Rosecrans* fought the Confederates several days at **Murfreesboro'**, in *Tennessee,* and was victorious after a loss of twelve thousand men. He drove the Confederates under *Bragg* toward *Georgia*.

25. In July, 1862, Congress gave President *Lincoln* authority to declare the **perpetual freedom** of the slaves in certain States. In September he issued a proclamation warning the people of those States that unless they should cease making war upon the government he would set their **slaves free.**

26. We have considered in this section—

(1) Military operations in *Kentucky, Tennessee, Northern Mississippi* and *Arkansas* in 1862; (2) the *Merrimack* and *Monitor;* (3) the grand *forward movement*

QUESTIONS.—22. What have you to say about Harper's Ferry, and a battle in Maryland? 23. What can you tell about General Burnside and his doings with the Army of the Potomac? 24. What have you to say about conflicts in Tennessee? 25. What did Congress authorize the President to do, and what did he do? 26. What have we considered in this section?

¹ *an-tee'-tum.*

of the armies; (4) surrender of *Fort Pulaski;* (5) capture of *New Orleans;* (6) a *general movement* toward *Richmond;* (7) Confederate *invasion of Maryland;* and (8) further military operations in *Virginia.*

SECTION III.

THE CIVIL WAR CONTINUED.

[1863.]

1. The warning of the President was unheeded, and on the 1st of January, 1863, he issued a **proclamation** of **emancipation** for about three million slaves. In 1864, fully two hundred thousand of the freedmen were **soldiers** in the National Army.

2. Late in January, 1863, General *Joseph Hooker* became the commander of the Army of the Potomac. Toward the end of April he led them across the *Rappahannock,*[1] and on the edge of the *Wilderness,* at **Chancellorville,** they had a severe battle on the 2d and 3d of May. The Nationals were driven back beyond the *Rappahannock* with a heavy loss.

3. Early in June, General *Lee,* with about a **hundred thousand** men, moved down the *Shenandoah Valley* and crossed the *Potomac* into *Maryland.* *Hooker* followed him on his flank. On the 28th of the month General *George*

QUESTIONS.—1. What have you to say about the Emancipation Proclamation? 2. What can you tell about General Hooker, and the doings of his troops? 3. What can you tell about the movements of General Lee, and about Generals Hooker and Meade?

[1] *rap'-pa-han'-ok.*

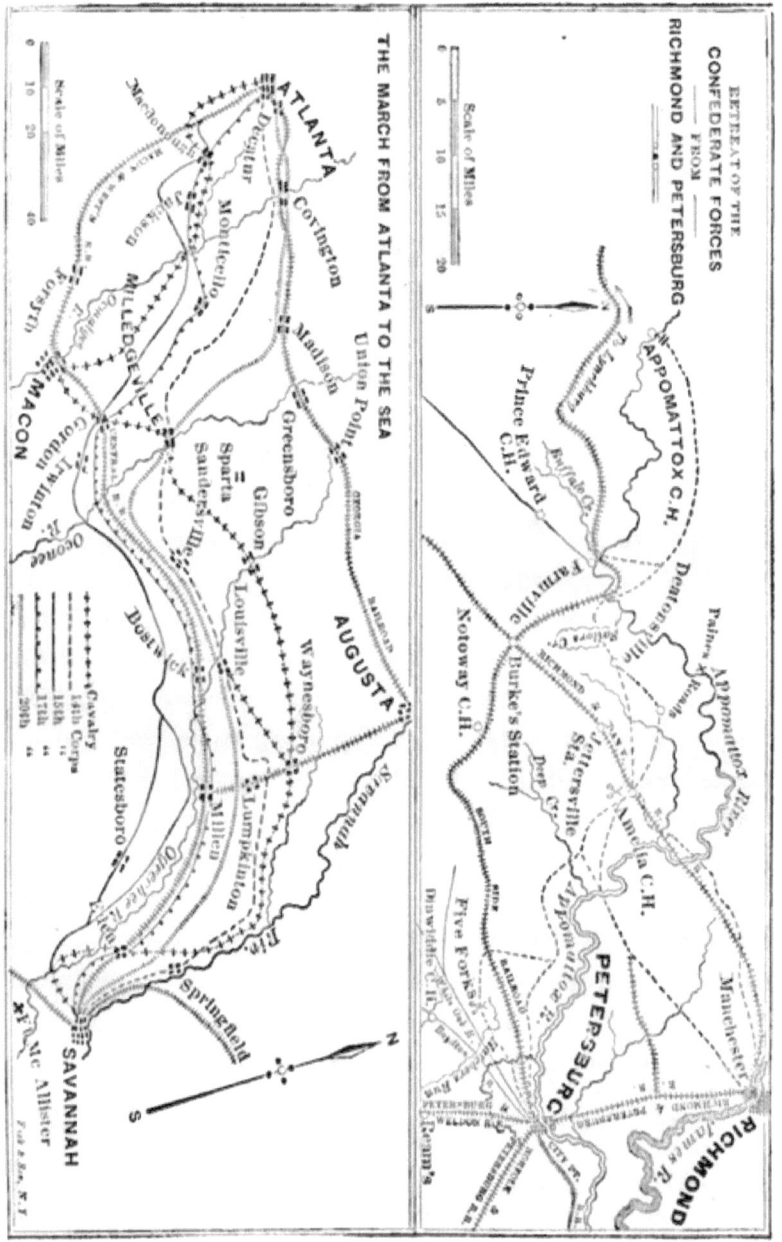

C. Meade succeeded *Hooker* as commander of the Army of the Potomac.

4. About this time *Lee* pushed forward into *Pennsylvania*, being disappointed because so few *Marylanders* joined his army. From the 1st to the 3d of July, a desperate battle was fought at **Gettysburg**, and the Confederate army was defeated with terrible loss. General *Lee* retreated on the 4th of July, and escaping into *Virginia* with his army, moved rapidly toward *Richmond*.

5. Meanwhile General *J. G. Foster* was struggling with General *A. P. Hill* for the mastery of the coast-region of *North Carolina*. At the same time General *Longstreet*, of *Lee's* army, was unsuccessfully trying to drive the National forces from *Norfolk*.

6. In April Admiral *Dupont*[2] and General *Gillmore* began a siege of *Charleston*, S. C., which lasted almost two years. Bombardments were frequent. National bomb-shells reduced **Fort Sumter** to a heap of ruins, and the city was terribly shattered by them.

7. At the same time, General *Banks*, in command of the Department of the Gulf, with his headquarters at *New Orleans*, drove the Confederates out of portions of *Louisiana* westward of the *Mississippi*. In July he captured **Port Hudson** on that stream, taking six thousand Confederates prisoners of war.

8. At the close of the year 1862 General *Grant* entered

QUESTIONS.—4. What did Lee do? What can you tell about a severe battle? 5. What have you to say about operations in North Carolina and near Norfolk? 6. What have you to say about the siege of Charleston, and the effects of bombardments? 7. What have you to tell about General Banks' movements in Louisiana and on the Mississippi? 8. What can you tell about General Grant's operations on the shores of the Mississippi?

[1] *get'-tez-burg.*   [2] *du-pont'.*

upon the task of **clearing the banks of the Missis-sippi** River of Confederate forces. Their chief stronghold was at *Vicksburg,* and he proceeded to attack that city, from which General *Sherman* had been repulsed on the 27th of December.

9. Grant was aided by Admiral *Porter* with a fleet of gun-boats. A decided victory at **Port Gibson** by the Nationals on the first of May led to others, and on the 4th of July the Confederate General *Pemberton* **surrendered Vicksburg** and his army to Grant. More than thirty thousand Confederates were made prisoners.

ADMIRAL PORTER.

10. *Rosecrans* had driven *Bragg* into *Georgia,* where the latter was joined by troops from *Lee's* army under General *Longstreet.* South of *Chattanooga,*[1] on *Chickamauga*[2] *Creek,* the Nationals and Confederates had a very severe battle on the 19th and 20th of September.

11. In the **battle of Chickamauga,** *Rosecrans* was beaten and his army was driven back to *Chattanooga.* *Grant* had hastened to help him, and arrived just in time to relieve him from great peril.

12. General *George H. Thomas* was placed in command of the Army of the *Cumberland.* General *Sherman*

QUESTIONS.—9. By whom was Grant aided? What was accomplished? 10. What have you to say about General Rosecrans, and a severe battle? 11. What can you tell about the battle of Chickamauga? What did Grant do? 12. What have you to say about General Thomas, his associates, and a severe battle?

[1] *chat'-a-noo'-gah.* [2] *chik-a-maw'-gah.*

joined him late in November, and with the assistance of General *Hooker* these officers gained a decided victory over the Confederates on the 25th of that month, after a conflict of three days known as the **battle of Chattanooga.**

13. At this time General *Burnside* was in command of National troops at *Knoxville,* in *East Tennessee,* where he was besieged by *Longstreet.* *Sherman* went to the relief of *Burnside,* and the Confederates, having been repulsed on the 29th of November, fled into *Virginia.*

14. During 1863 the war raged in *Missouri* and *Arkansas,* but no great battle was fought in either State. On the 1st of September General *Blunt* took *Fort Smith* from the Confederates. On the 10th General *Steele,* at the head of National troops, captured *Little Rock,* the capital of *Arkansas,* from the Confederates.

15. In June, a noted leader of a roving band, named *Morgan,* with three thousand horsemen, crossed the *Ohio River* into *Indiana,* and swept through the southern portions of that State and of *Ohio,* expecting to join *Lee* in *Pennsylvania.* He was captured on the 26th of July with nearly the whole of his command.

16. The **National Navy,** which had grown to be large and powerful, thoroughly blockaded the Southern ports during 1863, while fleets of gun-boats greatly assisted the National troops on the coasts and the rivers of the Southwest.

17. The President having been authorized to make a **draft** for three hundred thousand men for the army, ordered it in the spring of 1863. There was violent opposition to the measure ; and resistance to it, in the city of *New York,* led to a very serious **riot** there in July, which lasted four days. The rioters displayed the most fiendish disposition toward the harmless colored people.

18. On the 20th of June, 1863, a new State was added to the Union by the admission of *West Virginia. Kansas* had been admitted as a State on the 29th of January, 1861.

19. In this section we have considered—

(1) The *Emancipation Proclamation ;* (2) military operations in *Virginia, Maryland,* and *Pennsylvania ;* (3) operations in *North Carolina* and *Lower Virginia ;* (4) *siege of Charleston ;* (5) operations on the *Mississippi River ;* (6) events in *Northern Georgia* and *East Tennessee ;* (7) *Morgan's raid,* and (8) the *National Navy* and the *draft.*

SECTION IV.

THE CIVIL WAR CONTINUED.

[1864.]

1. At the beginning of 1864, the National armies were strong, hopeful and cheerful. The government was well supplied with **men** and **money.**

2. In February, General *Sherman* marched eastward from *Vicksburg* almost to *Alabama,* destroying an im-

QUESTIONS.—18. What can you tell about the admission of new States? 19. What have we considered in this section?

QUESTIONS.—1. What have you to say about the National armies? 2. Give an account of the movements of Generals Sherman and Seymour.

340   *THE CIVIL WAR.*

Events in Louisiana and Kentucky.   Large Armies put in Motion.

mense amount of property and **liberating ten thousand slaves.** At the same time General *Seymour* [1] was defeated by Confederates in a battle at *Olustee,* [2] in *Florida.*

3. In March, General *A. J. Smith* and Admiral *Porter* went up the *Red River* with gun-boats and troops, and were joined by soldiers under General *Banks*, who had marched from *New Orleans* across *Louisiana.*

4. Above *Alexandria* the Nationals under *Banks* fought sharp battles at **Sabine** [3] **Cross-roads** and **Pleasant Hill,** but were compelled to retrace their steps. It was with much difficulty that *Porter's* gun-boats descended the rapids at *Alexandria,* on account of low water there.

5. While these troops were up the *Red River,* Confederates under General *Forrest* invaded *Kentucky* and *Tennessee,* captured *Union* City, and afterward, on the 12th of April, captured *Fort Pillow,* on the *Mississippi,* where three hundred of its defenders were killed after its surrender. General *Steele* had met with misfortunes in *Arkansas.*

6. In March, 1864, General *Grant* was commissioned **Lieutenant-General,** and made commander-in-chief of all the National armies. At the beginning of May he ordered the larger bodies of troops to move against the Confederates at various points.

7. General *Meade,* in command of the Army of the *Potomac,* accompanied by Lieutenant-General *Grant,* moved toward *Richmond,* and fought the army of *Lee*

QUESTIONS.—3. Tell about an expedition up the Red River. What did General Banks do? 4. What can you tell about battles above Alexandria, and the passage of the Rapids there? 5. What happened in Kentucky, Tennessee and Arkansas? 6. What have you to say about General Grant? What did he order? 7. What have you to say about General Meade? What about two terrible battles?

[1] *see'-moor.*   [2] *o-lus-tee'.*   [3] *sa-bine'.*

much of the way to the *James River*. On the 5th of May the terrible battle of the **Wilderness,** which lasted two days, was begun. That of **Spottsylvania** took place on the 9th.

8. At the same time General *Sherman* moved from *Chattanooga* into the heart of *Georgia* to capture *At-lanta*. He was opposed by General *Joseph E. Johnston*. *Sherman* won battle after battle and drove the Confederates from their strongholds; and in July he crossed the *Chattahochee*[1] *River* with his whole army and appeared before **Atlanta.**

GENERAL SHERMAN.

9. General *Hood* succeeded General *Johnston* at *Atlanta*. After three sharp battles there in July, the Nationals **besieged the city.** *Hood* abandoned it at the beginning of September, and on the 2d of that month the Nationals took possession of the place. It was one of the most important military posts in the South.

10. At the beginning of June *Grant* had compelled *Lee* to fall back to the defences of *Richmond*. They had fought at the *North Anna* and **Cool Arbor.** Meanwhile General *Butler,* with the Army of the *James,* had secured a position at *Bermuda Hundred,* near the mouth of the *Appomattox*[2] *River*.

11. *Beauregard* was now coming up from *North Caro-*

QUESTIONS.—8. What can you tell about General Sherman's campaign in Georgia? 9. What can you tell about events at Atlanta? 10. What can you tell about the movements of Grant and Lee? What did General Butler do? 11. What did Beauregard do? What did Grant do, and what did he compel Lee to do?

[1] chat'-ta-hoo'-chee.   [2] ap'-po-mat'-tox,

lina to help *Lee.* *Grant* led his army successfully across the *James River,* and took a position before **Petersburg.** *Lee* was compelled to cross the river, also, to defend *Petersburg,* its safety being essential for the security of **Richmond.**

12. A force of Nationals under *Sigel,* in the *Shenandoah Valley,* intending to aid *Meade* in his march toward the *James,* was defeated at **New Market.** General *Hunter* then took command of this army, and was compelled to retire into *West Virginia,* after gaining a victory at *Piedmont*[1] on the 5th of June.

13. In July General *Early,* with about fifteen thousand Confederate troops, crossed the *Potomac* into *Maryland,* and threatened *Baltimore* and *Washington.* General *Wallace,* with a few troops, fought them at the **Monocacy**[2] **River,** and detained them until troops were thrown into *Washington.* Thus *Wallace* saved the National capital and *Baltimore.*

14. *Early* recrossed the *Potomac* with much plunder, closely pursued. He received a severe blow from National troops under General *Averill* near *Winchester.* Securing reinforcements, the Confederates pushed the Nationals back to the *Potomac,* and some of Early's cavalry again crossed, swept through *Maryland,* and burned **Chambersburg,** in *Pennsylvania.*

15. While *Grant* and *Sherman* were making their successful movements on the land, Admiral *Farragut* was

QUESTIONS.—12. What can you tell about General Sigel and troops? What have you to say about General Hunter? 13. Give an account of a Confederate invasion of Maryland. What did General Wallace accomplish? 14. What did General Early do? What can you tell about Early and Averill, and a cavalry raid into Maryland and Pennsylvania? 15. What did Admiral Farragut do?

[1] *peed-mont'.*   [2] *mo-nok'-a-se.*

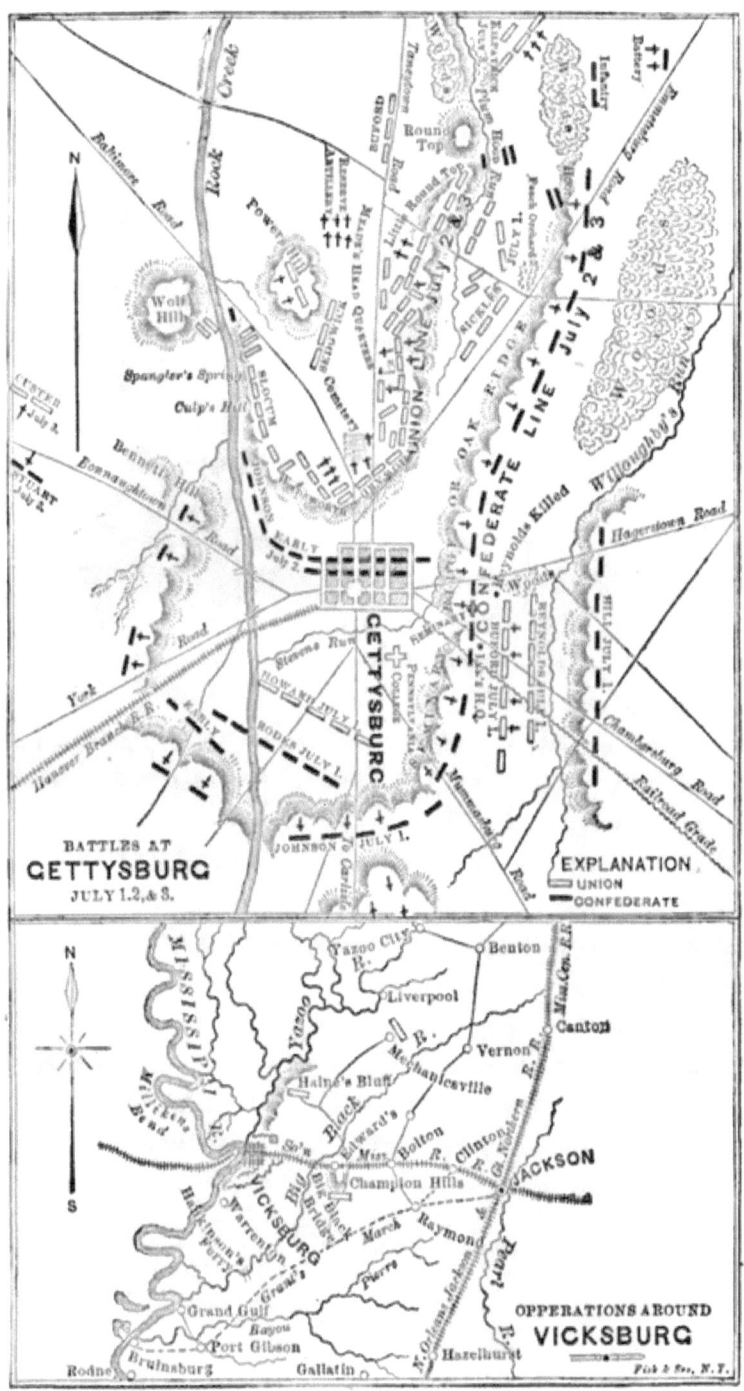

BATTLES AT
GETTYSBURG
JULY 1, 2, & 3.

EXPLANATION
UNION
CONFEDERATE

OPERATIONS AROUND
VICKSBURG

preparing to attack the forts below *Mobile*. This he did about the middle of August, and captured them on the 23d, with the assistance of troops under *General Granger*.

16. *Farragut's* fleet entered *Mobile Bay*, and so cut off *Mobile* and a vast region of country occupied by the Confederates from all communication with the sea. This was a heavy blow for them.

ADMIRAL FARRAGUT.

17. During the autumn, General *Philip Sheridan,* who succeeded *Hunter,* broke the power of the Confederates under *Early,* in the *Shenandoah Valley.* On the 19th of September he defeated them at **Winchester.** Three days afterward he routed them at **Fisher's Hill,** and a month later he beat them at **Cedar Creek.**

18. From the beginning of the war the *English* helped the Confederates. They built, manned, armed, and provisioned a ship-of-war for them, named the *Alabama.* She and the *Sumter* were the most destructive of the Confederate privateers.

19. The *Alabama* was commanded by *Raphael Semmes,*[1] of Alabama. She destroyed or captured sixty-four *American* merchant vessels. The estimated value of property destroyed by her was ten million dollars.

QUESTIONS.—16. What more did Farragut do? 17. What did Sheridan do, and where? 18. What have you to say about the English? How did they help the Confederates? 19. What have you to tell about the Alabama and her fate?

[1] *semz.*

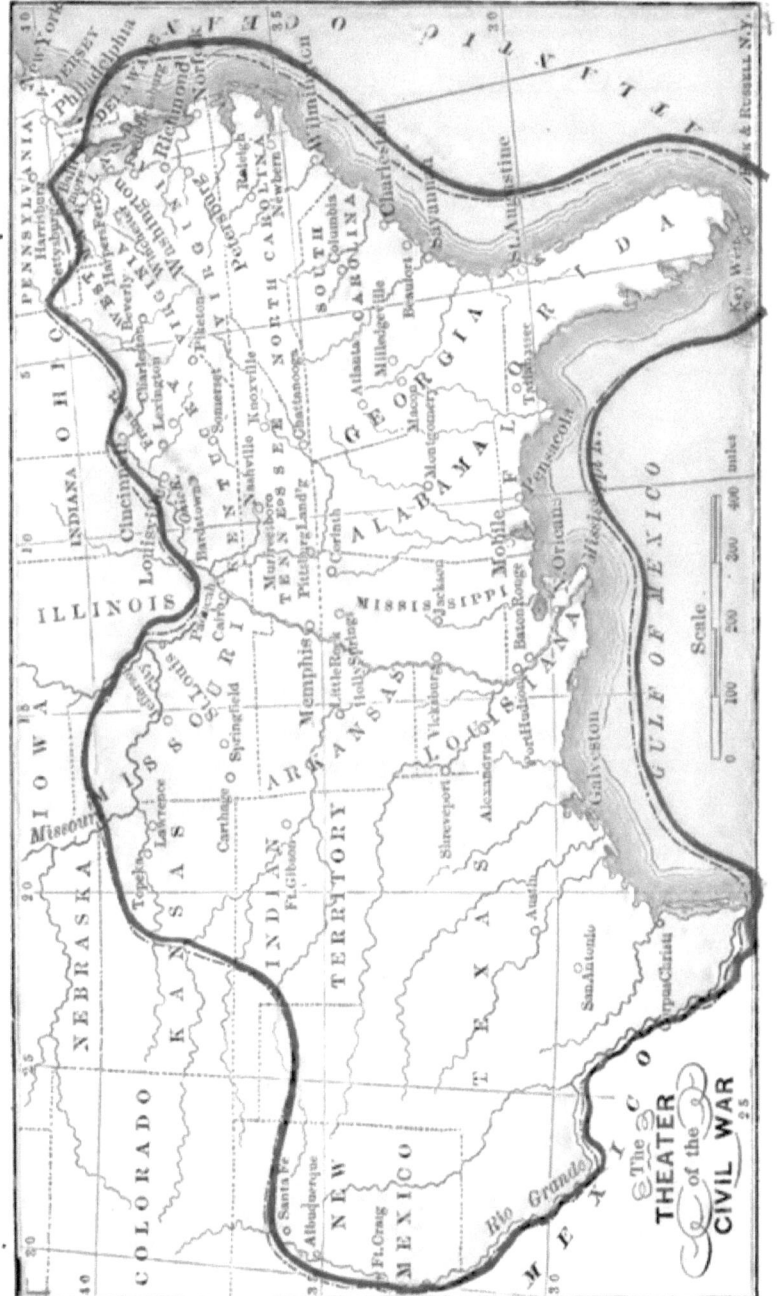

The
THEATER
of the
CIVIL WAR

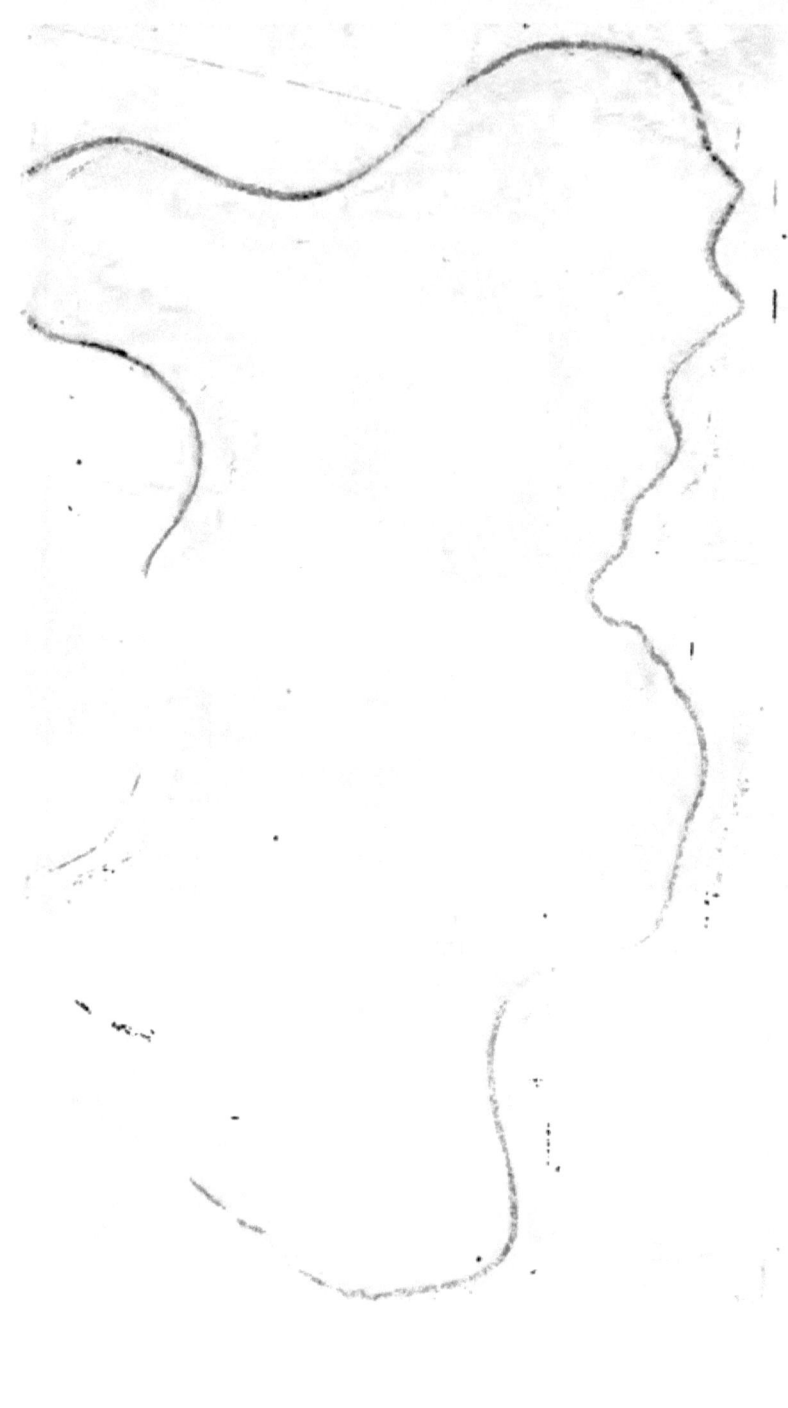

20. The *Alabama* always avoided National war vessels. Finally, when she was compelled to leave a *French* port, she encountered the *Kearsarge*,[1] a National vessel commanded by Captain Winslow. The **Alabama** was sunk by the *Kearsarge* on the 19th of June, 1864.

21. During the summer and autumn of 1864, and the ensuing winter, General *Grant* prosecuted the **siege of Petersburg** vigorously. Meanwhile General *Sherman*, leaving General *Thomas* to watch *Hood*, abandoned *Atlanta* and began his famous march toward the sea at the middle of November. He entered the city of **Savannah,** as a victor, on the 21st of December.

22. *Hood* invaded *Tennessee* and pushed up toward

Nashville. He had a sharp fight with Nationals under General *Schofield*,[2] at **Franklin,** drove them back, and then besieged **Nashville,** the capital of *Tennessee,* to which *Thomas* had retired.

23. On the 15th of December General *Thomas* marched out and attacked *Hood*, and drove him

GENERAL THOMAS.

back into *Alabama* with great loss.

24. On Christmas day, 1864, *Fort Fisher,* at the mouth of the *Cape Fear River,* was bombarded by Admiral *Porter's* fleet, and an attempt to capture the fort was made by troops under General *Weitzel*.[3] It failed. On the 15th of

QUESTIONS.—21. What did General Grant do? What can you tell about Sherman in Georgia? 22. Give an account of an invasion of Tennessee. 23. What did General Thomas do? 24. What have you to say about Fort Fisher?

[1] *keer'-sarj.*   [2] *sko'-feeld.*   [3] *wits'-zel.*

January, 1865, the fort was **captured** by the combined forces of *Porter* and General *Terry*. The National forces then took possession of *Wilmington*.

25. Meanwhile *Sherman* had crossed the *Savannah River* into South Carolina. On the 17th of February he captured **Columbia**, the capital of the State, and the Confederates abandoned *Charleston*. Colored troops then marched in and took possession of the latter city.

26. *Sherman* marched from *Columbia* into *North Carolina,* and was joined at *Goldsborough* by *Schofield* and *Terry,* who came from *Wilmington*. On the 16th of March *Sherman* **gained a victory** over the Confederates under General *Hardee*.[1]

GENERAL SHERIDAN.

27. During the early part of the spring of 1865 *Sheridan* had greatly weakened *Early's* army ; and by quick movements had cut off supplies of food from *Richmond*. *Lee's* army was thus threatened with **starvation.**

28. Grant had compelled *Lee* to remain and defend *Petersburg* since June of the previous year. Seeing his peril from want of supplies, *Lee* **attempted to escape** by breaking through *Grant's* lines and joining the Confederates under *Johnston* in *North Carolina*.

29. In this attempt *Lee* did not succeed. Encompassed

QUESTIONS.—25. What can you tell about Sherman in South Carolina? What occurred at Charleston? 26. What did Sherman do? Who joined him, and what happened? 27. What have you to say about the movements of Sheridan, and their results? 28. What did Grant compel Lee to do? What did Lee attempt to do?

[1] *hard'-ee.*

by the Nationals he was finally compelled to surrender his whole army to *Grant* at **Appomattox Court-House.**

30. On the night of the 2d of April, 1865, *Jefferson Davis* and other members of the Confederate government fled from *Richmond* into *North Carolina,* and on the morning of the 3d, colored troops under General *Weitzel* marched into and took possession of the Confederate capital.

31. The surrender of *Johnston's* army in *North Carolina* soon followed that of *Lee.* Already the power of the Confederates in *Alabama* and the adjacent regions had been broken by a cavalry force under General *J. H. Wilson,* who operated in aid of *Canby.*

32. The Confederate troops in *Mobile* had been captured or dispersed, and peace was assured. The last conflict of the **Civil War** did not occur until more than a month later, when a severe skirmish occurred near the **Rio Grande**, in Texas.

33. On the surrender of *Lee* the people rejoiced because of the assurance of peace. This event was followed by one which caused wide-spread mourning. **Abraham Lincoln,** the President of the Republic, was **assassinated** in the National Capital on the evening of the 15th of April, 1865.

34. According to the provisions of the Constitution the Vice-President, *Andrew Johnson,* of *Tennessee,* now became President of the Republic. In the autumn of 1864, Mr. *Lincoln* had been re-elected President, and was inaugurated on the 4th of March, 1865.

QUESTIONS.—29. What have you to say further about General Lee? 30. What did the Confederate government do? What occurred at Richmond? 31. What have you to say about Johnston's army, and the Confederate power elsewhere? 32. What have you to say about Mobile, and the last battle in the Civil War? 33. What events caused rejoicing and mourning? 34. What have you to say about Mr. Lincoln's successor? What was done in the autumn of 1864, and spring of 1865?

35. In this section we have considered—

(1) *Military operations* in *Mississippi*, *Red River* region and *Kentucky;* (2) *Grant's new commission*, and advance of the Army of the *Potomac;* (3) *Sherman's campaign* against *Atlanta* and in *Georgia;* (4) the *siege of Petersburg*, and events in the *Shenandoah Valley* and in *Maryland;* (5) capture of forts near *Mobile;* (6) the *Alabama*, and her fate ; (7) *Hood* and *Thomas* in *Tennessee;* (8) *capture of Fort Fisher;* (9) *Sherman's campaign in the Carolinas*, and (10) *closing events of the Civil War.*

SECTION V.

JOHNSON'S ADMINISTRATION.

[1865–1869.]

1. *Andrew Johnson* took the oath of office as President on the 15th of April, 1865.   He was the sixteenth chief magistrate of the Republic.   He immediately offered large rewards for the arrest of *Jefferson Davis* and his official associates.

2. Mr. *Davis* was captured in *Georgia* on the 10th of May, 1865, while making his way to the *Gulf of Mexico*, and after a long confinement in *Fortress Monroe*, was released.

3. The Civil War left much confusion in the States wherein

QUESTIONS.—35. What have we considered in this section ?

QUESTIONS.—1. What have you to say about Andrew Johnson ? 2. What can you tell about Jefferson Davis ? 3. What have you to say about the condition of certain States and the duty of the National government ?

insurrection had existed. The first business of the government was to bring order out of this confusion, and to have

ANDREW JOHNSON.

all the States **represented
in Congress.**

4. It was soon apparent
that the Congress and the
President would not agree
upon a plan for the perfect
reorganization of the Union.
Congress wished to give all
citizens of the United States,
without distinction of **race
or color,** equal privileges
as citizens. The President
opposed this proposition, and
a final settlement was long
delayed.

5. Congress was strongly
supported by the people, and
went forward in the execution of its plan for **reorganization.** By an amendment (the Thirteenth) of the National
Constitution, approved by the people and proclaimed on the
18th of December, 1865, **slavery was forbidden to
exist** in the Republic forever.

6. Another amendment (the Fourteenth) was adopted by
Congress on the 13th of June, 1866, which guaranteed
civil rights to the emancipated slaves ; enforced the payment of the **National Debt,** then amounting to about three

---

QUESTIONS.—4. What was apparent in relation to the President and Congress?
What did Congress wish to do? What did the President do? 5. What have you to
say about Congress and the people? What about an amendment to the Constitution?
6. What about another amendment?

THE HOUSE OF REPRESENTATIVES IN SESSION.

thousand million dollars, and prohibited the payment of the public debt of the Confederate States.

7. Acts were passed for securing to the freedmen their rights as free citizens, and placing them on an equality with other citizens. These various measures were termed Reconstruction Acts. They were properly **Reorganization Acts,** for the Union had remained perfect from the beginning in all its essential elements.

8. The President steadily vetoed the reorganization acts of Congress, believing them to be unconstitutional ; but they all became laws without his signature, by a vote of two-thirds of the members of each House of Congress in their favor.

9. On account of the attempts of the President to frustrate the action of Congress, and his public declaration that the National Legislature, as then organized, was an **illegal body,** he was put upon his trial on the 30th of March, 1868, charged with high crimes and misdemeanors.

10. On the 22d of February, 1868, the House of Representatives made the charges, in the form of **Articles of Impeachment.** These were adopted, on the 2d of March, and the President was arraigned for trial before the Senate of the Republic, which sat as a **High Court of Impeachment.** He was, after a long trial, acquitted.

11. On the 1st day of March, 1867, the Territory of **Nebraska**[1] was admitted into the Union as a State. The Territory of **Nevada**[2] had been admitted on the 31st of October, 1864.

[1] *ne-brah'-ska.*   [2] *ne-vah'-dah.*

12. We have observed that the telegraphic cable stretched across the Atlantic was broken in 1858, after only two messages had passed over it. In the summer of 1865 a new and lasting one was laid. The first communication through it was made on the 29th of July. Other ocean cables have since been laid in various parts of the world.

13. By a treaty with *Russia* in the autumn of 1867, a large domain in the northwestern extremity of North America was purchased by the United States for the sum of **seven million two hundred thousand dollars** in gold, and annexed to the Republic as the **Territory of Alaska.**[1]

14. In the autumn of 1868, the Republican party named *Ulysses S. Grant* as their candidate for President of the United States, and *Schuyler Colfax* for Vice-President. The Democratic party named *Horatio Seymour* for President and *Francis P. Blair* for Vice-President. *Grant* and *Colfax* were elected.

15. In this section we have considered—

(1) The *inauguration of President Johnson* and the *capture of Jefferson Davis;* (2) the *Reorganization measures;* (3) *amendments to the Constitution;* (4) the *impeachment of the President;* (5) admission of *new States;* (6) a permanent *Atlantic cable;* and (7) the *purchase of Alaska.*

QUESTIONS.—12. What have you to say about ocean telegraphic cables? 13. What can you tell about a new Territory? 14. What have you to say about nominations for President and the election? 15. What have we considered in this section?

[1] *a-lask'-a.*

SECTION VI.

GRANT'S ADMINISTRATION.

[1869–1875.]

1. On the 4th of March, 1869, *Ulysses Simpson Grant,* the seventeenth President of the United States, was inaugurated. He was then forty-seven years of age. He was chosen by a large majority of the people.

2. During the first year of *Grant's* administration *Virginia, Mississippi,* and *Texas,* having complied with the requirements of Congress, were allowed representatives in that body. So the **reorganization of the Republic** was finally perfected. It now consists of **thirty-eight States** and **ten Territories.**

3. On the 30th of March, 1870, a **Fifteenth Amendment** to the Constitution was adopted and proclaimed, which guaranteed the

PRESIDENT GRANT AND HIS BIRTHPLACE.

stitution was adopted and proclaimed, which guaranteed the

QUESTIONS.—1. What have you to say about President Grant? 2. What can you tell about the perfecting of reorganization? 3. What did the Fifteenth Amendment secure?

right of suffrage to all citizens of the *United States,* without regard to race or color.

4. In May following an organized band of *Irishmen,* styled *Fenians,* associated for the avowed purpose of liberating *Ireland* from the political control of *Great Britain,* invaded *Canada* from the *United States,* in violation of our **neutrality laws.** The movement was a failure.

5. The fitting out of the privateer *Alabama* by *British* subjects, and her depredations, had produced a serious dispute between the governments of the *United States* and *Great Britain.* It was finally agreed to settle the matter by **negotiation.** Early in 1871 each government appointed commissioners for the purpose.

6. This **High Commission,** as it was called, met in the city of *Washington* in the spring of that year, and soon agreed to submit the whole matter to arbitrators appointed by the two governments, whose decision should be final.

7. The arbitrators met in *Geneva, Switzerland.* Their decision was that the *British* government should pay to the *United States,* for indemnity to American citizens for losses sustained by the depredations of the *Alabama* and other privateers, the sum of **fifteen million five hundred thousand dollars.** This was done, and so an apparent cause for war was removed by the more sensible and Christian-like way of peaceful negotiation.

8. In the autumn of 1872 President *Grant* was re-elected, with *Henry Wilson* as Vice-President. His opponent was

QUESTIONS.—4. What have you to say about the Fenians? 5. What can you tell about a dispute between the United States and Great Britain? 6. Tell what you know about a High Commission, and their doings. 7. What did the arbitrators do? 8. What can you tell about an election in the autumn of 1872?

Horace Greeley. Grant and *Wilson* were inaugurated on the fourth of March, 1873.

9. Indian affairs and political troubles in the South occupied much of the public attention during a greater portion of Grant's second term of office. A peace policy with the Indians was yet only an experiment.

10. The Modoc Indians gave special trouble. At a friendly conference they treacherously murdered General Canby and a clergyman in April, 1873. Four of the leaders were hanged in October following.

11. By judicious measures our country has been kept at peace with other nations. Many of them will probably have official representatives at our National Centennial celebration at Philadelphia in 1876. The Territory of Colorado was admitted as a State March 4th, 1875.

12. Our internal troubles, chiefly growing out of social changes in the South, seem in a fair way for adjustment, and our future appears cheerful.

13. In this section we have considered—

(1) The *inauguration of President Grant;* (2) the perfected *reorganization of the Republic;* (3) a *Fifteenth Amendment* to the Constitution; (4) a *Fenian movement;* (5) the *settlement of the dispute* caused by the depredations of the *Alabama,* and (6) *troubles with the Indians,* and in the *South.*

QUESTIONS.—9. What attracted much public attention? What have you to say about a peace policy? 10. What can you tell about the Modoc Indians? 11. What did judicious measures effect? What have you to say about other nations and our Centennial celebration? 12. What have you to say about internal troubles? 13. What have we considered in this section?

OUTLINE OF IMPORTANT EVENTS FROM 1857 TO 1875.[1]

1857. James Buchanan inaugurated President in *March*.

1858. Quiet restored in Utah in *April*. First communication by telegraph sent across the Atlantic in *September*. The people of Kansas vote to have a free-labor State.

1859. John Brown's raid into Virginia in *October*.

1860. Embassadors from Japan, and the Prince of Wales visit the United States. Abraham Lincoln elected President in *November*. South Carolinians pass an ordinance of secession in *December*.

1861. South Carolinians fire on the *Star of the West;* secession ordinances passed in five States in *January*. Texans pass an ordinance of secession, and Confederate States government formed in *February*. Lincoln inaugurated President in *March*. Fort Sumter attacked and evacuated by National troops, and the President calls for 75,000 men to put down the insurrection; Davis offers commissions to privateersmen; Virginians pass an ordinance of secession, and Southern ports declared to be blockaded in *April*. Arsenal at Harper's Ferry and navy-yard at Gosport destroyed; National troops enter Virginia, and ordinances of secession passed in Arkansas, Tennessee, and North Carolina in *May*. Battles at Big Bethel and Romney in *June*. Richmond made the Confederate capital; the National Congress meet and vote men and money for war; battles at Bull Run, Carthage, and Dug Springs in *July*. Battle won by Confederates at Wilson's Creek, and forts at Hatteras Inlet captured by Nationals in *August*. Lexington surrendered to the Confederates, and battle at Carnifex Ferry in *September*. Confederates victorious at Ball's Bluff in *October*. Nationals capture forts at Port Royal entrance, and Mason and Slidell; Confederates victorious at Belmont in *November*. A large amount of paper money authorized in 1861.

1862. Confederates defeated at Mill Spring, and the great National armies ordered to advance upon the Confederates in *January*. Roanoke Island and Fort Donelson captured by the Nationals in *February*. National victory at Pea Ridge; *Merrimack* destroys U. S. ships; fight between the *Merrimack*

[1] See foot-note on page 32.

and *Monitor*, and **New** Berne captured by the Nationals in
March. Victory of Nationals at Shiloh, and they capture
Island No. 10, Fort Pulaski, Huntsville, and New Orleans, in
April. Confederates defeated at Williamsburg; Norfolk
captured by the Nationals, and battle at Fair Oaks, in *May*.
Destructive battles near Richmond in *June*. Battle of Cedar
Mountain, and severe battles near Bull Run in *August*. Na-
tionals victorious at Iuka Springs ; Lee invades Maryland and
is defeated at South Mountain and Antietam in *September*.
Confederates repulsed at Corinth in *October*. Confederates
successful at Fredericksburg in *December*, and defeated at
Murfreesboro' in *January*.

1863. Emancipation proclamation issued in *January*. Siege of
Charleston begun in *April*. Confederates defeated at Port
Gibson, and victorious at Chancellorville in *May*. West
Virginia admitted into the Union, and Lee invades Maryland
in *June*. The Nationals victorious at Gettysburg ; Vicksburg and Port Hudson surrender to the Nationals; draft riots
in New York, and Morgan raids and is captured in Ohio in
July. Confederates victorious at Chickamauga in *September*. The Confederates defeated near Chattanooga, and repulsed at Knoxville in *November*. The Confederate ports
thoroughly blockaded in 1863.

1864. Sherman liberates about ten thousand slaves, and the Nationals
are defeated at Olustee in *February*. Grant appointed
Lieutenant-General and chief commander of all the National
armies; the Red River expedition in *March*. Battles at
Sabine Cross-roads and Pleasant Hill ; Confederates capture
Fort Pillow in *April*. The large National armies move forward ; and battles in the Wilderness, and Spottsylvania won
by the Nationals ; Nationals repulsed at Cool Arbor, and
routed at New Market, in *May*. The Confederates defeated
at Piedmont, and the *Alabama* sunk by the *Kearsarge* in
June. The Confederates invade Maryland ; they are checked
at the Monocacy ; they sack and burn Chambersburg, and are
defeated before Atlanta in *July*. The Nationals capture the
forts below Mobile in *August*. Atlanta surrendered to the
Nationals; the Confederates defeated near Winchester, and
routed at Fisher's Hill in *September*. The Nationals victorious at Cedar Creek ; Nevada admitted into the Union in
October. Hood invades Tennessee with a Confederate army,
is repulsed at Franklin, and besieges Nashville in *Novem-

ber. Confederates defeated and driven from Nashville; Nationals, after crossing Georgia, enter Savannah; Fort Fisher bombarded in *December.*

1865. Fort Fisher captured by Nationals in *January.* Nationals capture Columbia; Charleston occupied by colored troops, and the Nationals take possession of Wilmington in *February.* The Nationals defeat the Confederates under Hardee in North Carolina in *March.* Lee attempts to evade Grant, but surrenders his army at Appomattox Court-House; Jefferson Davis and Confederate associates flee from Richmond; President Lincoln is murdered, and Andrew Johnson succeeds him; General Johnston surrenders his troops, and the Nationals capture Mobile in *April.* Jefferson Davis captured, and the last conflict of the war occurs in Texas in *May.* Slavery proclaimed to be abolished by the Thirteenth Amendment of the National Constitution in *December.*

1866. Fourteenth Amendment adopted in *June.* First communication sent over a permanent Atlantic Cable in *July.*

1867. Nebraska admitted into the Union in *March.* Alaska purchased of Russia in *June.*

1868. Articles of Impeachment of President Johnson presented in *February.* His trial begins in *March,* and he is acquitted in *May.*

1869. Ulysses S. Grant inaugurated President in *March.* Reorganization of the Union perfected.

1870. Fifteenth Amendment declared adopted in *March.* Fenians invade Canada in *May.*

1871. A treaty concerning the depredations of the *Alabama* concluded in *May.*

1872. President Grant re-elected, with Henry Wilson as Vice-President, in *November.*

1873. Grant inaugurated in *March.* Modoc Indians murder Peace Commissioners in *April.* Modoc murderers hung in *October.*

1874, 1875. Internal troubles prevail in some of the Southern States.

LIST OF THE MOST IMPORTANT BATTLES OF THE CIVIL WAR.

NAME.	DATE.	NAME.	DATE.
1861.		Chancellorville, Va...... .... May 2	
Attack on Fort Sumter, S. C.... April 12		Vicksburgh, Miss., siege, May 19 to July 4	
Big Bethel, Va. ....June 10		Port Hudson, La., siege, May 27 to July 8	
Bull Run, Va.... ....July 21		Gettysburgh, Pa.... ....July 1	
Wilson's Creek, Mo.. . ...Aug. 10		Little Rock, Ark.............. Sept. 10	
Lexington, Mo............. ..... Sept. 12		Chickamauga, Ga.......... ......Sept. 19	
Ball's Bluff, Va. ....Oct. 21		Chattanooga, Ga..................Nov. 25	
1862.		Knoxville, Tenn.................Nov. 29	
Mill Spring, Ky................Jan. 19			
Roanoke Island, N. C..... .. ....Feb. 8		**1864.**	
Fort Donelson, Tenn............Feb. 16			
Pea Ridge, Ark...... ....March 8		Olustee, Fla......................Feb. 20	
Merrimack and *Monitor*, Va.... March 9		Sabine Cross-Roads, La..........April 8	
Pittsburgh Landing, Tenn........April 6		Pleasant Hill, La... . ...April 8	
Shiloh, Tenn.................. ....April 7		Fort Pillow, Tenn.... ....April 12	
Forts below New Orleans, La... April 18		The Wilderness, Va........... ... May 5	
Williamsburgh, Va.............. .....May 5		Spottsylvania, Va.... ....May 9	
Fair Oaks, Va. ... .May 30		Resacca, Ga.......................May 15	
Cross Keys, Va...................June 7		Dallas, Ga.......................May 28	
Mechanicsville. ... .June 26 ⎫		Cool Arbor, Va.... ....June 3	
Gaines' Mill........June 27 ⎪ Near		Around Kenesaw Mountain, Ga.. June	
Savages Station.... June 28 ⎬ Richmond,		*Kearsarge* and *Alabama*.........June 19	
Glendale..... ...... June 29 ⎪ Va.		Monocacy, Md ....July 9	
Malvern Hill.........July 1 ⎭		Atlanta, Ga.....................July 22	
Cedar Mountain ....Aug. 9		Forts below Mobile, Ala.........Aug. 22	
Groveton, Va.. .... Aug. 29		Winchester, Va.................Sept. 19	
Bull Run (second), Va.... ...... Aug. 30		Cedar Creek, Va......... ....Oct. 19	
South Mountain, Md......... .. Sept. 14		Franklin, Tenn...................Nov. 30	
Antietam, Md....................Sept. 17		Nashville, Tenn.................Dec. 15	
Iuka Springs, Miss.............Sept 19		Fort Fisher, N. C.................Dec. 25	
Corinth, Miss....... ....Oct. 4			
Perryville, Ky........ ....Oct. 8		**1865.**	
Fredericksburg, Va..............Dec. 13		Fort Fisher, N. C.... ....Jan. 15	
Murfreesboro', Tenn............Dec. 31		Averysboro', N. C.............March 16	
1863.		Near Petersburgh, Va... Feb. and March.	
Port Gibson, Miss.... ....May 1		Five Forks, Va...................April 1	

SECTION VII.

THE NATIONAL CONSTITUTION.

We have here, and also on page 231, considered the **causes** which led to the construction of the **National Constitution**, in 1787; its adoption by the people of the *United States* as the organic law of the land, and the establishment of a **National Government** in accordance with its plan. Let us now take it up and study it carefully, for it is the **Great Charter of our Liberties.** We will begin with the introductory remarks, or

PREAMBLE.

Objects.

WE the People of the *United States,* in order to form a more perfect union, establish justice, insure domestic tranquillity, provide for the common defence, promote the general welfare, and secure the blessings of liberty to ourselves and our posterity, do ordain and establish this **Constitution** for the **United States of America.**

ARTICLE I.

SECTION I.

Legislative Powers.

All legislative powers herein granted shall be vested in a Congress of the *United States,* which shall consist of a senate and house of representatives.

SECTION II.

House of Representatives.

1st Clause.—The House of Representatives shall be composed of members chosen every second year by the people of the several States, and the electors in each State shall have the qualifications requisite for electors of the most numerous branch of the State legislature.

Qualification of Representatives.

2d Clause.—No person shall be a representative who shall not have attained to the age of twenty-five years, and been seven years a citizen of the *United States,* and who shall not, when elected, be an inhabitant of the State in which he shall be chosen.

QUESTIONS.—What have we considered? What are the remarks introductory to the National Constitution called? Recite the Preamble to the Constitution. Who ordained and established the Constitution? For what purposes?

ART. I. *Legislative Department.* SEC. I. Recite Section I. In what body are all legislative powers vested? Of what does Congress consist?

SEC. II. Recite the *1st Clause.* How is the House of Representatives composed? How often and by whom are the Representatives chosen? What are the qualifications for an elector or voter? Recite the *2d. Clause.* What is said about the age of a Representative? How long must he have been a citizen of the United States? What is required in regard to his residence? What three qualifications must a Representative possess?

Apportionment of Representatives.   *Number of Senators.*

3d Clause.—Representatives and direct **taxes shall** be apportioned among the **several** States which may be included within this **Union,**
according to their respective **numbers,** which shall be de-   **Apportionment of**
termined by adding to **the whole number** of free persons,   **Representatives.**
including those bound **to service for a** term of years, and
excluding Indians not taxed, **three-fifths of** all other persons. The actual enumeration shall be made within three years after the first meeting of the Congress of the
United States, and within every subsequent term of ten years, in such manner as
they shall by law **direct.** The number of representatives shall not exceed one for
every **thirty thousand, but** each **State** shall have at least one representative; and
until such **enumeration** shall be made, the State of *New Hampshire* shall be entitled to choose three, *Massachusetts* eight, *Rhode Island* and *Providence
Plantations* one, *Connecticut* five, *New York* six, *New Jersey* four, *Pennsylvania* eight, *Delaware* one, *Maryland* six, *Virginia* ten, *North Carolina*
five, *South Carolina* five, and *Georgia* three.

    4th Clause.—When vacancies happen in the representa-
tion from any State, the executive authority thereof shall   **Vacancies, how**
issue writs of election to fill such vacancies.   **filled.** .

    5th Clause.—The House of Representatives shall choose
their speaker and other officers; and shall have the sole   **Speaker, how**
power of impeachment.   **appointed.**

SECTION III.

1st Clause.—The Senate of the *United States* shall be
composed of two senators from each State, chosen by the **Number of Senators**
legislature thereof, for six years; and each senator shall   **from each State.**
have one vote.

    2d Clause.—Immediately after they shall be assembled in consequence of the first
election, they shall be divided as equally as may be into
three classes. The seats of the senators of the first class   **Classification of**
shall be vacated at the expiration of the second year, of the   **Senators.**
second class at the expiration of the fourth year, and of the
third class at the expiration of the sixth year, so that one-third may be chosen every
second year; and if vacancies happen by resignation, or otherwise, during the recess
of the legislature of any State, the executive thereof may make temporary appointments until the next meeting of the legislature, which shall then fill such vacancies.

QUESTIONS.—SEC. II. Recite the *3d Clause.* How are Representatives and direct
taxes apportioned among the several States? How are the respective numbers of
the representative population to be determined? When was the first enumeration
or census to be made, and how often thereafter? How many inhabitants, at least,
are required for one representative? What number shall each State have? What
number of representatives respectively were the States then in the Union entitled
to? Of how many members, consequently, did the first House of Representatives
consist? Recite the *4th Clause.* How are vacancies in the representation of a State
to be filled? Recite the *5th Clause.* Who shall choose the officers of the House of
Representatives?
    SEC. III. Recite the *1st Clause.* Of whom shall the Senate be composed? By
whom are the Senators chosen, and for what space of time? How many votes is
each Senator entitled to? Recite the *2d Clause.* Into how many classes were the
Senators at first divided? In what order were their seats vacated? What proportion of Senators are chosen every second year? Under what conditions may the
Executive or Governor of a State fill a vacancy in the Senate? How long may a
Senator so appointed fill the office? How shall the vacancy then be filled?

Qualification of Senators.

3d Clause.—No person shall be a senator who shall not have attained to the age of thirty years, and been nine years a citizen of the *United States,* and who shall not, when elected, be an inhabitant of that State for which he shall be chosen.

Presiding Officer of the Senate.

4th Clause.—The Vice-President of the *United States* shall be president of the Senate, but shall have no vote, unless they be equally divided.

5th Clause.—The Senate shall choose their other officers, and also a president *pro tempore,* in the absence of the Vice-President, or when he shall exercise the office of President of the *United States.*

Senate, a court for trial of impeachment.

6th Clause.—The Senate shall have the sole power to try all impeachments: When sitting for that purpose, they shall be on oath or affirmation. When the President of the *United States* is tried, the chief-justice shall preside: and no person shall be convicted without the concurrence of two-thirds of the members present.

Judgment in case of Conviction.

7th Clause.—Judgment in cases of impeachment shall not extend further than to removal from office, and disqualification to hold and enjoy any office of honor, trust or profit under the *United States:* but the party convicted shall nevertheless be liable and subject to indictment, trial, judgment, and punishment, according to law.

SECTION IV.

Elections of Senators and Representatives.

1st Clause.—The times, places, and manner of holding elections for senators and representatives, shall be prescribed in each State by the legislature thereof; but the Congress may at any time, by law, make or alter such regulations, except as to the places of choosing senators.

Meeting of Congress.

2d Clause.—The Congress shall assemble at least once in every year, and such meeting shall be on the first Monday in December, unless they shall by law appoint a different day.

SECTION V.

1st Clause.—Each house shall be the judge of the elections, returns, and qualifications of its own members, and a majority of each shall constitute a quorum to

---

QUESTIONS.—SEC. III. Recite the *3d Clause.* At what age is a person eligible to be a Senator? How long must he have been a citizen of the United States? What is required concerning his residence? What are the three requisites of a Senator? Recite the *4th Clause.* Who shall be the President of the Senate? When may he vote? Recite the *5th Clause.* What officers shall the Senate choose? What officers may they choose *pro tempore,* or for the time being, and under what conditions? Recite the *6th Clause.* What sole power has the Senate? What sole power is given to the House of Representatives by the 5th Clause, Section II., Article I., of the Constitution? Under what conditions shall the Senate sit for the trial of impeachment? When shall the Chief-Justice of the United States preside in the Senate? What proportion of the Senate shall be necessary to a conviction? Recite the *7th Clause.* In cases of impeachment, how far may judgment extend? To what is the convicted person further liable?

SEC. IV. Recite the *1st Clause.* What prescription is allowed to each State legislature in regard to elections for members of the Congress? What may the Congress do in the matter? Recite the *2d Clause.* How often and at what time shall the Congress assemble? How may a different day be appointed?

SEC. V. Recite the *1st Clause.* Of what may each House of Congress be the judge? What proportion shall constitute a quorum to do business? What power is given to a smaller number? What power is given these concerning absent members?

do business; but a smaller number may adjourn from day to day, and may be authorized to compel the attendance of absent members, in such manner and under such penalties as each house may provide.

Organization of Congress.

2d *Clause.*—Each house may determine the rules of its proceedings, punish its members for disorderly behavior, and, with the concurrence of two-thirds, expel a member.

Rules of proceeding.

3d *Clause.*—Each house shall keep a journal of its proceedings, and from time to time publish the same, excepting such parts as may in their judgment require secrecy, and the yeas and nays of the members of either house on any question shall, at the desire of one-fifth of those present, be entered on the journal.

Journal of Congress.

4th *Clause.*—Neither house, during the session of Congress, shall, without the consent of the other, adjourn for more than three days, nor to any other place than that in which the two houses shall be sitting.

Adjournment of Congress.

SECTION VI.

1st *Clause.*—The senators and representatives shall receive a compensation for their services, to be ascertained by law, and paid out of the treasury of the *United States.* They shall in all cases, except treason, felony, and breach of the peace, be privileged from arrest during their attendance at the session of their respective houses, and in going to and returning from the same; and for any speech or debate in either house, they shall not be questioned in any other place.

Compensation and privileges of members.

2d *Clause.*—No senator or representative shall, during the time for which he was elected, be appointed to any civil office under the authority of the *United States,* which shall have been created, or the emoluments whereof shall have been increased during such time; and no person holding any office under the *United States,* shall be a member of either house during his continuance in office.

Plurality of offices prohibited.

SECTION VII.

1st *Clause.*—All bills for raising revenue shall originate in the House of Representatives; but the Senate may propose or concur with amendments as on other bills.

Bills, how originated.

QUESTIONS.—SEC. V. Recite the 2d *Clause.* What powers are given each House over its rules of proceedings? What power is given to each for enforcing its own rules? Recite the 3d *Clause.* What is required of each House concerning its proceedings? What discretionary power is given to each House concerning its journals? When shall the yeas and nays in each House be entered on the journal? Recite the 4th *Clause.* What requirement is made concerning the adjournment of either House? How are they restricted as to the place to which either may adjourn?

SEC. VI. Recite the 1st *Clause.* What provision is made for the compensation of the members of Congress? What privileges are members of Congress entitled to? What are the exceptions? How is freedom in speech and debate secured to members of Congress? Recite the 2d *Clause.* How are members of Congress restricted concerning the holding of civil offices? What will prevent a person being a member of Congress?

SEC. VII. Recite the 1st *Clause.* In which House of Congress shall revenue bills originate? What may the Senate do?

How bills become laws.

2d Clause.—Every bill which shall have passed the House of Representatives and the Senate, shall, before it becomes a law, be presented to the President of the United States. If he approve he shall sign it, but if not he shall return it, with his objections, to that house in which it shall have originated, who shall enter the objections at large on their journal, and proceed to reconsider it. If, after such reconsideration, two-thirds of that house shall agree to pass the bill, it shall be sent, together with the objections, to the other house, by which it shall likewise be reconsidered, and if approved by two-thirds of that house, it shall become a law. But in all such cases the votes of both houses shall be determined by yeas and nays; and the names of the persons voting for and against the bill shall be entered on the journal of each house respectively. If any bill shall not be returned by the President within ten days (Sundays excepted) after it shall have been presented to him, the same shall be a law, in like manner as if he had signed it, unless the Congress by their adjournment prevent its return, in which case it shall not be a law.

Approval and veto powers of the President.

3d Clause.—Every order, resolution, or vote to which the concurrence of the Senate and House of Representatives may be necessary (except on a question of adjournment) shall be presented to the President of the *United States*; and before the same shall take effect shall be approved by him, or being disapproved by him, shall be repassed by two-thirds of the Senate and House of Representatives, according to the rules and limitations prescribed in the case of a bill.

SECTION VIII.

Powers vested in Congress.

1st Clause.—The Congress shall have power to lay and collect taxes, duties, imposts and excises, to pay the debts and provide for the common defence and general welfare of the *United States*; but all duties, imposts and excises shall be uniform throughout the United States;

2d Clause.—To borrow money on the credit of the United States;

3d Clause.—To regulate commerce with foreign nations, and among the several States, and with the Indian tribes;

4th Clause.—To establish an uniform rule of naturalization, and uniform laws on the subject of bankruptcies throughout the United States;

5th Clause.—To coin money, regulate the value thereof, and of foreign coin, and fix the standard of weights and measures;

QUESTIONS.—SEC. VII. Recite the *2d Clause.* What shall be done with a bill after it has passed both Houses of Congress? What must the President do with it? What shall the House to which the bill may be returned with the President's objections or *veto* do? When shall the bill be sent to the other House? What shall accompany the bill? What shall the other House do? If the bill shall be approved by two-thirds of both Houses, what then? How shall the votes of the Houses be determined, in such cases? What shall be entered in the journals? Under what other conditions may a bill become a law? What is the exception? Recite the *3d Clause.* What must be done with every order, resolution, and vote, requiring the concurrence of both Houses, before they shall take effect? What is the exception? How may such orders, resolutions, and votes be made effective, notwithstanding the President's veto?

SEC. VIII. Recite the *1st Clause.* What powers are given to the Congress concerning taxes, duties, imposts, excises, debts, and the common defence of the United States? What is said about the uniformity of duties, imposts, and excises? What power is given to Congress by the *2d Clause?* What power is given to Congress by the *3d Clause?* What power is given to Congress by the *4th Clause?* What power is given to Congress by the *5th Clause?*

Powers of Congress.   *Admission of Immigrants.*

6th Clause.—To provide for the punishment of counterfeiting the securities and current coin of the *United States ;*

7th Clause.—To establish post-offices and post-roads;

8th Clause.—To promote the progress of science and useful arts, by securing for limited times, to authors and inventors, the exclusive right to their respective writings and discoveries;

9th Clause.—To constitute tribunals inferior to the Supreme Court;

10th Clause.—To define and punish piracies and felonies committed on the high seas, and offences against the law of nations;

11th Clause.—To declare war, grant letters of marque and reprisal, and make rules concerning captures on land and water;

12th Clause.—To raise and support armies, but no appropriation of money to that use shall be for a longer term than two years;

13th Clause.—To provide and maintain a navy;

14th Clause.—To make rules for the government and regulation of the land and naval forces;

15th Clause.—To provide for calling forth the militia to execute the laws of the Union, suppress insurrections and repel invasions;

16th Clause.—To provide for organizing, arming, and disciplining the militia, and for governing such part of them as may be employed in the service of the *United States,* reserving to the States respectively, the appointment of the officers, and the authority of training the militia according to the discipline prescribed by Congress;

17th Clause.—To exercise exclusive legislation in all cases whatsoever, over such district (not exceeding ten miles square) as may, by cession of particular States, and the acceptance of Congress, become the seat of the government of the United States, and to exercise like authority over all places purchased by the consent of the legislature of the State in which the same shall be, for the erection of forts, magazines, arsenals, dockyards, and other needful buildings;—And

18th Clause.—To make all laws which shall be necessary and proper for carrying into execution the foregoing powers, and all other powers vested by this constitution in the government of the *United States,* or in any department or officer thereof.

SECTION IX.

1st Clause.—The migration or importation of such persons as any of the States now existing shall think proper to admit, shall not be prohibited by the Congress prior to the year one thousand   **Immigrants, how** eight hundred and eight, but a tax or duty may be imposed   **admitted.** on such importation, not exceeding ten dollars for each person.

QUESTIONS.—SEC. VIII. What power is given to Congress by the *6th Clause?* What power is given to Congress by the *7th Clause?* What power is given to Congress by the *8th Clause?* What power is given to Congress by the *9th Clause?* What power is given to Congress by the *10th Clause?* What power is given to Congress by the *11th Clause?* What power is given to Congress by the *12th Clause?* What power is given to Congress by the *13th Clause?* What power is given to Congress by the *14th Clause?* What power is given to Congress by the *15th Clause?* What power is given to Congress by the *16th Clause?* What is reserved to the States respectively? What power is given to Congress by the *17th Clause?* What power is given to Congress by the *18th Clause?*

SEC. IX. Recite the *1st Clause.* What restrictions were imposed upon Congress concerning the migration or importation of certain persons, meaning slaves, from Africa or elsewhere? What was the limit of that restriction? What tax or duty might be laid?

Habeas Corpus. *2d Clause.*—The privilege of the writ of habeas corpus shall not be suspended, unless when in cases of rebellion or invasion the public safety may require it.

Attainder. *3d Clause.*—No bill of attainder or ex post facto law shall be passed.

Taxes. *4th Clause.*—No capitation, or other direct tax shall be laid, unless in proportion to the census or enumeration hereinbefore directed to be taken.

5th Clause.—No tax or duty shall be laid on articles exported from any State.

Regulations regarding duties. *6th Clause.*—No preference shall be given by any regulation of commerce or revenue to the ports of one State over those of another; nor shall vessels bound to, or from, one State, be obliged to enter, clear, or pay duties in another.

Money, how drawn. *7th Clause.*—No money shall be drawn from the treasury, but in consequence of appropriations made by law; and a regular statement and account of the receipts and expenditures of all public money shall be published from time to time.

Titles of nobility prohibited. *8th Clause.*—No title of nobility shall be granted by the *United States:* And no person holding any office of profit or trust under them shall, without the consent of the Congress, accept of any present, emolument, office, or title, of any kind whatever, from any king, prince, or foreign state.

SECTION X.

Powers of States defined. *1st Clause.*—No State shall enter into any treaty, alliance, or confederation; grant letters of marque and reprisal; coin money; emit bills of credit; make anything but gold and silver coin a tender in payments of debts; pass any bill of attainder, ex post facto law, or law impairing the obligation of contracts, or grant any title of nobility.

2d Clause.—No State shall, without the consent of the Congress, lay any impost or duties on imports or exports, except what may be absolutely necessary for executing its inspection laws; and the net produce of all duties and imposts, laid by any State on imports or exports, shall be for the use of the treasury of the *United States;* and all such laws shall be subject to the revision and control of the Congress.

3d Clause.—No State shall, without the consent of Congress, lay any duty of tonnage, keep troops or ships-of-war in time of peace, enter into any agreement or compact with another State, or with a foreign power, or engage in war, unless actually invaded, or in such imminent danger as will not admit of delay.

QUESTIONS.—SEC. **IX.** Recite the *2d Clause.* What is said concerning the suspension of the privilege of the writ of *habeas corpus?* What does the *3d Clause* prohibit? What is said in the *4th Clause* about taxation? What does the *5th Clause* prohibit concerning exportations from any State? What does the *6th Clause* provide concerning the commerce between the States? What is provided in the *7th Clause* in relation to the drawing of money from the Treasury, and a statement and account of receipts and expenditures? Recite the *8th Clause.* What is said concerning titles of nobility? What restrictions concerning favors from foreigners are laid upon National officers?

SEC. X. What restrictions are laid upon each State by the *1st Clause?* What restrictions are laid upon each State by the *2d Clause?* What restrictions are laid upon each State by the *3d Clause?*

ARTICLE II.

SECTION I.

1st Clause.—The executive power shall be vested in a President of the *United States of America.* He shall hold his office during the term of four years, and, together with the Vice-President chosen for the same term, be elected as follows:

  Executive power, in whom vested.

2d Clause.—Each State shall appoint, in such manner as the legislature ther.of may direct, a number of electors, equal to the whole number of senators and representatives to which the State may be entitled in the Congress; but no senator or representative, or person holding an office of trust or profit under the United States, shall be appointed an elector.

  Presidential electors.

3d Clause.—The Congress may determine the time of choosing the electors, and the day on which they shall give their votes; which day shall be the same throughout the *United States.*

  Time of choosing electors.

4th Clause.—No person except a natural born citizen, or a citizen of the *United States* at the time of the adoption of this Constitution, shall be eligible to the office of President; neither shall any person be eligible to that office who shall not have attained to the age of thirty-five years, and been fourteen years resident within the *United States.*

  Qualifications of the President.

5th Clause.—In the case of the removal of the President from office, or of his death, resignation, or inability to discharge the powers and duties of the said office, the same shall devolve on the Vice-President, and the Congress may by law provide for the case of removal, death, resignation, or inability, both of the Presi-

  Resort in case of his disability.

QUESTIONS.—ART. **II.** *Executive Department.* SEC. I. Recite the 1*st Clause.* In whom is the executive power of the Republic vested? What is the term of office of the President and Vice-President? Recite the 2*d Clause.* What shall each State do? What shall be the number of electors? Who may not be an elector?

Now turn to the Twelfth Amendment of the Constitution, on page 374. Where shall the electors meet? How shall they vote? What restriction is made? How shall their ballots be made out? What lists shall they make? What shall they do with them? What shall the President of the Senate do? Who shall be declared the President under certain conditions? What are those conditions? When no choice shall be made by the electors, by whom is the President chosen? From how many and what candidates must the House of Representatives choose a President? How shall the votes be taken? What shall constitute a quorum? What is necessary to a choice? In the event of the House not choosing a President before the 4th of March following, who shall act as President? How shall the Vice-President be chosen? In the event of no choice by the electors, how shall he be chosen? Under what conditions may the Senate make the choice? What is said about the eligibility of a person for Vice-President? Recite the 3*d Clause* of Section I., Article II. What may Congress determine concerning electors? What is said about the day on which electors shall vote? Recite the 4*th Clause.* What is said about the birthplace of a person being eligible for the office of President? What shall be his age, at least, and the time of his residence in the United States? Recite the 5*th Clause.* On whom shall the office of President devolve, in the event of the death or disability of that officer? What power is given to Congress for filling the places of President and Vice-President?

---

dent and Vice-President, declaring what officer shall then act as President, and such officer shall act accordingly, until the disability be removed, or a President shall be elected.

Salary of the President.

6th Clause.—The President shall, at stated times, receive for his services, a compensation, which shall neither be increased nor diminished during the period for which he shall have been elected, and he shall not receive within that period any other emolument from the *United States,* or any of them.

Oath of office.

7th Clause.—Before he enter on the execution of his office, he shall take the following oath or affirmation:—"I do solemnly swear (or affirm) that I will faithfully execute the office of President of the United States, and will, to the best of my ability, preserve, protect, and defend the Constitution of the *United States."*

SECTION II.

Duties of the President.

1st Clause.—The President shall be commander-in-chief of the army and navy of the *United States,* and of the militia of the several States, when called into the actual service of the United States; he may require the opinion, in writing, of the principal officer in each of the executive departments, upon any subject relating to the duties of their respective offices, and he shall have power to grant reprieves and pardons for offences against the *United States,* except in cases of impeachment.

His power to make treaties, appoint ambassadors, judges, etc.

2d Clause.—He shall have power, by and with the advice and consent of the Senate, to make treaties, provided two-thirds of the senators present concur; and he shall nominate, and by and with the advice and consent of the Senate, shall appoint ambassadors, other public ministers and consuls, judges of the Supreme Court, and all other officers of the *United States,* whose appointments are not herein otherwise provided for, and which shall be established by law: but the Congress may by law vest the appointment of such inferior officers as they think proper, in the President alone, in the courts of law, or in the heads of departments.

May fill vacancies.

3d Clause.—The President shall have power to fill up all vacancies that may happen during the recess of the Senate, by granting commissions which shall expire at the end of their next session.

SECTION III.

Power to convene Congress.

He shall from time to time give to the Congress information of the state of the Union, and recommend to their consideration such measures as he shall judge necessary and expedient; he may, on extraordinary occasions, convene both houses, or either of them, and in case of disagreement between them, with

---

QUESTIONS.—SEC. I. Recite the *6th Clause.* What is said concerning the President's compensation? What restrictions are laid upon him? What does the *7th Clause* declare that the President shall do?

SEC. II. Recite the *1st Clause.* Of what, and under what circumstances, shall the President be a commander-in-chief? What may he require of the officers of the executive departments? What powers are given him concerning reprieves and pardons? What is the exception? What power is given to the President by the *2d Clause?* What proviso is made? What officers of the government shall he nominate, and, by and with the advice of the Senate, appoint? What may the Congress do concerning appointments? Recite the *3d Clause.* What power is given to the President for filling vacancies? What is the duration of such commission?

respect to the time of adjournment, he may adjourn them to such time as he shall think proper; he shall receive ambassadors and other public ministers; he shall take care that the laws be faithfully executed, and shall commission all the officers of the United States.

SECTION IV.

The President, Vice-President and all civil officers of the *United States,* shall be removed from office on impeachment for, and conviction of, treason, bribery, or other high crimes and misdemeanors.

How officers may be removed.

ARTICLE III.

SECTION I.

The judicial power of the *United States* shall be vested in one supreme court, and in such inferior courts as the Congress may from time to time ordain and establish. The judges, both of the supreme and inferior courts, shall hold their offices during good behavior, and shall, at stated times, receive for their services a compensation, which shall not be diminished during their continuance in office.

Judicial power, how vested.

SECTION II.

1st Clause.—The judicial power shall extend to all cases, in law and equity, arising under this Constitution, the laws of the United States, and treaties made, or which shall be made, under their authority;—to all cases affecting ambassadors, other public ministers, and consuls;—to all cases of admiralty and maritime jurisdiction;—to controversies to which the *United States* shall be a party;—to controversies between two or more States;—between a State and citizens of another State;—between citizens of different States;—between citizens of the same State claiming lands under grants of different States, and between a State, or the citizens thereof, and foreign states, citizens or subjects.

To what cases it extends.

2d Clause.—In all cases affecting ambassadors, other public ministers and consuls, and those in which a State shall be party, the supreme court shall have original jurisdiction. In all the other cases before mentioned, the supreme court shall have appellate jurisdiction, both as to law and fact, with such exceptions and under such regulations as the Congress shall make.

Jurisdiction of the Supreme Court.

QUESTIONS.— SEC. III. What information is the President required to give to the Congress? What recommendations shall he make? What may he do on extraordinary occasions? When may the President adjourn the Congress? What is his duty respecting ambassadors? What is his duty concerning the execution of the laws, and the commissioning of government officers?

SEC. IV. For what crimes may all civil officers of the Government be removed, and by what method?

ART. III. *Judicial Department.* SEC. I. In what body or bodies is the judicial power of the Republic vested? By what tenure do the judges hold their offices? What is said about compensation for their services?

SEC. II. Recite the *1st Clause.* How many subjects are named in which the United States courts have jurisdiction? Name the 1st. Name the 2d. Name the 3d. Name the 4th. Name the 5th. Name the 6th. Name the 7th. Name the 8th. Name the 9th. Recite the *2d Clause.* In what cases shall the Supreme Court have original jurisdiction? What is its jurisdiction, both as to law and fact, in all the other cases mentioned? What may be exceptions?

Rules respecting trials.

3d Clause.—The trial of all crimes, except in cases of impeachment, shall be by jury; and such trial shall be held in the State where the said crimes shall have been committed; but when not committed within any State, the trial shall be at such place or places as the Congress may by law have directed.

SECTION III.

Treason defined.

1st Clause.—Treason against the *United States* shall consist only in levying war against them, or in adhering to their enemies, giving them aid and comfort.

2d Clause.—No person shall be convicted of treason unless on the testimony of two witnesses to the same overt act, or on confession in open court.

How punished.

3d Clause.—The Congress shall have power to declare the punishment of treason, but no attainder of treason shall work corruption of blood, or forfeiture, except during the life of the person attainted.

ARTICLE IV.
SECTION I.

Rights of States to public faith defined.

Full faith and credit shall be given in each State to the public acts, records, and judicial proceedings of every other State. And the Congress may by general laws prescribe the manner in which such acts, records and proceedings shall be proved, and the effect thereof.

SECTION II.

Privileges of citizens.

1st Clause. The citizens of each State shall be entitled to all privileges and immunities of citizens in the several States.

Executive requisition.

2d Clause.—A person charged in any State with treason, felony, or other crime, who shall flee from justice, and be found in another State, shall on demand of the executive authority of the State from which he fled, be delivered up, to be removed to the State having jurisdiction of the crime.

Law regulating service or labor.

3d Clause.—No person held to service or labor in one State, under the laws thereof, escaping into another, shall, in consequence of any law or regulation therein, be discharged from such service or labor, but shall be delivered up on claim of the party to whom such service or labor may be due.

QUESTIONS.—SEC. II. Recite the *3d Clause*. By whom shall all crimes be tried? What is the exception? Where shall such trials be held? What may the Congress direct?

SEC. III.—Recite the *1st Clause*. In what does treason consist? Recite the *2d Clause*. What is required to convict a person of treason? Recite the *3d Clause*. What power is given to Congress in the matter of treason? How are the consequences of attainder of treason limited?

ART. IV. SEC. I. Recite this section. How are the public acts of the several States to be treated in each State? What may Congress do in relation to them?

SEC. II. What does the *1st Clause* declare concerning the privileges and immunities of citizens? Recite the *2d Clause*. Who shall be delivered up for removal from one State to another, on the demand of the executive authority of the State from which he fled? Where shall he be removed to? What does the *3d Clause* declare about fugitives from service or labor, meaning slaves, and apprentices bound by indentures?

SECTION III.

1st Clause.—New States may be admitted by the Congress into this Union ; but no new State shall be formed **New States, how** or erected within the jurisdiction of any other State ; nor **formed and ad-** any State be formed by the junction of two or more States, **mitted.** or parts of States, without the consent of the legislatures of the States concerned as well as of the Congress.

2d Clause.—The Congress shall have power to dispose of and make all needful rules and regulations respecting the territory or other property belonging to the *United States ;* and nothing in **Power of Congress** this Constitution shall be so construed as to prejudice any **over public lands.** claims of the *United States,* or of any particular State.

SECTION IV.

The United States shall guarantee to every State in this Union a republican form of government, and shall protect each of them against invasion, and on application of the legislature, or of the ex- **Republican govern-** ecutive (when the legislature cannot be convened), against **ment guaranteed.** domestic violence.

ARTICLE V.

The Congress, whenever two-thirds of both houses shall deem it necessary, shall propose amendments to this Constitution, or, on the application of the legislatures of two-thirds of the several States, **Constitution, how** shall call a convention for proposing amendments, which, **to be amended.** in either case, shall be valid to all intents and purposes, as part of this Constitution, when ratified by the legislatures of three-fourths of the several States, or by conventions in three-fourths thereof, as the one or the other mode of ratification may be proposed by the Congress, provided that no amendment which may be made prior to the year one thousand eight hundred and eight shall in any manner affect the first and fourth clauses in the ninth section of the first article ; and that no State, without its consent, shall be deprived of its equal suffrage in the Senate.

ARTICLE VI.

1st Clause.—All debts contracted and engagements entered into, before the adoption of this Constitution, shall **Validity of debts** be as valid against the United States under this Constitu- **recognized.** tion, as under the Confederation.

QUESTIONS.—SEC. III.—Recite the *1st Clause.* By whom may new States be admitted into the Union ? What restrictions are applied in the formation of new States ? Recite the *2d Clause.* What power is given to Congress by this clause ? What construction, as to claims, is not to be put upon any part of the Constitution ?

SEC. IV. Recite this section. What shall the United States, or National Government, guarantee to every State ? In what two ways is the National Government bound to protect each State ?

ARTICLE V. Of what does this article treat ? In what ways may amendments to the Constitution be proposed ? How shall amendments be made a part of the Constitution ? What restrictions were imposed concerning the *1st* and *2d Clauses* of the ninth section of the first article ? Recite those clauses. Have those restrictions any force now ? Why not ? What is said of the equality of the States in the Senate ?

ARTICLE VI. Recite the *1st Clause.* What is said of the validity of former public debts ?

2d Clause.—This Constitution, and the laws of the *United States* which shall be made in pursuance thereof; and all treaties made, or which shall be made, under the authority of the *United States,* shall be the supreme law of the land; and the judges in every State shall be bound thereby, anything in the Constitution or laws of any State to the contrary notwithstanding.

Supreme law of the land defined.

3d Clause.—The senators and representatives before mentioned, and the members of the several State legislatures, and all executive and judicial officers, both of the *United States* and of the several States, shall be bound by oath or affirmation to support this Constitution; but no religious test shall ever be required as a qualification to any office or public trust under the *United States.*

Oath, of whom required, and for what.

ARTICLE VII.

Ratification.
The ratification of the conventions of nine States shall be sufficient for the establishment of this Constitution between the States so ratifying the same.

Done in convention by the unanimous consent of the States present, the seventeenth day of September, in the year of our Lord one thousand seven hundred and eighty-seven, and of the independence of the *United States of America* the twelfth. In witness whereof we have hereunto subscribed our names. [Signed by the members of the convention.]

AMENDMENTS.

At the first session of the First Congress, begun and held in the city of *New York*, on Wednesday, the 4th of March, 1789, many amendments to the National Constitution were offered for consideration. The Congress proposed ten of them to the legislatures of the several States. These were ratified by the Constitutional number of State legislatures by the middle of December, 1791. Five other amendments have since been proposed and duly ratified, and have become with the other ten a part of the National Constitution. The following are the amendments:

ARTICLE I.

Freedom in religion and speech, and of the press.
Congress shall make no law respecting an establishment of religion, or prohibiting the free exercise thereof; or abridging the freedom of speech, or of the press; or the right of the people peaceably to assemble, and to petition the government for redress of grievances.

ARTICLE II.

Militia.
A well-regulated militia, being necessary to the security of a free state, the right of the people to keep and bear arms shall not be infringed.

QUESTIONS.—ART. VI. Recite the *2d Clause.* What is declared to be the supreme law of the land? By what are the judges in every State bound? Recite the *3d Clause.* Who shall be bound by oath or affirmation to support the National Constitution? What is said concerning religious tests?

ARTICLE VII. What does this article declare? Where, and by whose consent, and when was the National Constitution formed? Who were the witnesses to it?

AMENDMENTS. When and where were amendments to the Constitution offered to the Congress? What did the Congress do? How many amendments were ratified? What others were proposed, and when were they ratified? What can you tell about a thirteenth amendment?

ARTICLE I. Recite the first amendment to the Constitution. What subjects are the Congress prohibited from making laws upon?

ARTICLE III.

No soldier shall, in time of peace, be quartered in any house, without the consent of the owner, nor in time of war, but in a manner to be prescribed by law.   **Soldiers.**

ARTICLE IV.

The right of the people to be secure in their persons, houses, papers, and effects, against unreasonable searches and seizures, shall not be violated, and no warrants shall issue, but upon probable   **Search-warrants.** cause, supported by oath or affirmation, and particularly describing the place to be searched, and the persons or things to be seized.

ARTICLE V.

No person shall be held to answer for a capital, or otherwise infamous crime, unless on a presentment or indictment of a grand jury, except in cases arising in the land or naval forces, or in the   **Capital crimes.** militia, when in actual service in the time of war and public danger; nor shall any person be subject for the same offence to be twice put in jeopardy of life or limb; nor shall be compelled in any criminal case to be a witness against himself, nor to be deprived of life, liberty, or property, without due process of law; nor shall private property be taken for public use, without just compensation.

ARTICLE VI.

In all criminal prosecutions, the accused shall enjoy the **right to a speedy and public trial**, by an impartial jury of the State and district wherein the crime shall have been committed, which district shall have been previously ascertained by law, and to   **Trial by jury.** be informed of the nature and cause of the accusation; to be confronted with the witnesses against him; to have compulsory process for obtaining witnesses in his favor, and to have the assistance of counsel for his defence.

ARTICLE VII.

In suits at common law, where the value in controversy shall exceed twenty dollars, the right of trial by jury shall   **Suits at common** be preserved, and no fact tried by a jury shall be otherwise   **law.** re-examined in any court of the *United States,* than according to the rules of common law.

QUESTIONS.—ARTICLE II. Recite this article. What is declared concerning the militia, and rights of the people?

ARTICLE III. Recite this article.

ARTICLE IV. Recite this article. What right are the people to be secure in? What is declared concerning warrants?

ARTICLE V. What is declared concerning the holding of persons to answer for alleged offences? What is said about a second trial for the same offence? In what case shall a person not be compelled to testify in court? What guarantee of protection is promised? When only can private property be taken for the public use?

ARTICLE VI. What right shall a person accused of crime enjoy? What right as to the witnesses that may appear against him? What method is secured to him for obtaining witnesses in his favor, and the obtaining of counsel?

ARTICLE VII. In what civil cases shall the right of trial by jury be preserved? In what way shall the re-examination of facts tried by a jury be made?

ARTICLE VIII.

Bail.

Excessive bail shall not be required, nor excessive fines imposed, nor cruel and unusual punishments inflicted.

ARTICLE IX.

Certain rights defined.

The enumeration in the Constitution of certain rights shall not be construed to deny or disparage others retained by the people.

ARTICLE X.

Rights reserved.

The powers not delegated to the *United States* by the Constitution, nor prohibited by it to the States, are reserved to the States respectively, or to the people.

ARTICLE XI.

Judicial power limited.

The judicial power of the *United States* shall not be construed to extend to any suit in law or equity, commenced or prosecuted against one of the *United States* by citizens of another State, or by citizens or subjects of any foreign State.

ARTICLE XII.

Amendment respecting the election of President and Vice-President.

The electors shall meet in their respective States, and vote by ballot for President and Vice-President, one of whom, at least, shall not be an inhabitant of the same State with themselves; they shall name in their ballots the person voted for as President, and in distinct ballots the person voted for as Vice-President, and they shall make distinct lists of all persons voted for as President, and of all persons voted for as Vice-President, and of the number of votes for each, which lists they shall sign and certify, and transmit sealed to the seat of Government of the *United States,* directed to the President of the Senate;—the President of the Senate shall, in the presence of the Senate and House of Representatives, open all the certificates, and the votes shall then be counted;—the person having the greatest number of votes for President, shall be the President, if such number be a majority of the whole number of electors appointed; and if no person have such majority, then from the persons having the highest numbers not exceeding three on the list of those voted for as President, the House of Representatives shall choose immediately, by ballot, the President. But in choosing the President the votes shall be taken by States, the representation from each State having one vote; a quorum for this purpose shall consist of a member or members from two-thirds of the States, and a majority of all

---

QUESTIONS.—ARTICLE **VIII.** What does this article declare?
ARTICLE **IX.** What does this article declare?
ARTICLE **X.** What does this article declare?
ARTICLE **XI.** What does this article declare?
ARTICLE **XII.** What does this article declare? In what connection have we considered the Twelfth Article of the Constitution, which relates to the election of President and Vice-President of the United States?

the States shall be necessary to a choice. And if the House of Representatives shall not choose a President whenever the right of choice shall devolve upon them, before the fourth day of March next following, then the Vice-President shall act as President, as in the case of the death or other constitutional disability of the President. The person having the greatest number of votes as Vice-President, shall be the Vice-President, if such number be a majority of the whole number of electors appointed, and if no person have a majority, then, from the two highest numbers on the list, the Senate shall choose the Vice-President; a quorum for the purpose shall consist of two-thirds of the whole number of senators, and a majority of the whole number shall be necessary to a choice. But no person constitutionally ineligible to the office of President shall be eligible to that of Vice-President of the *United States.*

ARTICLE XIII.

SECTION I.

Neither slavery nor involuntary servitude, except as a punishment for crime, whereof the party shall have been **Slavery** prohibited. duly convicted, shall exist within the *United States,* or any place subject to their jurisdiction.

SECTION II.

Congress shall have power to enforce this article by appropriate legislation.

ARTICLE XIV.

SECTION I.

All persons born or naturalized in the *United States,* and subject to the jurisdiction thereof, are citizens of the United States and of the State wherein they reside. No State shall make or enforce **Citizens and their** any law which shall abridge the privileges or immunities of **rights.** citizens of the *United States;* nor shall any State deprive any person of life, liberty, or property, without due process of law, nor deny to any person within its jurisdiction the equal protection of the laws.

SECTION II.

Representatives shall be appointed among the several States according to their respective numbers, counting the whole number of persons in each State, excluding Indians not taxed. But when the right to vote at any election for the choice of electors for President and Vice-Pres- **Adjustment of re-** ident of the *United States,* representatives in Congress, **presentation to the** the executive or judicial officers of a State, or the members **elective franchise.** of the Legislature thereof, is denied to any of the male inhabitants of such State, being twenty-one years of age, and citizens of the *United States,* or in any way abridged, except for participation in rebellion or other crime, the basis of representation therein shall be reduced in the proportion which the number of such male citizens shall bear to the whole number of male citizens twenty-one years of age in such State.

SECTION III.

No person shall be a Senator or Representative in Congress, or elector of President and Vice-President, or hold any office, civil or military, under the *United*

ARTICLE XIII. What does this article declare?
ARTICLE XIV. What does this article declare?

Disabling conditions. *States,* or under any State, who, having previously taken an oath as a member of Congress, or as an officer of the *United States,* or as a member of any State Legislature, or as an executive or judicial officer of any State, to support the Constitution of the *United States,* shall have engaged in insurrection or rebellion against the same, or given aid or comfort to the enemies thereof. But Congress may, by a vote of two-thirds of each House, remove such disability.

SECTION IV.

The validity of the public debt of the *United States,* authorized by law, including debts incurred for payment of pensions and bounties for services in suppressing insurrection or rebellion, shall not be questioned. **Treatment of public debts.** But neither the United States nor any State shall assume or pay any debt or obligation incurred in aid of insurrection or rebellion against the *United States,* or any claim for the loss or emancipation of any slave; but all such debts, obligations, and claims shall be held illegal and void.

SECTION V.

Congress shall have power to enforce, by appropriate legislation, the provisions of this article.

ARTICLE XV.

SECTION I.

The right of the citizens of the *United States* shall not be denied or abridged by the *United States,* or by any State, on account of race, color, or previous condition of servitude.

SECTION II.

The Congress shall have power to enforce this article by appropriate legislation.

------◆●◆------

OUR NATIONAL PROGRESS.

No nation ever showed such *marvellous growth* as ours has done, since it was established under a national constitution, in 1790. In *expansion of area, increase in population, development of resources* of every kind, *growth* of *its manufactures, commerce, arts, science* and *literature,* and in *moral* and *political influence* among the family of nations, its progress has been most remarkable.

New States added to the original thirteen, have become members of the Union by a simple process. After a wild region has acquired a certain number of permanent inhabitants, it is organized into a Territory. When the population reaches another prescribed number, it may be admitted into the Union as a State, by an act of Congress, with a State constitution for its local government. The following table shows the date of settlement of each State in the Union, by whom settled, and the date of admission of each.

Order.	Name.	Date of Settlement.	Where first Settled.	By whom Settled.	Date of admission.
1	Virginia	1607	Jamestown ...	English.....	
2	New York.....	1614	New York ...	Dutch......	
3	Massachusetts..	1620	Plymouth.....	English.....	
4	New Hampshire	1623	Little Harbor.	"	
5	Connecticut....	1633	Windsor.....	"	
6	Maryland.......	1634	St. Mary's....	"	
7	Rhode Island ..	1636	Providence...	"	
8	Delaware	1638˙	Wilmington..	Swedes.....	
9	North Carolina.	1650	Chowan River	English.....	
10	New Jersey....	1664	Elizabeth.....	"	
11	South Carolina.	1670	Ashley River.	"	
12	Pennsylvania...	1682	Philadelphia .	"	
13	Georgia........	1733	Savannah	"	
14	Vermont.......	1724	Fort Dummer.	"	1791
15	Kentucky......	1775	Boonesboro'..	"	1792
16	Tennessee	1757	Fort Loudon .	"	1796
17	Ohio	1788	Marietta	"	1802
18	Louisiana......	1699	Iberville	French.	1812
19	Indiana........	1730	Vincennes....	"	1816
20	Mississippi.....	1716	Natchez......	"	، 1817
21	Illinois	1720	Kaskaskia ...	"	1818
22	Alabama ,......	1711	Mobile.......	"	1819
23	Maine	1625	Bristol	"	1820
24	Missouri	1764	St. Louis.....	"	1821
25	Arkansas	1685	Arkansas Post	"	1836
26	Michigan	1670	Detroit..... .	"	1837
27	Florida........	1565	St. Augustine.	Spanish.....	1845
28	Texas..........	1692	San Antonio..	"	1845
29	Iowa.....,.....	1833	Burlington...	English.....	1846
30	Wisconsin	1669	Green Bay...	French......	1848
31	California	1769	San Diego ...	Spanish.....	1850
32	Minnesota......	1846	St. Paul......	Americans..	1858
33	Oregon	1811	Astoria	"	1859
34	Kansas.........	....	....	"	1861
35	West Virginia..	....	....	English.....	1863
36	Nevada........	....	....	Americans..	1864
37	Nebraska.......	...;	....	"	1867
38	Colorado.	....	....	"	1875

QUESTIONS. —Name the original thirteen States in the order of their settlement. When was Virginia first settled? Where? By whom? When was New York first settled? Where? By whom? Ask the same questions about all of the thirty-eight States.

When was the first State admitted, into the Union formed by the original thirteen States? What State was it?

Give the names of the other States in the order of their admission. When was Vermont admitted? When Kentucky? Ask the same questions about all the other States. How many States are there now in the Union?

THE following Table shows the national progress in population. *The Census,* or enumeration of the inhabitants, is taken every ten years.

Census.	Date of Census.	Number of States.	Population of the States.	Population of the Tritoerries.	Total Population.
1	1790	13	3,894,136	35,691	3,929,827
2	1800	16	5,231,992	73,949	5,305,941
3	1810	17	7,036,474	203,340	7,239,814
4	1820	23	9,515,397	122,794	9,638,191
5	1830	24	12,729,429	136,591	12,866,020
6	1840	26	16,897,207	172,246	17,069,453
7	1850	31	23,047,891	143,985	23,191,876
8	1860	33	31,040,842	402,479	31,443,321
9	1870	37	38,113,253	442,730	38,555,983

QUESTIONS.—When was the first Census of the United States taken? How often is the Census taken? How many States were there in the Union when the first Census was taken? How many States were admitted before the next Census? Before the next? What was the population of the United States when the first Census was taken in 1790?* In 1800? In 1810? And so on. What was the increase in population from 1790 to 1800? From 1800 to 1810? From 1810 to 1820?

TABLE OF PRESIDENTS AND VICE-PRESIDENTS OF THE UNITED STATES.

No.	Presidents.	Residence when elected.	Born.	Died.	When inaugurated.	Vice-Presidents.
1	George Washington.	Va.....	1732	1799	1789	John Adams.
2	John Adams.........	Mass..	1735	1826	1797	Thomas Jefferson.
3	Thomas Jefferson ...	Va.....	1743	1826	1801	Aaron Burr. / George Clinton.
4	James Madison......	Va.....	1751	1836	1809	George Clinton. / Elbridge Gerry.
5	James Monroe.......	Va.....	1758	1831	1817	Daniel D. Tompkins.
6	John Quincy Adams.	Mass..	1767	1848	1825	John C. Calhoun.
7	Andrew Jackson	Tenn..	1767	1845	1829	John C. Calhoun. / Martin Van Buren.
8	Martin Van Buren ..	N. Y..	1782	1862	1837	Richard M. Johnson.
9	W. H. Harrison.....	Ohio ..	1773	1841	1841	John Tyler.
10	John Tyler..........	Va.....	1790	1862	1841	
11	James K. Polk......	Tenn..	1795	1849	1845	George M. Dallas.
12	Zachary Taylor	La.....	1784	1850	1849	Millard Fillmore.
13	Millard Fillmore....	N. Y..	1800	1874	1850	
14	Franklin Pierce.....	N. H..	1804	1869	1853	Wm. R. King.
15	James Buchanan....	Penn..	1791	1868	1857	J. C. Breckinridge.
16	Abraham Lincoln...	Ill. ...	1809	1865	1861	Hannibal Hamlin. / Andrew Johnson.
17	Andrew Johnson....	Tenn..	1808	....	1865	
18	Ulysses S. Grant ...	Ill, ...	1822	... .	1869	Schuyler Colfax. / Henry Wilson.

QUESTIONS.—Name in their order the Presidents of the United States. Name those who served two terms, or eight years. Name those who served but one term, or four years. Name those who died before their term of office expired.

---

* It probably will not be best to require the scholar to give the exact population at each of these dates. "The population in 1790 was nearly four million," would be a sufficient answer, and would fix an important fact in the mind. To say that the increase of population for the first ten years was about 1,300,000 would be a good answer, and thus fixing these figures approximately in the mind will give some idea as to our wonderful growth as a nation. The increase in population may be stated at about thirty-three per cent. every ten years.

BIOGRAPHICAL NOTES.

Among the multitude of persons mentioned in this work, who bore a part in the discovery, settlement, planting of the colonies, or assisted in laying the foundations of our Republic, a few appear conspicuous because of their more palpable achievements. From these I have selected the following as subjects for brief biographical notices, and placed their names in alphabetical order for convenient reference. Students are recommended to read more extended histories of their lives in other books. These notes indicate only the most conspicuous services of each.

Adams, John. Born in Quincy, Massachusetts, in 1735; was a lawyer by profession; was an early and earnest champion of the rights of the people; a signer of the Declaration of Independence; a representative of his country at foreign courts, and second President of the Republic. Died at Quincy in 1826.

Adams, Samuel. Born in Boston in 1722. A powerful advocate of the rights of the people. A legislator without blemish; firm in resisting British oppression; a signer of the Declaration of Independence: a member of the convention which adopted the National Constitution, and Lieutenant-Governor of Massachusetts. Died in Boston in 1803.

Baltimore, Lord, Cecil Calvert, son and heir of George Lord Baltimore. Sent a colony to settle Maryland, and became the founder of that commonwealth. Born in England about 1613, and died there in 1676. He never came to America.

Bradford, William. Born in Yorkshire, England, in 1588. Came to America in the May-Flower, and became the second governor of Plymouth. He ruled wisely and well. Died in 1657.

Cabot, Sebastian. Born at Bristol, England, about 1472. Son of an Italian merchant and navigator; he made a voyage westward, and discovered North America at about the time Columbus discovered South America. Died in 1557.

Cartier, Jacques. Born at St. Malo, France, in 1494. An eminent navigator; he was sent out by the king of France to the coasts

of North America. He discovered the Gulf and River St. Lawrence, and named them. He ascended the St. Lawrence to
Montreal. Died about the year 1555.

Coligni, Gaspard de. Born in 1517. Admiral of France, and a leader
of the French Protestants. He attempted to form a colony of
these people in Florida. They were murdered or driven away.
He was killed in Paris on St. Bartholomew's Eve, 1572.

Columbus, Christopher. Born at Genoa about 1435. A navigator of
great skill and engaged in scientific research, he came to the con-
clusion that the earth was a sphere, and that India, then difficult
to reach by merchants of western Europe, might be found by
sailing westward. Whilst seeking a westward passage to that
country, he discovered America. Died at Valladolid, Spain, in
1506.

De Soto, Fernando. Born in Estramadura, Spain, about 1500. An
adventurer, who accompanied Pizarro in the conquest of Peru.
Attempted the conquest of Florida, and failed; but he was the
first European discoverer of the Mississippi River. Died in 1542.

Elizabeth, Queen. Born in the palace at Greenwich, in 1533. Daughter of Henry the 8th and Anne Boleyn. Ruled England with
vigor for forty-five years. Encouraged efforts to make settlements in America. An unmarried sovereign. Died in 1603.

Franklin, Benjamin. Born in Boston in 1706. By trade a printer.
Became a philosopher and statesman, legislator and foreign em-
bassador. Was one of the foremost men in civil life, in the War
of the Revolution, and was a signer of the Declaration of Independence. Helped negotiate the treaty for peace and independence. Died in Philadelphia in 1790.

George, King. The Third George was born in London in 1738. He
ascended the English throne in 1760. It was from his rule that
the Americans declared themselves to be independent; and
against him the charges in the Declaration of Independence
were made. He reigned fifty years. Died at Windsor Castle
in 1820.

Greene, Nathaniel. Born in Warwick, Rhode Island, in 1742. A
member of the Society of Friends. Became one of the foremost
of the major generals of the Revolution. President of the court
that tried and condemned Major André. Died in Georgia in
1786.

Hamilton, Alexander. Born on the island of Nevis in 1757. Eminent for oratory and logic. A good soldier and acute statesman. First Secretary of the Treasury of the Republic and chief author of our Financial system. Killed in a duel with Aaron Burr in 1804.

Henry, Patrick. Born in Hanover Co., Virginia, in 1736. He was an idle youth, but finally became a lawyer, when it was discovered that he possessed great powers of oratory. He was one of the most powerful of the patriots who stirred the Americans to rebel against Great Britain. Was governor of Virginia. Died in 1799.

Hudson, Henry. Born late in the sixteenth century in England, and was a skillful navigator. Employed by the Dutch to find a sea passage around northern Europe; he failed, turned westward, and discovered the river now known by his name, in the State of New York. He sailed to the head of its tide-water. Set adrift in an open boat in the great bay that bears his name, he was never heard of afterwards.

Isabella, Queen. Born in Madrigal in 1451. Monarch of Castile and Leon. She assisted Columbus in fitting out his expedition for seeking India by sailing westward, and shares with him the honor of discovering America. Died in 1504.

James, King. The first King James of England was a son of Mary Queen of Scots. The first English settlements in America were made during his reign of more than twenty years. Our translation of the Bible was made in his reign. Born in Scotland in 1566. Died in London in 1625.

Jefferson, Thomas. Born at Shadwell, Va., in 1743. Was a lawyer by profession. Served in the Virginia legislature. Wrote the Declaration of Independence; was American Minister at the French court, and third President of the Republic. He was a keen politician, an able statesman, versed in the sciences, and an elegant writer. Died at Monticello in 1826.

Jones, John Paul. Born in Scotland in 1747. Was a mariner, and settled in Virginia. Appointed commander in the Continental Navy, he performed the most signal service on the ocean for the patriots. Afterward in the service of Russia. Died in Paris in 1792, when the National Assembly decreed him a public funeral.

Lafayette, Marquis de. Born in Auvergne, France, in 1757. Espoused the cause of the American patriots, and joined them in their war for independence. He was the most useful foreign friend the Americans had, and was always revered by them. A leader in the beginning of the French revolution. Died in Paris in 1834.

Liesler, Jacob. Born in Frankfort, Germany. A merchant in New York. Led a democratic party there in opposition to the aristocracy, and was hanged in 1691, by virtue of a death-warrant issued by a drunken governor.

Morris, Robert. Born in Liverpool, England, in 1733. Was a merchant in Philadelphia, a signer of the Declaration of Independence, and leading financier during the Revolution. His personal credit sustained that of the country at one time. Died in Philadelphia in 1806.

Oglethorpe, James Edward. Born in London in 1698. A soldier and philanthropist. He founded the colony of Georgia, by procuring the release of debtors from prisons, and sending them to settle in America. Died in London in 1785.

Penn, William. Born in London in 1644. Became a leading "Friend" or "Quaker," and the founder of Pennsylvania. He was the first of the English proprietors who treated the Indians justly. Laid out the city of Philadelphia. Died at Rushcourt, England, in 1718.

Pitt, William. Born at Westminster, England, in 1708. Eminent for oratory and statesmanship, he was called the "Great Commoner of England." Created Earl of Chatham. The constant friend of the Americans in their struggle with the British aristocracy. Died at Hayes, England, in 1778.

Pocahontas. Born about 1595. An American Indian princess. She saved the life of Captain Smith, and also those of the settlers at Jamestown. Married an Englishman named Rolfe. Died in England in 1617.

Raleigh, Walter. Born in Devon, England, in 1552. Was a soldier, statesman and courtier. He promoted and assisted the fitting out of expeditions to plant colonies in America, but failed. He was a favorite of Queen Elizabeth, but King James caused him to be beheaded in 1618.

Rochambeau, Count de. Born in Vendome, France, in 1725. A marshal of France, he led the French army in America which assisted in the campaign against Lord Cornwallis. He suffered during the French Revolution, but escaped with his life. Bonaparte pensioned him. Died in 1807.

Schuyler, Philip. Born in Albany in 1733. As commander of the Northern Army and Indian Commissioner, he exercised great influence, and did more than any other man to save the cause of the patriots from ruin, by restraining invasion on the northern frontiers. A pure patriot, wise legislator, and honest citizen. Died at Albany in 1804.

Smith, John. Born in Lincolnshire, England. Chief founder of Virginia. He had fought the Turks as a soldier before coming to America. He explored the coasts and made a map of New England. Died in London in 1631.

Steuben, Baron de. Born in Magdeburg, Prussia, in 1730. An officer under Frederick the Great. Came to America in 1777, and became Inspector-general of the Continental Army. In that position he rendered important service to the cause. Died at Steubenville, N. Y., in 1794.

Stuyvesant, Peter. Born in Holland in 1602. He was a good soldier, brave and honest. Made governor first of the Island of Curaçoa, and then of New Netherland (New York). He ruled with vigor, and was the last Dutch governor of that province. Died in New York in 1682.

Washington, George. Born in Westmoreland, Virginia, in 1732. Learning the military art in the Colonial service during their wars with the Indians, he became commander-in-chief of the Continental Army, and won the independence of the United States. First President of the Republic. Died at Mount Vernon in 1799.

William, King. Born at the Hague, Holland, in 1650. With a fleet and army he entered England by invitation of the people there, and became their sovereign jointly with Mary his wife. His reign had much influence on the destinies of America. Died at Kensington in 1702.

Williams, Roger. Born in Wales in 1599. A Puritan clergyman. Settled at Salem, in Massachusetts. Banished from that colony, he founded Rhode Island, and was the first to ordain absolute religious freedom in America. Died at Providence in 1683.

Winthrop, John. Born in Suffolk, England. Bred a lawyer, he was one of the most useful of the colonists who settled Massachusetts. Governor of that colony, he ruled with prudence. Died in Boston in 1649.

FACTS TO BE SPECIALLY REMEMBERED.

In the following tables are noted some of the more important events in our history, arranged according to the different periods into which that history naturally divides. These are facts which the pupil should especially endeavor to retain in memory.

Discoverers and Discoveries.

Columbus discovers American Islands 1492
Columbus discovers South America.................... ⎱ 1498
Sebastian Cabot discovers North America.............. ⎰
Americus Vespuccius discovers South America 1499
Juan Ponce de Leon discovers Florida...... 1512
Vasco Nunez de Balboa discovers the Pacific Ocean 1513
Cartier discovers Canada................................1534
De Soto discovers the Mississippi River. 1541
Hudson discovers New York Bay and the Hudson River..1609

A desire to find a western or north-western passage to India, and for personal wealth and power, were the chief causes which led to these discoveries.

Settlers and Settlements.

English emigrants land in Virginia........................1607
English Puritans settle on the coast of Massachusetts..........1620
French Protestants from Holland settle in New Netherland
　　　　(New York)..1623
English emigrants settle in New Hampshire 1629
Puritans from Massachusetts settle in Connecticut.............1633
Roman Catholics and Protestants settle in Maryland...........1634
Rhode Island settled.. .. 1636
Swedes settle in Delaware 1638
English from Long Island settle in New Jersey 1664
The Carolinas settled by the English......................1650, 1670
Penn founds Philadelphia and treats with the Indians..........1682
Georgia settled by the English............................ 1733

The desire to escape from persecution and intolerance were the principal causes which led to permanent settlements here.

The Colonies.

Representative government established in Virginia..............1619
Virginia made a royal province.............................1624
Charter of Massachusetts transferred to the colony.... 1629
First legislature of Maryland assemble. .... ⎱ 1635
Roger Williams banished from Rhode Island.................. ⎰
War with the Pequods 1637
New England Confederacy formed 1643
Charter for Rhode Island given................................1644
Silver money first coined in the United States...................1652
Charter for Connecticut given... ... .1662
Representative assembly in New Netherland (New York)........1663
Surrender of New Netherland (New York) to the English.........1664
King Philip's war...1675
First legislative assembly in New Jersey....................1681
First legislative assembly in Pennsylvania 1682
Attempt to seize the Connecticut charter......................1686
King William's war...1689
Queen Anne's war 1702
King George's War 1744
French and Indian War 1755
Canada conquered by the English 1760

Aspirations for the enjoyment of civil and religious liberty, were the chief causes which promoted the growth of feeble Settlements into vigorous Colonies.

The Revolution.

Stamp Act passed by the British parliament...... .... } 1765
Stamp Act Congress meets in New York........................ }

Tax-gatherers and troops sent to Boston...................... 1768
The "Boston Massacre".......................................1770

A British cruiser burned in Narraganset Bay.................... } 1773
Cargoes of tea destroyed in Boston harbor.................... }

Port of Boston closed to commerce............................ } 1774
First Continental Congress assembles at Philadelphia.......... }

Skirmishes at Lexington and Concord......................... }
Capture of Ticonderoga..................................... }
Battle of Bunker Hill....................................... } 1775
Washington appointed Commander-in-chief.................... }
Canada invaded by the Republican troops.................... }

British troops driven from Boston........................... }
Declaration of Independence .... } 1776
New York taken by the British.............................. }
Washington made Dictator for six months.................... }

The British plan measures for dividing the colonies........... }
Lafayette joins the Americans............................... } 1777
Surrender of Burgoyne and his army to the Americans......... }

Treaty of alliance between the U. S. and France................1778

War chiefly in the Southern States.......................... } 1779
Exploits of Paul Jones on the ocean......................... }

The British overrun the Carolinas.......... .... }
Treason of General Arnold...... .... } 1780
Capture and execution of Major André...... .... }

Surrender of Cornwallis and his army........................ } 1781
A national league formed........... .... }

Preliminary treaty of peace signed 1782

British troops leave the country............................ } 1783
Washington resigns his commission .... }

National Constitution framed................................1787

The Nation.

A National Government established............................ } 1789
Washington inaugurated first President of the U. S............. }

National Bank established 1791
National Mint established....................................1792
A Navy authorized..1794
Treaty with Great Britain negotiated by John Jay.... 1795
Washington retires from the Presidency 1797
Washington dies...1799
City of Washington made the seat of the National Government.....1800

Louisiana purchased from France............................ } 1803
War with the Barbary States................................ }

First navigation by steam................................... } 1807
First Embargo Act passed by Congress .... }

Fight between an American and British vessel................. } 1811
War with Indians in the northwest .... }

The United States declare war against Great Britain .... } 1812
Americans invade Canada.................................... }

Americans victorious on Lake Erie 1813

Americans victorious on Lake Champlain...................... }
Washington City captured and burnt by the British............. } 1814
Treaty of peace signed at Ghent............................ }

Oppressive restrictions upon commerce and manufactures; the imposition of taxes on the colonists without their consent by representatives in parliament, and a determination to maintain local self-government, were the chief causes which impelled the Americans to revolt.

From 1789 to the war of 1812 was the period when the National Government was put into operation, its policies defined, and its resources made manifest.

The Nation—continued.

Battle of New Orleans..	} 1815
War with Algiers..	
Lafayette visits the U. S. as the nation's guest.................	1824
Erie canal completed...	1825
Death of John Adams and Thomas Jefferson on the same day..	1826
Trouble with South Carolinians settled by compromise........	} 1833
Government funds withdrawn from U. S. Banks..............	
War with Indians in Florida	1835
Electro-magnetic telegraph established......................	1844
Texas annexed to the United States............................	1845
War with Mexico...	1846
Battle of Buena Vista...	} 1847
Scott's battles and triumphant march to Mexico.............	
Treaty of peace with Mexico......................................	} 1848
Gold found in California..	
Fugitive Slave law passed...	1850
Civil war in Kansas...	1855
John Brown's raid into Virginia..................................	1859
Abraham Lincoln elected President..............................	1860

The war of 1812 was a successful Second War for independence of Great Britain. From that time until the Civil War was a period of great national growth and development of internal dangers.

The Civil War and its consequences.

South Carolinians pass an ordinance of secession	1860
South Carolinians fire on the *Star of the West*.................	
Other slave-labor States pass ordinances of secession	
Confederate States Government formed...........................	
Lincoln inaugurated President......................................	
Fort Sumter attacked and evacuated.............................	
The President calls for 75,000 volunteers........................	} 1861
National troops invade Virginia...................................	
Richmond made the Confederate Capital.........................	
Nationals defeated at Bull Run....................................	
Congress makes provision of men and money for war............	
Confederate ambassadors taken from a British ship.............	
Roanoke Island and Fort Donelson captured by the Nationals....	
The Confederate "ram" *Merrimack* destroys National war-vessels...	
The *Merrimack* defeated by the *Monitor*	} 1862
Nationals victorious at Shiloh.....................................	
New Orleans captured by Nationals...............................	
Seven days battles near Richmond	
Confederates defeated at Antietam...............................	
The President proclaims the freedom of the slaves..............	
Charleston besieged...	
Confederate victory at Chancellorsville..........................	
West Virginia admitted into the Union............................	} 1863
Nationals victorious at Gettysburgh	
Vicksburg surrendered to the Nationals..........................	
Draft riots in New York	
Confederate ports thoroughly blockaded.........................	
General Grant placed in chief command..........................	
The great National armies ordered to move simultaneously....	
Army of the Potomac moves on Richmond........................	} 1864
Sherman penetrates Georgia to Atlanta	
The *Alabama* sunk by the *Kearsarge*...........................	

The Civil War was produced by a difference of opinion which had long existed between the people of the slave-labor and free-labor States concerning the institution of slavery in this country.

The Civil War and its Consequences—continued.

Petersburg besieged ....
Atlanta surrendered to the Nationals.................................
Sherman marches to the sea 1864
Confederates invade Tennessee...............................
Nationals victorious at Nashville ....
National land and naval forces attack Fort Fisher................
National troops capture Columbia, S. C. ....
Charleston occupied by colored troops............................
Sherman marches through the Carolinas.................. ....
Lee surrenders the Confederate army to Grant. ....
Jefferson Davis and associates flee from Richmond..... ....
President Lincoln assassinated.................................. 1865
General Johnson surrenders his army..... ....
National forces capture Mobile....................................
Last conflict of the civil war occurs in Texas....................
Thirteenth Amendment to the Constitution, forbidding slavery,
    adopted............... . ...
Fourteenth Amendment guaranteeing civil rights to the freed-
    men adopted. 1866
Atlantic Telegraph cable permanently laid........................
Alaska purchased from Russia..... 1867
President Johnson impeached and acquitted 1868
Fifteenth Amendment, guaranteeing the right of suffrage to the
    freedmen, adopted 1870
Treaty with England concerning the depredations of English-Con-
    federate cruisers 1871
The dispute with England settled by arbitration.................. 1872

The chief consequences of the civil war were the destruction of slavery as an institution, and a social revolution in the late slave-labor States.

TOPICAL REVIEW.

* This and the smaller maps may not only be used for references, but any pupil or pupils in a class, may make an outline on the blackboard or on paper. Such an exercise, even though very rudely performed, will greatly assist the memory.

SETTLERS AND SETTLEMENTS.

THE COLONIES.

THE STRIFE FOR FREEDOM, OR THE REVOLUTION.

THE CONSTITUTION.